Rivers of WIND

A Western Boyhood Remembered

GARY PENLEY

FILTER PRESS
Palmer Lake, Colorado

Publisher's Cataloging-in-Publication
(Provided by Quality Books, Inc.)

Penley, Gary N.
    Rivers of wind : a Western boyhood remembered / Gary
Penley. -- 1st ed.
    p. cm.
    Preassigned LCCN: 98-85764
    ISBN: 0-86541-044-5

    1. Penley, Gary N.--Childhood and youth. 2. Blizzard,
George. 3. Lamar (Colo.)--Biography. 4. Ranchers--
Colorado--Lamar--Biography. I. Title.

CT275.P46A3 1998   978.8'98'092 [B]
                              QBI98-987

Publisher's Note: In an effort to protect individual privacy, yet depict events in the truest form possible, some names in this story have been changed.

Printed in the United States of America

10   9   8   7   6   5   4   3   2   1

To Karen,
for walking through fire with me.

Nothing in the world can take the place of persistence. Talent will not; nothing is more common than unsuccessful men with talent. Genius will not; unrewarded genius is almost a proverb. Education will not; the world is full of educated derelicts. Persistence and determination alone are omnipotent.
—Attributed to Calvin Coolidge

Life is either a daring adventure, or nothing.
—Helen Keller

ACKNOWLEDGMENTS

I wish to thank everyone who helped make this book a reality:

Dr. Edward Geary, Brigham Young University, for editing and evaluating the story in an historical context.

Luis Alberto Urrea, University of Southern Louisiana, for reading, critiquing, and ever encouraging.

Paul Lindquist, my wild, crazy, intelligent friend, for everything.

Trevor Casper, for ideas, critiques, and listening when I just needed to rattle on.

Stan Kolodzie, for imaginative ideas, advice, and endless encouragement.

Jim Holdeman, for reading the entire manuscript twice, but mostly just for being Jim.

David Buthman, for detailed editing and sound advice.

Nina Harun, for sharing her deepest feelings on the story.

Mike Elwood and Larry Voss, for insightful and objective critiques.

Neal Coats, for hours of lively discussion, sound ideas, and keeping me sane.

The Cow Creek Boys, Fred Birch, Donnie Hughes, Jerry Melvin, and Mike Kolodzie, the greatest friends, trail buddies, and cheerleaders an author could have.

Kim and Jessica Benge, Jim and Sharon Ruby, for encouraging me to tell the story.

Dr. Levi Peterson, Weber State University, for teaching me the elements of writing many years ago and sharing with me his love of language.

Mrs. Dixie Munro, an inspiring, compassionate English teacher who wouldn't give up on me in high school when I was in danger of giving up on myself.

Karen, my wife and best friend, for encouraging me to tell this story, putting up with more during two and a half years of writing than I could have in fairness asked, and cheering me on every step of the way. Thanks, Easter Bunny.

And a special tribute to Jigs, a noble horse and the greatest friend this child ever knew. With no regard for his own life, he proudly stood in harm's way to save mine.

CONTENTS

Geo. Blizzard

PROLOGUE

Life's adventure has carried me far from my roots, but I am a man of the prairie at heart, the grandson of a fiercely determined man who had the boldness to reach for his dream, the tenacity to pursue it through a lifetime of disappointment, and the courage to grab for it once more as old age set in. He became the central figure of my life, the man I called Dad.

He never seemed old to me. He stood with the intensity of a coiled spring, a compact bundle of energy and fierce determination. His dark, piercing eyes challenged the world; his stubborn jaw defied it. The years hadn't mellowed him much. Even in his seventies he wore his hat cocked.

He belonged here. He and this hard prairie were alike—rugged, fierce, and enduring. Each stood ready to battle the other every day.

He carried a scar on the right side of his forehead, a crease midway between his heavy eyebrow and snowy hair. When I was twelve I asked him about it. "Dad, what made that dent in your head?"

A narrow grin crossed his leathery face, and his gray eyes brightened a little. "A rock," he said, "about the size of your fist." He'd got it in a fight when he was young. A man had gripped a rock and slugged him with it. The rock had cracked his skull. He chuckled as he reminisced about that old battle.

"Did it knock ya down?" I asked.

The grin faded, and his eyes darkened. "Yeah, it did," he grumbled. He'd been knocked down only a few times in his life.

I grew up with this rare man and his daughter, my mother, a brave woman who chose hardships, harsh weather, and isolation to place her sons in the care of the best man she knew.

This is their story. Between the lines you'll find mine.

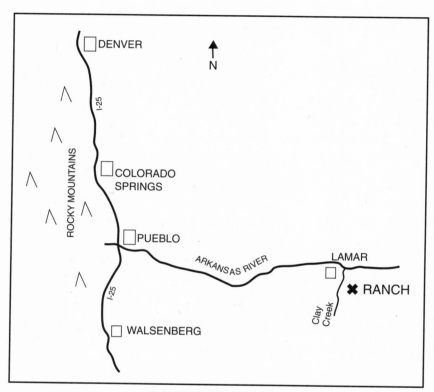

EASTERN COLORADO

Chapter 1

THE CHALLENGE

When my grandfather, George Blizzard, arrived in the frontier town of Lamar, Colorado, back in 1913, it was a wild and half lawless cow town. The streets were hard-packed dirt and filled with horses, cars largely a thing of the future. My grandfather, the man I would call Dad, had quickly earned a reputation for hard work and honesty after his arrival, but he would soon gain fame for his fists as well. Witnesses would long remember the day of the big fight on Main Street, and tell and retell the story.

Every Western town in those days had a man known as the town tough. Lamar's town tough was a scrapper named Hank Stoner. Stoner was not only a street fighter, he was a seasoned expert in the boxing ring who sported his reputation proudly. In public boxing matches held in Lamar for a decade, Stoner was a featured attraction. He reportedly finished those years undefeated. People called him the King, and most were afraid of him.

But Dad considered Hank a bully, and he couldn't abide bullies. Of course, Dad never went out of the way to avoid a fight himself, whatever the reason. Although he was a relatively short man, five feet eight inches tall, he was stocky and powerfully built, his body hardened early in life by hard physical labor. Dad being Dad, and Hank being Hank, it was probably inevitable that the two would come to battle.

Dad said the fight started that day over Hank bullying a boy. Dad was thirty-eight years old at the time. Stoner was ten to fifteen years younger.

In the years following, my mother and her sisters always talked about how Dad had "whipped Hank Stoner," presumably with ease. Neighbors and townspeople continued to marvel at the duration of the fight and its outcome. They told how it had taken place in the middle of Main Street with most of the town watching, but aside from that I'd never heard many details.

Years after Dad passed on, I met an old man who had lived in Lamar all his life. When I told him I was George Blizzard's grandson his face lit up. "When I was about twenty years old I saw your grandpa in a hell of a fight down on Main Street, with a guy named Hank Stoner." His eyes danced with the memory.

"You mean you saw that fight?" I practically shouted.

"Yep, every bit of it, start to finish," he said with pride.

"All I ever heard was that Dad whipped him," I said excitedly. "Will you tell me about the fight?" He grinned with delight. We sat down, and he told me what he had seen that day.

The fight started in the upstairs of a building that faced Main Street, just north of the railroad tracks. A door opened directly from the sidewalk to a narrow stairway that led to a gambling house on the second floor. A loud ruckus broke out up there one afternoon. People on the street below stopped to listen, wondering what all the hollering and cussing was about. The ruckus became louder as it neared the stairwell, and soon the source of the commotion tumbled into view. Locked in combat, Dad and Hank Stoner crashed down the stairs, through the door, across the board sidewalk, and out into the dirt street. There they picked themselves up, squared off, and charged into each other.

Both men were near the same size and both stoutly built, but their fighting methods differed greatly. His years in the boxing ring had made Stoner a style fighter. He first began throwing calculated punches to test Dad's skills—to see how aggressive he was, how hard he could hit, how well he could take a punch. He soon learned that Dad wasn't a style fighter at all, that he really didn't do anything predictable. Dad could hit like a sledgehammer, he could take a blow, and he was sure as hell aggressive, but as for style he just did whatever came naturally, as he had done hundreds of times before.

Dad drove in hard, viciously pounding Hank's head and body. In the face of this attack Stoner gave up experimenting and started throwing the best he had. Countering with heavy blows of his own, he drove Dad back down the street. Dad soon stopped him, and neither could move the other. They stood toe to toe, jaws clenched, and rained shattering blows on each other. Neither could knock the other down. The style fighter and the instinctive fighter—both were good, and both were bulls.

News of the event spread, and people ran from all over town to watch. Some grinned and shook their heads. Some laughed and shouted at the fighters. Some simply stared as Dad and Hank stood in the dirt and hammered each other.

Open cuts lined their bleeding faces. Blood dripped from bruised fists. They grunted and roared their rage.

Dad caught him with a tremendous uppercut to the jaw, and Stoner went down. But he quickly jumped back to his feet and, with a roundhouse swing to the chin, knocked Dad down. Then he fell on top of him.

No longer a contest of different techniques, now the fight became basic, primal. They fought standing up. They fought on their knees. They fought on the ground. They fought in every position, tearing at each other with all the strength they had. Both knew the other would never give up.

The battle roared down Main Street for three city blocks, the fighters slugging, shoving, wrestling, and plowing their way through the dirt. The excited crowd could hear their fists smack flesh a block away and see the blood fly. Their shirts were ripped nearly off; torn shreds flapped from their bodies. Covered with mud and blood, they knocked each other down, fell down, got up, and knocked each other down again. When one swung and hit the other, he fell to the ground with him, carried by the momentum of his own swing. The first one to regain his feet swung and hit the other before he could regain his.

They finally both lay on the ground, too exhausted to rise. But through swollen eyes they glared at each other—wild animals, intent on the kill, not finished yet. Dad clenched his jaw tightly, and with a terrible effort heaved himself to his feet. Hank tried. He was halfway up when Dad lurched toward him and slammed the side of his head with everything he had left. Stoner fell on his back, and Dad managed to stay on his feet.

Dad stood over him, swaying like a drunken man, bloody shirt hanging in shreds, face swollen beyond recognition, battered fists still clenched. Hank Stoner could not rise again. The fight was finished.

The old man telling me the story had a distant look as he recalled the end of that battle. "Bloody mess," he said, shaking his head. "Bloody mess." Then a wide grin crossed his face, and his eyes danced again. "Yeah, your grandpa whipped him all right, but he took a hell of a beatin' doin' it!"

Mary Josephine, my grandmother, was home with two small children and a third on the way when the fight took place. The family was still fairly new in town, and she was concerned with their social standing and reputation. She wasn't aware that Dad was downtown establishing a reputation of his own, nor was she prepared for the sight of her husband when he came plodding home, bruised, bleeding, and caked with mud.

A few days after the fight, a stranger walked up to Dad on Main Street, stopped, and stared at him.

"What're you lookin' at?" Dad asked.

"I just wanted to see what the new King looked like," the man replied.

Chapter 2

THE ROAD TO THE RANCH

Dad was born in Kentucky in 1875, the oldest of eight children. He attended school only through third grade, then had to go to work to help support the family. His mother, Nancy, was a feisty little frontier woman who worked hard, cared for all those kids, and provided stability to the family. Squire Blizzard, his father, was an obstinate, hard-nosed character, neither ambitious nor hard working. Dad worked to support the family until he was grown, while his father pursued endeavors such as fishing and whittling. Dad hated that idleness. He protested all his life, forcefully and often, "I'm not a bit like my dad!"

Squire began to feel some pioneer yearnings when Dad was still a little boy, so he had Nancy get the family ready to go west. They left Kentucky in a covered wagon pulled by oxen, and after a six hundred-mile trek they stopped in southwest Missouri. After staying in Missouri only a short while, Squire decided to return to Kentucky. So Nancy got everything ready again, they hitched up the oxen and made the long trip back in the covered wagon.

Back in Kentucky, Squire decided Missouri wasn't so bad after all. Nancy was probably getting pretty confused by now, and the oxen could surely have walked the route blindfolded back to southwest Missouri. Either the wagon wouldn't make the trip again, or Nancy had had enough. At any rate, they stayed in Missouri, settling near present-day Joplin.

They homesteaded on would-be farmland, and Dad and his mother set about trying to make a living for them all. Wood was scarce, so like other settlers in the area they built a house of sod. They hitched up their mule and plowed rows of sod from the hard prairie ground, cut it into rectangles, and built walls with it. The roof was made of boards covered with the same sod blocks, and as a result the ceiling constantly leaked dirt down onto their heads. That didn't bother the floor; it was also dirt.

Little one-room houses like theirs were known as sod shanties. Dad grew up in that sod shanty with his parents and seven siblings, all ten of them living in one room, with dirt sifting into their hair.

Nancy made all their clothes by hand and washed them by hand. She helped raise pigs and chickens too, and grew a garden to provide the slender meals she cooked for them on a coal stove, the same stove that provided heat in winter.

Dad wasn't just the oldest son, he was a serious boy. At the age of ten or eleven, when other kids had mostly fun and mischief on their minds, he felt a sense of responsibility for the family. Besides working on the farm at that age, he sought outside jobs to help bring in a little more money.

Life on the unsettled prairie was dangerous, especially for children. Medical treatment was scarce and often inadequate, and many people couldn't afford it anyway.

Dad once told me the story of his little sister Mary, a memory he relived with difficulty. Mary was three years old and loved to sing. She always sang to herself while she played, and to anyone else who would listen. Mary wandered outside one morning while Nancy was busy. Nancy missed her and ran outside in time to see her in the corral, singing to herself as she walked behind a horse. Too late to save her, Nancy watched in horror as the horse kicked Mary in the head.

A country doctor came and did what he could, but her injuries were too severe. That night as the family stood around her bed, Mary sang a little song, smiled a faint smile, and died.

Dad dug Mary's grave and helped Squire bury her near the sod shanty.

Dad also buried his younger brother Charlie. An epidemic of spinal meningitis hit when Charlie was a teenager. He woke up one morning complaining about his back, failed rapidly through the day, and died that evening.

As he grew older and stronger, Dad looked for higher paying work. He found his first adult job in mining, a rapidly growing industry in the area. He didn't work underground, however; he hauled lead ore from the mouths of mines in horse-drawn wagons.

Lead ore, a mineral called galena, is extremely heavy. One shovelful of galena weighed thirty pounds, and Dad loaded and unloaded it all day long. He proudly said he could shovel a wagonful without stopping. As he put it, "I could load a wagonful without lookin' up."

A song about mining became popular when I was a kid. It talked about loading sixteen tons a day. Dad laughed when he heard the song. "Hell, sixteen tons in a day wasn't nothin' at all."

Another line in the song went, "I owe my soul to the company store." Dad said that part was certainly true. The mining companies provided meager housing for the miners and their families, and the company always ran a store that was easily accessible to them. According to Dad it worked this way. The companies didn't pay enough to raise a family on, so they extended credit to the miners for the rest of the bare necessities they needed to get by. The catch was, a miner couldn't quit his job and move on as long as he owed anything to the company store. This policy virtually enslaved the miners.

"I hardly ever bought a thing at the company store," Dad said, "and if I did I paid cash."

His stocky frame hardened into a hundred and eighty pounds of pure muscle from shoveling galena. His short, rippling arms looked like thick clubs, and his body was shaped like a wedge—broad shoulders narrowing down to small hips and short, powerful legs.

He worked in a rugged environment where injuries were common. Hard, coarse men cussed, tore muscles in two, sweated, bled, and fought each other. Physical strength and prowess separated men in that culture. A man had to fight to protect himself from bullies, to dominate others, or to become the boss. Dad was defiant by nature, and he hated bullies. He was young, powerful, and fierce.

He used to tell me about those younger days when he worked at the mines. "If a man decided to single ya out, to start hollerin' at ya or pickin' on ya, ya might as well stop it right then and there," he said. "I always liked to knock a man down if I hit 'im. And if he didn't go down the first time I hit 'im, then I knew I really had to lay into 'im."

His reputation for fighting followed him always, the stories of his battles becoming legend in our family. He prided himself in not having been knocked down many times in his life; in fact, the only time he was ever defeated was when he had his skull cracked with a rock. Dad underestimated his opponent that time, and didn't see the rock in his hand. The man was a stranger, and never again seen at the mines. He walked away and left Dad sitting on the ground, holding his broken skull and bleeding terribly. I asked Dad if he jumped up and tried to catch him. "Hell, no!" he said.

Dad's brother Sam was Dad's opposite. A short, slender fellow with a big nose, a wry grin, laughing eyes, and a lazy, stoop-shouldered posture, Sam didn't care to fight anybody. The most fluent cusser I've ever heard, he cussed constantly wherever he happened to be, lacing every sentence with two, three, or four cuss words. Yet somehow it was strangely inoffensive. He didn't emphasize the cuss words as most people do, and it all came out so naturally it didn't even sound like cussing. When he came to visit us later in his life he'd walk off the train saying, "Rode that goddam train sittin' up all the damn night. My goddam back feels like I died and went to hell. Wish they'd put softer seats in them goddam things. How in hell are ya, George? Ya look goddam fit as a fiddle." This would all be coming out as he walked through a crowd of people but in a normal voice that wouldn't even attract attention.

Sam had a penchant for telling funny stories, and he always looked for the humor in a situation or created it. When he was about eighteen, he and a buddy concocted a plan to seek their fortunes in Denver, eight hundred miles west of Joplin. They worked and saved their money until they each had a new hat, a new suit, and enough for a train ticket, and not much more.

The big day of their departure, Dad hitched up a horse and buggy and drove them to town to catch the train. On the way to town, as the two adventurers reveled in their upcoming exploits out West, they happened onto a crap game in progress under a big tree. Recognizing an opportunity to pick up some more cash for their trip, Sam and his buddy asked Dad to stop so they could get in the game.

Dad liked to gamble himself, and he was usually pretty smart about it, so all three joined in the crap game. Within a short while Sam and his friend lost a considerable amount of money. Dad, however, won steadily. By the time they got back in the buggy Dad had won more money than the other two had lost.

The travelers were in great spirits the rest of the way to town, ecstatic with relief that Dad had won their money back for them.

They did notice, however, that he hadn't given it to them yet, or said anything about it for that matter.

At the train station they learned the sad truth. "I didn't win your money. I won my money," Dad told them. He hadn't won their money back; he'd won different money. They had lost, and he had won. They boarded the train for Denver with long faces and less money.

Nobody heard from the big spenders for two weeks. Evidently they were busy cutting business deals and making names for themselves in the big city. Then late one night Squire woke to a meek knock at the door. "Who is it?" he hollered.

"It's Sam," said a tragic voice. "I've come home to die."

"Hell, you come home to get somethin' to eat," Squire replied. He opened the door, lit the lamp, and beheld his son, home from the big city. Sam stood slump shouldered in the light, his new hat scrunched sideways on his head, smashed and torn. Great ragged pieces of his new suit hung from him, exposing patches of lining, and black streaks of filth covered his face, his hands, and his clothes.

"Where the hell you been?" Squire asked.

Sam looked at the floor. "In a coal car," he said. "We rode back from Denver on a coal train." Dad, sitting up in bed, just grinned at Sam.

Sam never strayed again; he lived in Joplin the rest of his life.

Dad also had a desire to go west as he grew into his twenties, but he operated in a more controlled manner than Sam. He left Missouri sometime around the turn of the century, by himself, and moved to eastern Kansas. There he hauled ore, helped in wheat harvests, and took any other work he could find.

No one knows exactly where Dad lived during his years in Kansas, but he worked around the towns of Coffeyville, Arkansas City, and Galena, all in the southeast corner of the state.

Dad's hair turned steel gray in his twenties. His good looks and confident air often attracted the ladies' attention, and in spite of his rough ways he made it a point never to cuss in front of women or in the house, unless he lost his temper.

In Kansas he met a girl named Mary Josephine Noel. The circumstances that brought him to her house aren't known, but

Mary Josephine remembered all her life how handsome he appeared the day they met.

Dad noticed Mary Josephine too, a slender girl with dark hair, delicate features, and refined manners. She had grown up in Wisconsin and been raised with more money than Dad and in a more civil environment. She was a year older than him and much better educated, having finished high school and attended some college as well.

Regardless of their different backgrounds they soon became enthralled with each other, and Dad talked Mary Josephine into marrying him. He was twenty-eight; she was twenty-nine.

If Mary Josephine could have seen beyond Dad's good looks she might have realized that a life of hard work lay ahead of her. But this refined girl was up to that kind of life. Her delicate features belied her capabilities, the strength showing only in her keen, dark eyes. She proved to have plenty of stamina for the work and enough grit to put up with Dad.

Mary Josephine's mother was a pampered woman who had always gotten her way. Even as an adult she threw childish tantrums. Shortly after Dad and Mary Josephine were married, she threw a tantrum in their house. Dad disagreed with her over something, which prompted her to start bawling loudly and fall on the floor, kicking and screaming like a spoiled child. Dad walked to the kitchen, brought back a bucket of water, and threw it on her. Their relationship was never warm after that exchange, but she never threw another tantrum in his house either.

Dad had a desire, a drive, to become more than a simple laborer. Working horses became his master skill. Horses provided the power for farming, earth moving, construction, and most types of transport. He had learned to work horses and mules while growing up, and expanded those skills at the mines; now he learned to operate farm machinery and heavy earthmoving equipment. This entailed not only operating the machine but driving a team of two, four, or six horses pulling it.

He longed to go further west than Kansas, and sometime during those years Dad began to dream of cattle ranching. He once took a train trip to Pueblo, Colorado, just to look over the country. The prairie land around Lamar appealed to him, and when he returned he told Mary Josephine all about it.

Dad started his own livery stable in Kansas and made a success of it. Their first two girls, my aunts Mary and Helen, were born there—Mary in 1907 and Helen in 1908. The family appeared settled. His business success prompted the fledgling Ford Motor Company to offer him a dealership to market their new automobile, the Model T, but Dad declined the offer.

Two things prevented his taking the Ford dealership. Being a horse man, he guffawed the newly developed automobile, and he still wanted to go west to be a cattle rancher.

In 1913 he made his move. Dad took his family and his dream to Lamar.

The Arkansas River carves a wide path through eastern Colorado. Rushing east from the mountain front near the center of the state, it slows and meanders its way across the High Plains like a great, lazy snake, then glides on to lower climes in Kansas. The Santa Fe Trail, an artery for both cattle and commerce, ran beside the river in southeast Colorado. The first railroad there, aptly named the Santa Fe, ran along parts of the old trail.

An unusual birth took place beside those rails one night in 1886. I. R. Holmes, a former Santa Fe agent, intended to help populate the young country. Holmes was an ambitious land promoter and developer, and in collaboration with the railroad he planned to hold a land lot auction at a site just south of the Arkansas River on Monday, May 24, 1886. Both Holmes and the Santa Fe stood to profit if they developed a new town along the young railroad's track. He had advertised the sale widely and arranged for prospective buyers to arrive on a special train from the East the morning of the auction.

A railroad station was essential for the proposed new town. To ensure the success of the sale, the Santa Fe had ordered the relocation of a small station that sat at Blackwell, three miles east of the sale site. However, a problem arose a few days before the auction date.

An obstinate character named A. R. Black owned the little station and the land it sat on. Possibly with visions of his own for a new town, Black refused to allow the station's removal despite the railroad's authorization. This appeared to be a serious snag, but Holmes, the imaginative promoter, was undeterred.

On May 22, two days before the scheduled sale, Black received a telegram from Pueblo, Colorado, one hundred and ten miles to the west. The mysterious telegram insisted he come to Pueblo for important business that day. Black left as quickly as he could.

Holmes and the Santa Fe knew a court order could not be issued on the following day, Sunday. At one minute past midnight Saturday night, a Santa Fe work train pulled up to the station at Blackwell. The crew woke the astonished telegraph operator who lived upstairs over the station, told him to move out quickly, and began to uproot the building.

They picked up the entire building that night, loaded it onto flatcars, and moved it three miles west to the new town site. A switch was hastily installed in the tracks beside the station the same day, and Holmes met the train carrying his buyers the following morning.

A town was born.

They named the new town after Lucius Lamar, Secretary of the Interior at the time. Lamar sits on the south bank of the Arkansas, with Main Street running through the middle of town in the style of the Old West, and crossing the railroad tracks in the center. Some buildings on Main Street still sport false fronts dating back to those older, wilder times. Lamar became a Western crossroads, and not only its architecture but its colorful history is reminiscent of the Old West—dirt streets, dance halls, bordellos, street fights, shoot outs, bank robberies, an opera house, and an old saloon, still standing, where the legendary Tom Mix tended bar before becoming a star of silent Western movies.

The town of three thousand was not yet thirty years old when Dad arrived. He moved his family into a little rented house at the north edge of town, where my mother, Lois, was born the following year.

Dad tried to start another livery stable in Lamar, but economic times were hard in the newly settled West and his business soon failed. He looked for jobs relentlessly after that failure, working at anything he could find.

Shortly after Mom was born in 1914, Dad found a way to buy some prairie land. Under the Federal Homestead Act, in certain areas a person could still file a claim with the government for one hundred and sixty acres. This didn't involve an actual payment, but the prospective owner had to "prove up" the claim before ownership was granted. This required building a house and other improvements on the land, living on it, and cultivating it or raising livestock on it for five years.

Dad filed a claim for prairie land about twenty miles south of town. The following morning he hitched up a horse and buggy, and proudly took Mary Josephine and the girls to see it. Wide vistas rolled into distant view as they rode across the prairie for more than two hours. At times they could see thirty miles.

As they neared the claim the prairie rolled into greater relief, becoming more uneven and broken. Dad stopped the buggy on the brink of a steep hillside, and they looked down on their new home. Incised into the flatter prairie surrounding it, the rugged area was dominated by crags, bluffs, and rocky hillsides. A lazy creek wandered its way through the claim though. Pleasantly lined with big trees, it improved the scenery and provided a ready water supply.

At last he could start his ranch, his dream. Dad set about making improvements to the claim. Sleeping there much of the time and occasionally traveling back and forth in a buggy or on horseback to bring supplies from town, he built a crude rock house near the creek using sandstone blocks dug from a nearby hillside. Like most homesteaders' houses, it was a small, one-room dwelling with mud used to seal the cracks between the rocks. The flat roof was also covered with rocks, to keep the prairie wind from blowing it off. A cast-iron stove served for both heating and cooking.

A cave cellar was essential for food storage on the prairie. To make this he first dug a rectangular hole, six feet deep, ten feet long, and eight feet wide, then lined the walls with sandstone blocks. The roof was formed by laying boards over the hole and mounding dirt on top. A door at one end lay nearly flat on the ground, covering a rock stairway that led down into it much like a modern storm cellar.

When Dad finished the house and cellar, Mary Josephine and the girls moved to the claim. Mom was still a baby, but Mary and

Helen were seven and eight years old, and used to living in town. The country probably looked like a more rugged existence than they had in mind, and would prove so in the coming years.

One day as Mary Josephine walked down a little path, the three girls followed single file behind her. Mom walked last in line, followed by a baby chick. They passed a small bush standing to one side of the path but thought nothing of it. But as Mom looked around to see if the little chicken was still following, a rattlesnake struck from inside the bush and hit the chick, killing it in a matter of seconds.

Rattlesnakes were numerous on the claim, but snakes weren't their only worry. When Dad chose the location for their little house, he didn't judge the lay of the land very well. One quiet evening rain began to patter on the roof. Rain was a good sound, as they usually needed it. By bedtime the patter had increased to a downpour. That pleased Dad; a hard rain would really put some moisture in the ground.

Dad woke later in the night, and the sound of the rain had changed. Besides the pounding on the roof, he now heard a roar coming from outside. Getting up to investigate, he swung his feet off the bed and stepped into a foot of water. He hurriedly lit the lamp, and woke Mary Josephine. Water gushed into the house, and would soon reach the level of their beds.

They hadn't known how quickly conditions can change on the prairie. The roar that woke Dad was the creek. A handy distance from the house, it normally ran little more than a trickle, but while they slept the creek had overflowed its banks and become a torrent. And the water was still rising.

Dad swept Mom up in his arms and grabbed one of the girls by the hand. Mary Josephine grabbed the other girl as he forced the door open against the rushing water, and they ran for a nearby hill. Lightning flashes lit their way.

At the top of the hill they escaped the rising water, but found no shelter. Thunder rolled from horizon to horizon, and lightning flashes revealed the roaring creek, running wide as a river below them. They sat huddled in the downpour for hours. Dad and Mary Josephine shielded the girls from the rain as best they could, and prayed that a bolt of lightning wouldn't find them.

When the rain stopped and the water subsided, they trudged

back down the hill and looked over their mud-filled home and ruined belongings. Mary held her mother's hand, and stared at the wreckage. "Dad's trying to drown us out here!" she wailed.

Mary Josephine jerked her hand. "Hush that up," she said. "Your Dad's doing the best he can."

They dealt with the flood, the rattlers, and whatever else nature threw at them, but they couldn't combat the economy. Times grew worse, and Dad looked for outside work to supplement their income, but jobs were scarce. As the claim became more and more difficult to afford, he felt his dream slipping away. He'd been so proud of his claim, but after laboring for two years to prove it up he had to accept bitter defeat, and move the family back to town.

Dad rented another little house, this time on the southeast edge of town. For a while he worked as a security guard in a famous dance hall called the Bucket of Blood. Legend tells that the place got its name because a woman once stabbed a man to death there after hours, laid his body on a board between two sawhorses, and left a bucket under him to catch the blood.

A short while after Dad went to work at the Bucket of Blood, he was offered a police job. Though he had no previous experience in law enforcement, the city offered him the job of night marshal. The night marshal's job was not for the faint-hearted, as he was the only policeman on duty from sundown to sunrise. But the city officials remembered Dad's battle with Hank Stoner and felt confident of his abilities.

He didn't have to wear a uniform on duty, only a badge, and how he handled crimes or altercations was left to his own discretion. He carried a pistol and a blackjack, a small leather-covered club about eight inches long filled with lead.

One night Dad heard a commotion coming from an alley near the railroad tracks. Loud cussing and hollering carried for blocks. With the blackjack gripped in his hand, he ran to investigate. He found two men in the alley, drunk and fighting. Dad ran up to them hollering, "Hey, you boys stop that fightin'. You're makin' too much noise, raisin' a ruckus."

One of the men said, "All right, Mr. George," and backed off.

The other fellow wasn't so prudent. He turned on Dad. "Goddamit Mr. George, you keep outta this!" he hollered, and lunged at him. Dad swung the blackjack and caught him between the eyes. The man's head snapped back, he stopped, staggered, and bent over at the waist. A stream of blood poured from his forehead.

Dad liked to tell that story, especially the man's reaction after the blackjack hit him. As the blood ran from his forehead to the ground, he held the sides of his head with both hands and swayed back and forth, moaning, "Oh God, Mr. George. Oh God!"

When Dad found a chance to work horses again, which was always his preference, he quit the night marshal job. The economy continued to fluctuate in the following years, however, and he worked at whatever he could find. At times he had to leave Lamar to find a job, working on road-building crews in other parts of the state and even going back to eastern Kansas to help in wheat harvests again.

Around 1920 Dad bought a little one-story brick house just half a block north of the railroad tracks, forever to be known in the family as the red brick house.

He still thought about owning land and once tried to raise some livestock on a few acres he rented just outside of town. The land needed a fence, so he asked the landlord if he had any material he could use for fencing. The landlord told him, "Aw, just use anything you can find out there."

Dad had seen a stack of new lumber on the land, but he hadn't thought about using it until the landlord told him to use whatever was available. He built a fine fence from it. However, in spite of what he'd said, the landlord hadn't meant for Dad to use his new lumber, and when he saw the fence he went looking for Dad. First he went to the red brick house and banged on the door. Mary Josephine answered it. "Where's George Blizzard?" he demanded.

She told him she wasn't sure, but that he was probably downtown somewhere. "Why are you looking for him?" she asked.

"Because I'm mad at him," he spouted. "He used up my new lumber, and I aim to settle it with him."

Mary Josephine chuckled. "You might ought to calm yourself down a little before you find George Blizzard," she told him.

The man didn't take her advice. He stomped off in search of Dad. The landlord nursed his anger with a few drinks along the way, and somewhere he bought a loaf of bread. He was carrying the bread under his right arm when he spotted Dad walking across Main Street. He ran straight at Dad, shouting, "What the hell ya mean, usin' my new lumber to build your damn fence?!"

Dad stopped as the landlord charged up to him, but said nothing. The man jerked the loaf of bread from under his arm and started to shift it to the other. Dad sensed that he was about to swing, and punched him squarely on the point of the chin. He went limp and staggered backward, but didn't go down. Dad stepped forward and slugged him again, this time a roundhouse to the jaw. That put him down, sprawled on his back like a dead man.

Several bystanders had gathered by now. The man began to cough and wheeze, rolled his head to one side, and spit out four jaw teeth. Dad bent over, scooped up the teeth, calmly dropped them in his pocket, and walked away.

He kept the teeth for trophies, but Dad would pay for that one. The man sued him, and because the bystanders had seen Dad swing first, the judge fined him seventy-five dollars. That was to a lot of money in those days, and certainly more than he could afford, but Dad said it was worth it. When he told the story he'd grin and say, "Ya know, when I saw that guy down at the courthouse, his head was swelled so bad his nose was plumb over on the side of his face."

Dad fared much better another time when he was only a spectator at a fight. He was sitting in a dusty pool hall on Main Street, chatting with some other guys, when two men began to argue over a game of billiards. The argument soon became heated. The men began to holler and shove each other, and started throwing punches. Things got louder and the fight got rougher. The two knocked each other all over the pool hall, cussing, throwing chairs, falling down, and turning tables over. Dad folded his arms and watched from his seat, enjoying the show.

It got better. One of the men grabbed a cue stick off the rack and began whacking the other over the head. To Dad's amazement the fellow absorbed several punishing blows from the cue stick without going down. He did begin to tire of it, however, so he pulled out a big .45 revolver and retaliated. He didn't shoot the other guy though, instead he waded in and started clubbing him in the head with the gun.

The two men exchanged blows for several minutes as Dad watched. All three had hard heads. After a while Dad looked around and discovered that he and the two fighters were the only ones left in the pool hall. Everyone else had scattered when the pistol came out.

The man with the cue stick managed to whack the other one in the hand and knock his pistol to the floor. Dad saw where the gun slid, walked over, picked it up, and stuck it in his belt. He then sat back down and continued to watch the fight.

A few minutes later the sheriff came through the door, nodded at Dad, broke up the fight, and took the two off to jail. The next morning Dad told the sheriff about the .45 the fellow had dropped during the fight. By then the sheriff had learned that the man was a fugitive, and was holding him for federal authorities. "Keep the gun," he told Dad. "He won't need it where he's goin'."

Dad got himself a free pistol, the prize for being the most interested spectator. He said it had patches of hair and blood left in it from the fight. It was a huge gun, a Colt .45 army revolver. Dad kept it the rest of his life and carried it in his automobiles for years.

He loved that pistol, though his shooting prowess indicated he should probably have used it as a club himself. He did shoot it at times, his shots going pretty much in random directions when he did. Dad shot pistols and rifles all his life, and to my knowledge no one ever claimed to have seen him hit a thing.

Dad felt no attachments to any particular religion, but Mary Josephine had been raised Catholic. She was adamant that Mary and Helen attend Catholic high schools. Dad argued against it, but in the end Helen went to Pueblo, Colorado, and Mary to Denver. After Helen graduated she worked in a Pueblo hospital as a nurse's aide. Mary stayed in Denver, where she lived the rest of her life.

The economy continued to worsen, and work became harder and harder for Dad to find. Mary Josephine began doing other people's laundry and ironing to help keep food on the table.

One year when Mom was a little girl she badly wanted a Christmas tree, a luxury they couldn't afford. She found a piece of a broken one lying by the railroad tracks and carried it home. It was a pitiful sprig only a foot high, just the very top of a Christmas tree.

She happily carried it into the house and stood it up in the coal bucket, then ran to get her mother. "Look Mama, I found us a Christmas tree," she said. Mary Josephine wept as Mom beamed at the pathetic symbol of their poverty.

Hard times were on them, but harder ones were on the way. They would get far worse before they ever got better. No matter how bad the times became, however, Dad worked to pay off his debts. He never forgot one, even if it took him years to pay it off.

Buying land wasn't a possibility for Dad as they struggled through the next several years. In months when he couldn't make the house payment, the bank allowed him to just pay interest. He may have been poor and had little education, but through the years Dad earned the respect of the most influential men in town.

In 1928 Mary Josephine began to have abdominal pains that wouldn't go away no matter what she took to relieve them. She talked to Helen at the hospital in Pueblo and decided to go there to have some tests run.

Dad and Mom took her to the train station. She told them goodbye, not to worry about her, and waved through the window as the train set off for the three-hour trip west.

The following day Dad received a puzzling phone call from Helen. "Dad, Mother's taken sick," she said, "and I think you should come up here as soon as you can."

"What's wrong?" Dad asked with concern. "How bad is she?"

Helen's voice quavered, "They don't know what's wrong for sure. You just need to come up right away."

Dad and Mom hurried to catch the next train for Pueblo. When Mom asked him what was wrong with her mother, he told her he didn't know. Helen had just said she'd gotten sick and that they should come right away.

The excitement of a train trip distracted Mom, but Dad stared out the window, strangely quiet. Sometime along the way she looked over and saw tears in his eyes. She'd never seen him cry before. Suddenly distressed, she asked, "What's wrong, Dad?"

He burst into tears. "I think Helen just didn't want to tell me," he sobbed. "I'm afraid your mother's already gone."

And indeed she was. During the testing she'd had an allergic reaction to a test solution and died within a matter of minutes.

Mary Josephine was gone. Dad was stunned when he saw her body, and wouldn't leave her. He and Mom rode in the train with her casket back to Lamar, and when they arrived he wouldn't allow her to be taken to the mortuary. He brought Mary Josephine home to lie in their living room until the funeral. When Mom asked him why he'd brought her mother there, he said, "I can't stand to think of her layin' down there on a cold slab." Mom would wake up at night and see him in the living room sitting with her.

Mary Josephine's pallbearers represented a cross-section of people, from the wealthiest civic leaders to the poorest folk in town. Mom's sisters and family friends had to help her through the funeral. Dad wept uncontrollably, unable to contain his grief. He became so distraught at the graveside service that he asked to have her casket opened again, begging to see her one more time. Mary managed to console him and talked him out of it.

Mary, self-assured, forward, and outspoken, the one who inherited Dad's need to run the show, went back to Denver where she married and raised a family.

Helen, the plucky, spunky girl, went to school after her mother's death, first to become a registered nurse, then a nun. As a youngster she'd been fun-loving and mischievous, full of life. The adult Helen lived mostly in seclusion—devout, studious, and cynical. The laughing, daring eyes that dance from her teenage pictures became hard, stoic, and aloof. A lifetime later, years after Helen died at the age of seventy-three, we learned her astonishing secret. She had given her mother the injection that took her life, never guessing that a reaction would kill her within minutes. Helen lived with that dreadful secret all her life.

Dad was fifty-three years old when Mary Josephine died; Mom was fourteen. The Great Depression would be on them within a year. He managed to keep their house and provided what money he could, but Mom faced lonely years without her mother. During that time Dad often worked late or out of town, and she had to stay alone in the red brick house.

Dad brought his parents from Missouri to be with Mom after her mother died, but they stayed only about two weeks. He pleaded with them to stay longer for Mom's sake, but Squire refused, and they went back to Missouri.

Within months of Mary Josephine's death, Dad found a road-building job that would last for several months and provide some welcome money. Unfortunately it took him out of town and left Mom alone. Dad sent her money while he was gone, wrote letters to her, and signed them with love. He also visited her when he could, but he didn't get weekends off. She looked for him more often than he came.

Mom wasn't totally alone, however. Several families that knew Dad befriended her, sharing their meals, their homes, and their hearts with her. They included Mexican families, white families, a black family, and a single lady. They became her extended family and helped her through those lonely years.

Dad's new job took him to the town of Walsenburg in south-central Colorado, where he became the foreman of a large road-building project. Road construction was hard work and naturally attracted some pretty rough characters. As foreman, Dad had to hire men, train them to operate the equipment, and boss them. In order to supervise he had to physically dominate anyone who tried to buck his authority.

The main piece of earthmoving equipment used in road building was the fresno, a horse-drawn implement that scooped a load of dirt from one place, hauled it to another, and dumped it. The fresno was a tube-shaped iron bucket four to six feet wide, closed on the ends and open at the front. As a team of horses dragged the fresno along the ground, a blade at the bottom of the opening scooped earth into it. An iron lever five to six feet long extending from the back allowed the operator to tilt the bucket at various angles.

The operator walked behind the fresno, driving the horses with one hand and operating the lever with the other. By moving the lever up he could tilt the bucket forward and scoop dirt into it. Then he moved it down to tilt the bucket back and hold the dirt in while he hauled it to another location. Moving the lever back up tilted it forward again and dumped the load out. A skillful operator could manipulate the lever to leave a smooth surface where he scooped the earth in and spread it smoothly over a wide area when he dumped it out.

Fresno operation was an art form with Dad. He could drive four horses with one hand and operate a fresno with the other so smoothly that the entire process became a continuous, fluid motion.

Dad stood on a high mound of earth one day, smoking a cigar and watching the work in progress. He saw a dark-skinned boy approaching in the distance, barely a teenager. The boy walked up the mound, stopped in front of him, smiled politely, and asked, "Sir, do you have any jobs available?" Dad looked coolly down his cigar, studying the boy. He wasn't yet grown, not five and a half feet tall, and he looked neither stout nor tough. His bright eyes and full, tan face with high cheekbones looked more friendly than tough.

As Dad sized him up, the boy met his steady gaze. "How old are ya, son?" he asked.

"Fourteen, sir," came the honest reply.

"Ya ever done this kind of work before?"

"No, sir. I've never had a chance to learn anything like this."

"What nationality are ya, son?"

"I'm an Indian, sir."

"What's your name?"

"Jack Beatty, sir. What's yours?"

Dad paused. "George Blizzard," he said.

Something about the boy impressed Dad. He had an honest, straightforward manner, and he looked you dead in the eye when he talked to you. "What kind of job you lookin' for, Jack?" he asked him.

"Anything, George. I'll have to learn whatever you want me to do, but I'll do it."

"Follow me," Dad said, and walked toward the horse shed. He harnessed a team of horses while Jack watched his every move, then hitched them to a fresno and drove to an area where a crew was building a road grade. "Now watch what I do," he told Jack. The other operators pulled their teams to the side and stopped, staring at the pint-sized Indian boy getting a private lesson from the boss.

Dad put the team through its paces, scooping up a load of dirt, hauling it to the road, and dumping it evenly over the grade. He made several rounds with the fresno, each one an exact repeat of the one before. Jack watched him intently. Dad spread a final load, stopped the team beside the boy, and handed him the reins. Jack took the reins, stepped behind the fresno, and began a new life.

He had never held a set of reins in his hands before, but he snapped them at the team, hollered "Hee-yah," and started them off. Heedless of an entire crew of men watching, Jack concentrated on the reins in his left hand and the lever in his right. His first round was bumpy, and he didn't dump the load evenly, but the next one was better. Each round steadily improved. Within thirty minutes Jack was working the horses, filling the fresno, and spreading dirt over the roadbed like he'd been doing it for years. Dad and fifty men shook their heads as the boy mastered the craft before their eyes.

Jack needed a place to stay while he worked, so Dad shared his quarters with him. After he had worked for just a few weeks, Dad made him a crew boss. Jack was still only fourteen.

They were building the road in rugged terrain, and Dad had difficulty staying within the allotted time. He'd been meeting schedule though. He and Jack saved money by streamlining some procedures to speed up the work.

A pompous state inspector arrived one day and walked around the work site with Dad. He began to question the new procedures, so Dad explained that they worked fine and allowed them to build the road faster. The inspector swelled with importance. "No, no, no, Mr. Blizzard. This is not the way it's done. This will never do." That afternoon he called a halt to the operation.

Early the next morning the inspector continued his scrutiny and disparaging remarks. He questioned every detail imaginable while Dad followed him, addressing each question.

Jack and the other men sat idly watching the show. As the inspector strutted like a rooster, Jack wondered how long Dad would put up with him. Around noon that day he found out.

The two of them stood on the side of a road grade as Jack watched from a distance. Dad stood a foot or so below the inspector as the man criticized him and pointed at some infraction with an outstretched arm. Dad glared up at him, crouched low, and clenched his fist near the ground. Then he drove the fist upward in a long uppercut, catapulting his entire weight behind the swing. His fist connected under the man's jaw like a piston, driving him straight up off the ground. He came down like a limp rag, unconscious before he landed.

Jack jumped to his feet and ran to check the man's condition. His jaw lay wide open, split from chin to ear and bleeding badly, but miraculously it wasn't broken. Dad stared down at him, lit a cigar, and walked away.

The state sent another inspector, who stayed a prudent distance from Dad, spoke to him politely, and kept the job shut down for three more days while they tried to find another foreman to replace Dad. No one else would take the job though, so after wasting most of a week, Dad and the crew resumed work.

That job launched a career in heavy equipment for Jack. After he learned everything about horse-drawn machinery, he went on to learn mechanized equipment. His easygoing, congenial manner ultimately led to a senior sales position.

Jack visited Dad often for the rest of his life and spoke of him with reverence. Years after I was grown and Dad had passed on, I asked Jack how he had managed to boss a crew of rough men at the age of fourteen. He flashed a wide grin and told me what Dad had said when he put him in charge. "Now listen, you can boss 'em, but you can't whip 'em. If they give ya any trouble, I'll whip 'em."

1929, the Great Depression. The stock market crashed around the time Dad finished the road-building job. The hard times became harder. At fifty-four years old, he came home to stand in unemployment lines with hundreds of others. Morning after morning, month after month, he waited to see if he would be one of the few chosen to work the day for fifty cents. His debts mounted far beyond what he could pay.

The Depression ruined people, destroyed their dignity, killed their spirits. The most wretched of the hard times wore on for four years. Dad could seldom find any work. Mom said later it was the only time she ever saw him walk with his shoulders stooped.

Franklin D. Roosevelt became president in 1932 and set the government in motion to overcome the Depression. By 1933 Dad began to find more work—not a great amount, but more. In 1935 Roosevelt started the Works Progress Administration (WPA), a federally funded public works program designed to reduce unemployment. Dad quickly became a supervisor on the WPA, and though it didn't pay well it provided more security than he and Mom had known for years. Still using horse-drawn machinery, he helped build the city park, the high school stadium, and several other Lamar landmarks.

Dad once told a lazy man in his crew to get to work and stop loafing on the job. The man told him he didn't have to work if he didn't want to. "Then get outta here," Dad said. "You're fired." The man said Dad couldn't fire him from a WPA job.

"We'll see about that," Dad said, as he huffed into his car and drove to the WPA office.

As Dad sat in the office talking to the WPA administrator, the loafer walked in holding his hat in his hand. Looking at the floor, he said, "I'm sorry, Mr. George. I'll work for you."

"All right then, let's get back to work," he said.

Dad ended up far in debt as many did in those times, but some long-term relief became available to those in his situation. Due to a statute of limitations, many of the debts incurred during the Depression became legally invalid after seven years. If they hadn't been paid by that time the debts were taken off the books, the slate wiped clean to give people an opportunity to start over.

Dad kept his own records though, and his slate was never wiped clean until the debts were paid. It took him eighteen years to do it, but he paid off every dollar he owed.

When the first upswing from the Depression began in 1935, the faintest glimmer at the end of the tunnel, the old fighter reached up, grabbed the ropes, and pulled himself off the canvas. At the age of sixty, Dad rented a little piece of land outside of town, bought two cows, borrowed a bull, and aimed for his goal.

He went to work for the city of Lamar around the time he bought those two cows, and for the next eight years Dad worked, paid off debts, and built up a small herd on rental land. He attained the position of City Water Commissioner during those years, with responsibility for the city's water supply, streets, alleys, and cemeteries.

During the time Dad was working and building up his little herd, my brother and I came on the scene.

Mom and our father were married in 1934. Both in their early twenties and broke, they stayed in the red brick house with Dad until my brother, George, was born the following year. After George was born, they lived in little rental places for several years until World War II began in 1941, the year I was born.

Our father joined the navy and went off to war before I was a year old. In his absence Mom took George and me back to the red brick house to live with Dad again. We lived with him there for two years.

He had bought tiny cowboy boots for George and me when we were first born. He wasn't my Dad yet, but my earliest memories are of my grandfather. He took me everywhere with him, he let me puff on his cigars when I was barely big enough to hold one, and he called me Son.

Dad either anticipated the post-war boom or he got lucky, probably both. At the age of sixty-eight he took the plunge. He went to the bank president and told him he wanted to borrow enough money to buy four thousand acres of grassland and more cattle. The bank approved his loan, and Dad had his ranch at last. With that determined gleam in his eye that he'd carried a lifetime, he moved to the prairie.

He sold the red brick house when he bought the ranch, so Mom rented another little place and we waited for our father to return from the war.

The war years were hard on people, and hard on families. Two years after Dad moved to the prairie our father returned from the war, but not for long. He had difficulty coping with life when he came back, and he and Mom soon parted. He left Colorado when I was four and never returned. I would never know my father, or have any memory of him.

Mom had to make a decision about our lives after our father left. She had George and me to care for, and no means of support. She'd never worked at a full-time job, and had no special skills or job training. The thought of trying to make a living for us was surely a scary prospect, but that wasn't Mom's worst fear. She feared most for how George and I would grow up, for our future. If she worked full time, she knew we'd spend too much time alone as she had in her teens—that we would grow up "on the streets," in her words.

She had another option though, one that she knew would teach us values. Mom could take us to the prairie to live with Dad. She loved her father dearly, trusted him to provide financial security, and knew how to put up with his hard-driving ways. She knew that growing up with him would be a unique opportunity for George and me.

Mom didn't want to go to the prairie to live, however, and understandably so. Dad's ranch had few modern conveniences, and it lay three miles from the nearest highway. You couldn't see another house from his place, and a big hill blocked the view to the highway, completing the isolation. The prospect of living out there had little appeal for a single woman thirty-one years old. With practically no opportunity for social contact, it offered only isolation, hardships, and hard work.

But George and I had a chance to grow up under the influence of the best man she knew, and to Mom that outweighed all the drawbacks. She would spend countless hours, years, looking at that hill, wishing she were on the other side of it or hoping in vain to see company come over it, but she made the choice.

I was four the summer of 1945 when Mom took us to the prairie to live with her dad. He was seventy, and looked like he could fight a bear. His hair was snowy white, his face smooth and leathery, and those gray eyes meant what they said.

He wore a tall Stetson hat and high-heeled cowboy boots everywhere he went. An old weathered hat served for wearing on the ranch, but he kept a new one in a box to wear to town. Both were high-crowned Stetsons.

He wore a long-sleeved khaki shirt every day, and Levi denim pants with the cuffs rolled up several inches to accommodate his short legs. For special occasions he wore khaki pants and a khaki dress shirt. A worn leather jacket served for cool days, and an old wool sweater if he needed it. In cold weather he wore a great sheepskin-lined leather coat that reached to his knees.

George and I began to call him Dad about the time we moved to the prairie, and he was our Dad for the rest of his life.

Dad and Gary on the ranch, 1945

Chapter 3

HOME

The High Plains is prairie country, wild and remote, an endless sea of buffalo grass, skies that reach forever. A world of horizons—wide vistas roll into view thirty miles in the distance; rocky bluffs stand like fortresses. Broad hillsides glide into grassy bottoms half a mile wide—great troughs that drain the land when flash floods come—old-timers called them draws.

The land rolls in great waves—the coarse, grassy carpet dotted with sharp prickly pear, spiny yucca, patches of green thistles, and sand-blown fields of sage. A few scrub cedars, stunted and gnarled, cling to the rocky hillsides. Lone tree cactus, woody and wiry tough, stand solemn vigils over it all.

Sandy creeks nose through the prairie like wandering serpents. The creeks are too far apart to water herds of cattle, and they dry up between rains anyway. Great cottonwoods stand on the creek banks, willowy tamaracks hide in their bottoms. Trees seldom venture onto the prairie.

Whirlwinds spin high in the dry air, dancing their dusty jigs over the arid land. Wandering tumbleweeds roll by lean coyotes and over the backs of a million rattlesnakes. Keen-eyed hawks circle endlessly, hunting everything that moves: jackrabbits, cottontails, lizards, snakes, or careless prairie dogs that venture too far from their underground haven. Golden eagles soar higher, befitting their noble station, their primal screams piercing the miles. Dark vultures lurk to claim the waste.

The temperature range is extreme, from thirty below in the winter to one hundred ten in the summer—bitter cold to beastly hot. The weather is a demon, vicious and unpredictable; it can change in minutes. Natives watch the horizon on clear days.

Water, precious water. Rain is too rare, and when it does come it often falls in torrents, flooding the prairie and turning the draws into rivers hundreds of yards wide.

Wind. The wind and the prairie are one. The wind blows forever, too often and too hard. But thank God for the wind, and thank God for windmills. Windmills, those whirling sentinels played a lead part in the settling of the West. Neither people nor cattle could have survived without them.

Windmills. Those lone partners of the wild wind coaxed the precious fluid from deep underground. The lifeblood water flowed to the prairie on rivers of wind.

The High Plains—vast in size, hard in nature. One look tells you it's no place for the cowardly or the weak. If the pioneers couldn't read the land before they stopped, they quickly learned; they had to stand ready to battle it every day, or move on.

It isn't all harshness and hardships though; the prairie possesses a beauty of its own. Even in the hard winter a new-fallen snow is a wondrous sight, peaceful, serene, a million diamonds sparkling in the sun, an unmarred blanket of pure white stretching forever.

When the long winter ends, the prairie springs to life. The hearty prairie lark tends its tiny nest hidden in the grass and prickly pear. The meadowlark's joyous song welcomes the cactus blooms, brilliant reds, yellows, and golds that rival any rose. When that vast carpet turns from cold brown to spring's warm green, the land begs forgiveness for winter's travails.

And God's own sunsets. They set the western horizon ablaze at evening's last light. Crimson spires reach high into the dying sky, setting the undersides of clouds afire and igniting their rims in vermilion and gold. Prairie days may tire the body and test the soul, but their spectacular farewell renews the spirit, and reminds one of the honesty of it all.

Electricity had been around for generations by the time Dad became a rancher, and the age of television was about to dawn, but not on that prairie. No one had electricity, indoor plumbing, or telephones. The dim glow of kerosene lamps provided what light the houses had, and pot-bellied coal or kerosene stoves heated them. Windmills supplied water for people and livestock, and the outhouse stood a short run from the house.

Dad's ranch was south of town, fourteen miles on the highway, and three more east on a prairie road. Prairie roads were simply two parallel tracks, ruts worn into the ground by the wheels of vehicles passing over them.

The ranch was roughly rectangular in shape, around three miles long by two miles wide. The four thousand acres formed an irregular pattern broken into three pastures and two fields. The two largest pastures covered more than three thousand acres between them, while the third, much smaller, was only one hundred and sixty. The fields covered five hundred acres and one hundred and sixty acres respectively.

Three different prairie roads accessed the ranch, two from the highway to the west, and another from a graded county road to the east. We seldom used the east route, as it required driving nearly all the way to town on dirt roads before reaching the highway. The choice of roads didn't make much difference anyway; whichever you chose meant opening and closing three barbwire gates and driving through a creek to reach the highway.

The fourteen miles of highway ran absolutely straight all the way to town. The prairie roads ran straight in some portions and wound like snakes in others. They were passable in good weather, but a different matter in rain, snow, or melting snow.

Clay Creek ran between the ranch and the highway. Most of the time the creek was either dry or running a very small stream. Our roads all crossed the creek bed in one of its smoother portions. As the crossings tended to get soft and muddy, we'd sometimes haul truckloads of gravel to dump on them. That usually helped, until the next time the water rose and washed the gravel away.

The creek was on our minds at the first sign of rain or snow. How much rain would fall? How much snow would fall? The creek could rise and isolate us by running bank-full of water, or it could fill with several feet of snow.

Even after the water receded from flood stage, the creek bottom stayed too muddy to cross for at least a couple of days. If the crossing drifted full of snow, we had to either break through it with a tractor or a team of horses, or shovel a hell of a lot of snow. Even if the snow didn't completely fill the creek, when it began to melt, here came the mud.

It felt exhilarating the morning after a big snow, to drive up to the creek, stop, look down at a huge drift in the bottom, and wonder what your chances were of busting through. Maybe if you backed up and took a running start at it. Dad liked that method. He nearly always tried it first, instantly converting his pickup into a battering ram.

He'd back up about fifty yards, grip the wheel with both hands, clench his teeth, eye the drift narrowly, and run at it like a knight on a charger. It usually didn't work. Roaring down into the creek bed, his screaming pickup would ram the drift, plow a fountain of snow twenty feet in the air, and jolt to a stop, buried so deep the doors wouldn't open. No big problem though; we could usually dig it out within half a day.

The prairie soil—God must have been feeling impish the day he created it. Composed of extremely fine silt, it forms the slickest mud imaginable, almost like grease. The slick mud was always fun to work in, as it becomes nearly impossible to walk without falling down and sledding along on your backside ten or twenty feet. Its effect on the prairie roads and creek crossings didn't enhance the driving either. The challenge was like driving a vehicle on polished glass.

Two old houses stood on Dad's land, both built by homesteaders. The one he lived in was two miles from the highway; the other was three. Dad's house was a simple little three-room frame structure built around 1900. The kitchen was in the middle, with a living room and bedroom on either end. It was a very small house; all three rooms covered only about six hundred square feet.

A grove of trees surrounded Dad's house, an unusual sight on the prairie. Most houses had very few trees, if any. A cave cellar and a wooden outhouse sat close by. A barn, a long shed, three corrals, a feed storage building, a granary, chicken house, windmill, and two water tanks completed the place.

A mile north of Dad's place stood a crumbling rock house, probably built around the 1880s. It was considerably larger than Dad's house, but at around a thousand square feet it really wasn't that big itself. Austere and imposing on the stark prairie, the rock house had stood there alone for sixty or seventy years, and sat vacant for the last thirty or forty.

Three other deserted structures stood with the rock house: a dilapidated barn, a falling chicken house, and a creaky windmill.

Piles of tumbleweeds rested against them all. A forlorn little elm tree stood by the windmill. A twisted and battle-worn eight feet high, it was the only tree on the place. Rivulets of dust blew across the dirt yard that had never known a lawn. Not even buffalo grass grew there now.

As my four-year-old eyes took in the forsaken scene, I couldn't know that this house, this place, would forever mean home to me.

The house was made of sandstone blocks, stacked one on another and sealed with mud. Its six rooms included a living room, dining room, kitchen, and three bedrooms. The living room faced west, the kitchen east, and the dining room sat in the middle. A bedroom adjoined each one. The living room opened onto a crumbling front porch, while an awkward back porch clung to the other end of the house.

Some of the rocks had separated and fallen out. Portions of walls had fallen down, as well as most of the front porch. Dad hired some help from town to repair the stonework. They rebuilt the front porch, put the fallen rocks back in place, and cemented everything together.

The Rock House—home from 1945 to 1957

We received a grand welcome to the prairie the day we arrived, quite appropriately, from three rattlesnakes. Mom looked out the door and saw them lying only a few feet away, sunning themselves by the fallen front porch. She wasn't about to share her new home with rattlesnakes. She walked back in the house, loaded a rifle, and shot them all.

Those rattlers were practically an omen. We quickly learned how numerous they were, and that they were simply a part of life on the prairie. We had to watch for snakes constantly during the spring, summer, and fall.

The old place needed much improvement. We put up several new buildings during the first few years and repaired the old ones. Dad hired a man from town to do general work much of the time during those years, and on occasion he hired more than one.

Our most memorable hired man, and the one who worked for us the longest, was a good-natured, benign old guy named Bill Lock. Life hadn't treated Bill very well, and Bill didn't treat Bill very well. In town he spent most of his time drunk, and sometime in his life somebody had bitten off half of one of his ears, but when he came out to work for us he stayed sober. He nipped a little in the evening, but he was ready to work in the morning.

Bill was a capable man; he could do any job. He had only one speed, however, and that was slow. You couldn't hurry him. That about drove Dad nuts, but he grumbled and put up with him because he knew when Bill finished a job it would be done to perfection.

Of all the projects that needed to be done when we moved there, we had no trouble deciding which one came first. We didn't have an outhouse, and when you don't have one of those, you really need one. But even though we needed it badly, we didn't rush the job. We wouldn't compromise on quality. Our outhouse was special from the start.

A regular, everyday outhouse was a simple wooden building that sat over a hole about six feet deep. A wooden bench sat inside the outhouse with a toilet hole cut in the top. The purpose of the hole, of course, was to sit upon. The board walls of most outhouses had large cracks and knotholes in them. The extra ventilation was all right in the summertime, but terribly excessive in the winter.

We made our outhouse first-class, building the walls of tightly mortared cement blocks. Those stout walls would hold back the elements, at least more so than boards would. Some snow did get through the wooden door, and occasionally the wind blew it open when one least desired such exposure, but our outhouse was still the talk of the county. We even made it a "two-holer," installing a wide bench with two holes of different diameters, custom made to accommodate bottoms of various sizes and ages. Many folks settled for less; they had only a one-holer. Not us. We figured you only live once.

A new barn, chicken house, granary, and pigpens completed the place. I planted a second elm tree in the yard when I was six, a seedling. Some fifty years later, it and the original tree are still the only two there. The original stands around fifteen feet high now; the seedling I planted is ten feet. Those two little trees must hold some kind of endurance record on that dry prairie.

The interior of the rock house was not fancy by any measure: patched plaster walls, bare ceilings that had never known light fixtures, and linoleum-covered floors. Small throw rugs lay beside our beds for cold mornings. In order to keep the front and back doors from blowing open in high winds, we jammed the blade of a strong table knife between the door casing and the wall, leaving the handle to overlap the door and hold it shut. A hard wind would force the door open a finger width and make the knife hum like a tuning fork.

A tall kerosene heating stove stood in a corner of the dining room, the most central spot in the house. In winter when the wind whistled through the ill-fitting doors and windows, all the chairs were gathered around the stove.

The nicest thing in the house was an upright piano in a corner of the living room. Mary Josephine had bought the piano before she met Dad, and he'd had to finish paying for it after they were married. For as long as he lived, Dad never tired of pointing that out.

Dad lived in his little house for four more years, then moved into the rock house with us. We always called his old place "Dad's Place," even after he no longer lived there.

The weather on the High Plains is unpredictable, and can turn on you quickly. That first summer we learned how suddenly nature can bring on a storm.

Rain is a premium in arid country, so when clouds began to form that day we thought we might be in for some welcome moisture. The clouds started gathering faster, the sky darkened quickly, and the wind began to blow from the north. Within minutes the sky grew black and angry. Lightning bolts speared the ground, thunder cracked, and the wind blew harder and harder. The north windows began to rattle.

Hard rain began. Large drops smacked the windows loudly. The big raindrops landed far apart at first, a sign that often precedes hail. The drops grew dense, and the wind and rain pounded our north windows until water ran down the glass in sheets.

Then the hail came. Ice poured from the sky into the wind. Hailstones the size of golf balls fell by the ton, the hard wind catching them and whipping them sideways like a tremendous fan. As they neared the earth they flew parallel to the ground, coming at the house in a solid, white mass.

Loud crashes—shattering glass flying through the house—the hail took out our north windows, all of them. Hailstones filled the air, flying across the rooms and hammering the inside walls like machine-gun fire. Lampshades exploded, pictures fell from the walls; glass, magazines, and papers flew everywhere.

Mom grabbed me and dropped to the floor to shield me. I was not yet five, but I knew the world was coming to an end. She sat me behind a chest of drawers and ran to help Dad and George. They grabbed blankets off the beds and leaves from the table, and held them to the windows to deflect the hail.

The wind and hail began to die as quickly as they had come, and in a few minutes it was over. The clouds went away, the wind calmed, and the sun came out again.

We'd all been whacked by a few hailstones, but no flying glass had hit us. In that few minutes, however, the inside of our house had been wrecked. It was a jumble of broken glass, hail, and scattered belongings, and everything we owned was wet.

Hail wasn't our only surprise that summer. A wide gully ran just south of the house, a broad, shallow trough we called the draw. Simply a long, winding depression in the landscape, the draw was several hundred yards wide with a soft, grassy bottom.

When we built our first pigpens, the draw looked like the perfect place to locate them. We soon had nearly a dozen pigs living in pens and sheds in the draw, and it seemed to work well.

A few months after we built the pens, the pounding of hard rain woke me in the night. Over the pouring rain I could hear a faint roar in the distance. I got out of bed and saw Mom and George on the front porch. Lightning flashed, thunder clapped, and a strong wind whistled around the house. When I opened the door to join them on the porch, the roar and the storm were so loud we had to shout into each other's ears to be heard.

The roar was a torrent of water running in the draw. A flash flood had turned the draw into a raging river. Lightning flashes lit up the night, and by that light we could see the water running two hundred yards wide by our house, an eerie sight on the dry prairie.

We could see the edge of the running water fifty yards from us. We stayed up the rest of the night in case the water reached the house, but it never did.

The water roared on through the night. At dawn the rain had slowed, but the draw still ran full. Daylight revealed the flood's devastation. The pens, the sheds, and all the pigs had washed away. The water had carried everything a quarter of a mile, until it entered a flatter area in the field west of the house and lost its force.

From the front porch we could see torn remnants of the pigpens spread out over several acres of the field. Across the draw and downstream, at the water's far edge, we saw what appeared to be a line of dots. The dots turned out to be our pigs. A quarter of a mile away, the pigs sat in a line on the bank, staring at the running water. All had managed to swim to high ground, and all survived.

After the water receded, we saw that several rocks as big as barrels had washed down the draw and out into the field. The rocks weighed several hundred pounds each and had to be pulled from the field with a tractor.

Old-timers called those prairie floods gully washers. Had we known what to look for before we built the pigpens, we could have seen that a large area drained into the draw. Erosion from gully washers over the years is what had formed the draw in the first place.

The pigs were tired and dirty when the water receded, and homeless. We built new pens and sheds for them, this time on higher ground. They smiled and grunted their satisfaction, but I think some of them rolled their eyes too, wondering why we hadn't figured that out before the flood.

Chapter 4

MOM AND THE PRAIRIE

I was taking a nap one sunny afternoon that first summer. A window by the head of my bed stood open as I slept. The sharp crack of a gunshot woke me. I looked out the window and saw Mom, standing over a dead rattlesnake with a .22 rifle in her hand.

The snake had crawled into the window sill while I slept and coiled itself a foot from my head. Mom looked in the room and saw the rattler lying there by me. She knew it would arouse the snake if she woke me, and that it might strike before she could snatch me out of its reach. Instead she got the rifle and went outside. She reached into the window opening with the rifle barrel, dragged the rattler out, and shot it.

As the snake writhed in its death throes, she showed me where it had lain coiled by my head. I was only four, but I can still see her standing over that rattler with a rifle in her hand.

Mom's childhood photographs reflect a happy little girl with an impish grin. That grin came from deep within, from a sunny nature that life could never dampen.

She was a dark-haired, slender, attractive lady with lively eyes, a ready smile, and an easy laugh in familiar surroundings, but tempered with a quiet caution around strangers. Her unassuming manner belied a strength that even she didn't seem aware of, and a strong self-confidence that only adversity or a confrontation would bring to the surface.

Mom's indomitable spirit had helped her through a difficult childhood; now it would help her survive the prairie. She had felt that life on the ranch would be tough when she made the decision to go. Her premonitions soon proved correct.

The windmill, which was about thirty yards from the house, supplied our water. The windmill pumped the water into a wooden barrel that served as our water supply. When the barrel was full, it overflowed into a livestock watering tank.

Two or three buckets of water sat on a bench in the kitchen, where we dipped water from them for cooking, drinking, and washing. George and I had to carry the buckets out to the barrel and refill them as often as necessary, about a hundred times a day it seemed.

Though we didn't have electricity, we had a refrigerator. It stood tall and white, and in the top it had a cold compartment for ice the same as any other refrigerator. It didn't have a light in it, however, and one other difference—it burned kerosene. To my amazement, a fuel-saturated wick burned in the bottom, and if the flame went out the refrigerator wouldn't stay cold. Years later I learned how it worked, but it certainly didn't make any sense at the time.

The refrigerator was temperamental. Mom always looked at it with suspicion and checked the temperature often. When it started acting up, she could fix it. She'd eye it narrowly and say, "That damn thing," back up, and kick it. After she kicked it several times it usually started working. That amazed me too.

The lamps in every room also burned kerosene. They weren't as temperamental as the refrigerator, but they had to be refilled daily, the lampshade cleaned, and the wick trimmed.

The kitchen stove burned propane, piped in from two large metal bottles that sat beside the house. A little hole in the rock wall accommodated the copper gas pipe and let in the cold as well. That old gas range was the most modern thing in Mom's kitchen.

Although the heating stove sat in the middle of the house, it still didn't heat very well in the coldest part of winter. In order to concentrate the heat in the dining room and living room, we kept the bedroom doors closed until just before bedtime. That heated the rest of the house better by sacrificing the heat in the bedrooms. At bedtime we'd run in and jump under the covers. The bed felt like ice, so we'd lie perfectly still until our spot began to get warm. We used lots of blankets.

We turned the stove down low at bedtime; otherwise it would run out of fuel before morning. Our breath blew clouds of vapor when we woke, and on the coldest mornings we'd find the water buckets in the kitchen frozen over.

Mom's washing machine sat on the old back porch. A breezy, unpretty thing, the porch had partial walls only waist high. The space between the low walls and the roof was spanned by screen wire.

The wind just whipped on through. The washing machine was an old Maytag, powered by a noisy gasoline engine mounted between its four legs. The engine chugged and sputtered as it ran, and vibrated the entire machine. It had a kick starter that often kicked back, and a long exhaust pipe that extended off the porch. The pipe kept the engine from gassing the operator.

Washday was an all-day task and required a great amount of hot water. For Mom to get that much hot water took some innovation. Somewhere she found a big cast iron pot for sale, about four feet in diameter. The pot weighed around two hundred pounds, so heavy it took several men to load it in her pickup. Mom hauled it home, and we dumped it in the yard. Now she had a way to heat her wash water.

On washday George and I carried water from the barrel to fill the iron pot, about fifty buckets of it. Mom then banked wood around the base of the pot and built a fire under it. When the water was hot we bucketed it from the pot to the washing machine, twice. One machineful for washing, and another for rinsing.

Mom hung the laundry on an outdoor clothesline to dry. In the summer the clean clothes were plastered by duststorms, and in the winter they often froze stiff.

One washday morning Mom walked out to the big iron pot, looked in it, and hollered, "Who put these frogs in here?" She really didn't have to ask; I'd forgotten about the frogs. As she glared at me and my frogs, I quickly returned them to their natural habitat.

Mom ran a small side business to supplement our income. She sold cream, eggs, and frying chickens to regular customers in town. She raised the chickens, killed them and cleaned them herself; canned and sealed the cream in pint jars; and cleaned and boxed the eggs. Besides providing extra money, it ensured that she got to go to town at least once a week to make her deliveries.

She was happy to get to go to town for any reason. As most of her customers were also her friends, she'd sit down and chat with them for a few minutes when she had the time. They all had electricity, plumbing, television, and social lives. They didn't work as hard as she did, and they didn't make their own dresses from printed feed sacks.

Mom canned food every summer to help get us through the winter. Several things happened at canning time: the kitchen became a maze of pots, pans, and pressure cookers; Mom became short-tempered; and George and I had to bucket a hell of a lot of water to the house.

She didn't have the time, inclination, or shade to raise a garden, but she bought vegetables to can, and cucumbers to make pickles. Several neighbors and friends gave her vegetables from their gardens, and people who liked to fish but didn't eat them saved their fish for her.

She'd clean the fish, cook them in a pressure cooker, and can them. In the winter we had canned fish along with her vegetables and pickles. She made fried patties that looked much like salmon patties and tasted delicious. In Colorado they weren't salmon, however; they were catfish patties.

The few inhabitants of the plains lived so far apart they seldom saw each other, but once a year a popular event drew them together way out on the prairie, the Old Settler's Picnic.

Its name came from an event the homesteaders began in the 1800s. They all gathered in the summer to have a picnic, a social. Everyone ate lots of food, the kids played, the ladies talked and sewed, and the men sneaked drinks, laughed, argued, and occasionally bloodied each other up.

The Old Settler's Picnic was still a big thing when George and I were kids. It had grown somewhat from its original form but hadn't changed in spirit. No longer just a picnic, it was now a rodeo and a dance as well, and an all-day affair. People came from as far as sixty or seventy miles away in cars, trucks, pickups, and on horseback. They gathered at a wide creek bed with big shade trees, thirty miles south of the nearest town, Holly, Colorado, and forty-five miles from Lamar. A rustic rodeo ground sprawled on the prairie beside the creek, and an old dance floor made of rock and mortar hid under the big trees. A barbwire fence ringed the open dance floor; this kept cattle from walking on it, or leaving something on it.

The old rodeo ground made a perfect setting: rambling fences of loose boards and sagging wire; wooden chutes that threatened to burst as bulls and broncs reared and pawed inside them; a dusty, trampled arena overlooked by long, droopy bleachers that sat open to the elements.

Mom loved the rodeo. It featured every contest imaginable. The rodeo rules were variable, mostly unofficial, and sometimes made up on the spot. Anyone could enter any event; it took only courage to qualify. Spectators hollered from the bleachers and waved their hats as young cowboys with more guts than good sense climbed onto the backs of wild broncs and huge, fierce bulls, gave the motion to open the chute, and struggled to stay on their heaving backs until that interminable whistle blew. Then, whether or not they were still on the animal's back, they had one more small problem to deal with. They had to get to their feet and make it over the fence before the bull gored them or the bronc trampled them into the dirt. Even the animals had a chance to score.

One year Mom won the skillet-throwing contest. A man carried a straw-filled dummy out into the middle of the arena. It had on bib overalls, a red shirt, a straw hat, and a silly painted grin. The man leaned the dummy on a pitchfork to stand it up, walked about sixty feet away, and held a cast iron skillet in the air. "Ladies," he hollered, "this here's a skillet-throwin' contest. Stand over here and knock that guy down, and ya win two bucks."

Mom jumped up, waved her arm in the air, and hollered, "I'll do it."

She stepped off the bleachers and walked to the arena with a purpose. Mom was going for the gold. She took the skillet from the man, turned, and flashed a big grin to the crowd. Somebody hollered, "Get 'im, Lois." Mom turned toward the dummy, eyed it narrowly, and began to swing the skillet around and around her head.

She let fly. The heavy skillet winged across the arena and found its mark. It caught the dummy square in the stomach and knocked it flat. The crowd jumped to their feet, cheering, clapping, and hollering wildly. The man tipped his hat to Mom and handed her two dollars. She turned to the crowd, flashed another big grin, held the two dollars high, and bowed grandly.

Kerosene lanterns came out in the evening after the rodeo ended. That's when the dance started. Mom loved to dance, and somewhere she had learned to do it well. All the men knew she was good at it and danced with her until she was exhausted. Then she danced some more.

The band was made up of two, three, or four guys with guitars, fiddles, and beautiful singing voices. They stood on one corner of the hard dance floor, strummed, fiddled, tapped their feet, and wailed mournfully as folks in cowboy hats and boots shuffled past them, whirled around and around, swung their arms up and down, and seesawed their bodies back and forth in an exaggerated pumping action. Occasionally someone hollered, "Ah-haw!" overcome with the moment.

The men kept their bottles hidden under a sagebrush or yucca near the dance floor. Two or three at a time would be seen wandering out into the darkness, their serious faces indicating an important mission. Somehow their faces looked a bit less serious each time they returned.

Occasionally some loud hollering and cussing came from the darkness, accompanied by sharp whacks, shuffling feet, and falling bodies as old friends joined in knocking each other's teeth out.

The Old Settler's Picnic was a full day and had a little something for everybody. Mom was always tired when the day ended, but she smiled all the way home.

Mom and cooking never got along well. She was actually a good cook, but she didn't think so, and it wasn't her favorite thing to do anyway. Her meals tasted fine to us, but we stayed out of the kitchen when she prepared them.

One day when Bill Lock was working for us, Mom forgot several pie crusts baking in the oven until she smelled them burning. She ran into the kitchen, threw open the oven door, grabbed the baking sheet with the blackened crusts smoking on it, and ran for the back door, yelling her anger all the way. She ran out the door, through the back porch, hollered, "There, dammit!" and slung the crusts out into the yard.

Old Bill happened to be ambling up toward the house at that very minute. He heard Mom holler, looked up and saw those smoking missiles flying at him, whirled, and ran faster than I'd ever seen him move.

Mom was already stomping back toward the kitchen when she realized she'd caught a glimpse of Bill through the flying pie crusts. She went back out and saw him standing over against the yard fence, looking at her with suspicion, watching to see what else she might throw. A grin crossed her face, and then she broke out laughing. "I'm sorry, Bill," she said. "I just burned those pie crusts."

Bill grinned and shook his head. "I shore thought you was after me, Lois. I didn't know if I was gonna get back in the house again or not."

The unpredictable weather was always on our minds. It not only imposed hardships on us, it was hard on the cattle, horses, and other livestock as well. Regardless of how severe a storm became, we had to go out and feed the animals every day and see that they reached shelter.

Mom had an unusual fear of the weather, a fear she never overcame in all the years we lived on the prairie. She spent countless hours worrying about us when we were out fighting the storms. Several times each winter we became totally isolated in snowstorms. We called this being "snowed in." When we were snowed in we were completely on our own.

The sides of the dining room stove stayed very hot in cold weather; sometimes they glowed bright red. We were snowed in one cold evening when I was six years old. I backed up too close to the stove and swung my left arm against it. My entire lower arm, from wrist to elbow, stuck to the red hot stove. I screamed. I couldn't pull my arm away. Mom grabbed me, held me still to prevent tearing the skin, and slowly pulled my arm from the stove. Then she grabbed the butter off the table and rubbed it on my arm. Softening a burn with some sort of grease was an accepted treatment at the time.

It was not possible to get me to a doctor. Mom laid me in bed that night and held my arm so the bedcovers wouldn't touch the burn. She sat up all night beside the bed and held it while I slept. My arm healed with only a brown scar down the side, and even the scar faded away in a few years.

George contracted a serious ear infection when we were snowed in, and all Mom could do was try to comfort him and ease the pain. The infection finally broke in the middle of the night, and his fever went down, but he did suffer a slight hearing loss from it.

Mom gained years of experience in the practice of medicine while we were growing up. Working with cattle, horses, and machinery created prime conditions for accidents, and our own experiments didn't help either. George was smart and careful, so he didn't get hurt very often. I had a tendency to bore headlong into everything, however, which is not conducive to keeping yourself in one piece. I usually had several bruises and lacerations in various stages of healing at any given time. By the time I reached my teens, my body was about half covered with scar tissue, and Mom could handle anything short of open-heart surgery.

Our chicken house had burlap bags draped across the rafters for insulation. When I was eight, something in that unusual construction caught my attention. I noticed that one of the bags had a definite sag, as if weighted down by something on top. Curious as to what made it sag, I set about to solve the mystery. I knew that chickens often hid their nests and laid their eggs where they wouldn't be found, but that didn't occur to me at the time.

I dragged an old wooden box into the chicken house, positioned it under the sagging burlap bag, climbed onto the box, and pushed up on the sag. Sure enough, there was something in it. I had to know what it was. I took out my trusty pocket knife and slashed open the burlap. Eggs—rotten eggs—rained down on me. About a dozen broke all over me. Their green, slimy insides ran through my hair and down my clothes, all the way to my bare feet. The stench was horrible; they smelled like…rotten eggs.

Well, now I knew what had caused the sag, but I found myself in a curious condition. I walked to the house and in the kitchen door. Mom sniffed the air, looked at me, and hollered, "Get back out that door!" She followed me outside. "What happened to you?" she asked.

"Well," I began. I told her about spotting the sagging burlap and tried to explain why I had investigated it. She wasn't amused.

"You stay right here," she said, and stomped off. She came back with a washtub, dropped it beside me, and said, "Get those filthy clothes off and wait till I get back."

A few minutes later she returned with two buckets of hot water, a bar of soap, a wash cloth, and a towel. This was a first; I'd never taken a bath outside before. She poured the water into the tub, told me to get in, and set about scrubbing that nasty goo off of me. When she finished she handed me the towel. "Here, dry off," she said. "I'll be back." Then she stomped into the house to get me some clean clothes.

I dried myself off, picked up my clothes, still reeking from the eggs, and put them back on.

While Mom was inside getting clean clothes for me, it suddenly occurred to her that I might be out there putting the dirty ones back on. She came charging back out the door and stopped short.

I'd never had a spanking outside before either.

Mom was always determined that we learn to stand up for ourselves, even when we were little.

She was the only one who ever played the piano, except for a cat that liked to walk up and down the keyboard. When my cousin Wayne and I were both about six, we were sitting together listening to her play. We'd been told to sit still, of course, and to act like little gentlemen. We were sitting directly behind Mom, so she couldn't see us as she faced the piano. We had a problem; we were sitting side by side in two chairs, and only one of the chairs had arms on it. Having only a single armrest between us, we both wanted to use it. So while Mom played the piano, Wayne and I glared at each other and took turns pushing the other's arm off the armrest.

Wayne got tired of the arm shoving match, reached over, and socked me in the nose. Blood sprayed instantly. I howled, grabbed my nose, and ran for the kitchen. There I hung my head over the sink and continued to howl.

Mom followed me into the kitchen and asked me what had happened. "Wayne hit me in the nose!" I cried.

"Then why don't you go back in there and hit him in the nose?" she replied.

I cupped my bleeding nose again and walked back into the living room. There sat Wayne, with his arm on that armrest. I wound up and socked him in the nose, bloodied it, and we both went running back into the kitchen crying and holding our noses.

Mom couldn't help grinning as we both held our bleeding noses over the sink and howled.

Besides constantly worrying about the weather, Mom had another fear that made her life unpleasant on the ranch. She was afraid of horses, and especially afraid of riding them. As a child she'd fallen from a galloping horse, caught her foot in the stirrup, and been dragged a long way before her foot worked loose. Because of that experience, she always hollered at George and me as we rode away from the house, "Keep your feet out of the stirrups." And as ridiculous as it felt, and looked, we would ride off with our feet hanging down, the stirrups flapping against the horses' sides, until we were out of sight of the house.

Despite her fretting and worrying, Mom lent a peace to our lives and a tenderness that Dad seldom showed. Life with him was exciting, but it wasn't all that comfortable. Mom provided the comfort, an essential calm in the midst of Dad's intensity.

Mom in 1955

Mom in 1995

Chapter 5

GEORGE AND ME

George and I rode our horses every day, wild and free on the open prairie. We didn't have to play cowboys; we were cowboys. George loved that part of our life on the ranch. He rode beautifully, and he did cut a fiery figure charging across the prairie on a spirited horse.

His riding and roping impressed me, but the most memorable thing George ever roped was a yucca plant. Yucca plants, which abound on the prairie, are commonly called soap weeds because the Indians made soap from the roots. A yucca has a group of sharp spines one to two feet long radiating out from a central stem near the ground. The plant itself is only a foot or two high and two feet across, but it has a large root system designed to gather moisture in the arid climate.

On the surface a yucca plant gives no clue as to how well it is anchored to the ground. The root from a single yucca extends approximately four feet deep, beginning as a narrow neck near the surface and widening underground into a bulbous form three or four feet long and nearly a foot in diameter.

George had a spirited pinto named Champ at the time of the roping incident. He and his friend Larry were riding double on Champ that fateful summer day. In a single moment they would discover how strongly rooted a yucca is.

The whole thing began when George and Larry decided to see how fast Champ could run with both of them on his back. George rode in the saddle with Larry behind him, holding on with his arms around George's waist.

Champ was strong. Even carrying the two of them he could fly across the prairie. Things were going so well that George decided to try a little roping. He tied the end of his lariat to the saddle horn, so that whatever they roped couldn't get away from them, nor they from it. George leaned over Champ's neck as they charged along, holding the loop of the rope in his right hand, cowboy style.

Larry leaned with him, hanging on for dear life as they went galloping across the prairie, whooping and yahooing like wild buckaroos.

This home-grown Wild West show was traveling around thirty miles an hour when the lariat came into play. As they thundered past a big yucca, George coolly dropped the loop over it, figuring their forward momentum would simply yank the plant out of the ground. It didn't work exactly that way.

As Champ galloped on, the loop tightened around the base of the yucca, the rope pulled taut, and the plant didn't budge. It jerked Champ to a dead stop, whirled him sideways, and threw him to the ground. George and Larry continued to yell, the tone of their yells changing somewhat as they catapulted from Champ's back, flew wildly through the air, and hit the ground some twenty or thirty yards away.

With the wind knocked out of him and looking wild-eyed, Champ managed to climb back to his feet. The saddle no longer sat on his back. The rope had pulled it sideways and downward, forming the ridiculous picture of a horse with a saddle sticking straight out from his side. The taut lariat, still tied to the saddle horn, tethered him to the stout yucca.

George and Larry picked themselves up and tried to calm Champ down, telling him everything was okay. He wasn't buying any of that. He tried his best to run away, but the lariat and the stoic yucca wouldn't let him go. They had quite a time holding him while they loosened the saddle to straighten it back up.

The ride back to the house was far less glorious than the ride out. Champ wouldn't gallop, he wouldn't stand for any whooping and hollering, and he kept an eye on George to see that he didn't unwind that lariat again.

George received his own welcome to the prairie shortly after we arrived—from a rattlesnake, of course. In spite of rattlers and cactus, we often went barefooted in the summertime; all the kids who lived on the prairie did. George was running through the grass barefooted one day, only a hundred yards or so from the house, when he saw some old boards and other junk in his path. Dodging in and out to avoid them, he set his foot down on what he thought to be a shadow in the grass. His foot landed on something soft, and he felt movement. He bounded on a few more steps, stopped, looked back, and saw that it wasn't a shadow at all. It was a rattlesnake. He had stepped on a huge coiled rattler with his bare foot.

George surprised the rattler when he stepped on it, and didn't give it time to strike. Prairie rattlers are normally between two and four feet long, but that snake measured a full six feet. It was the biggest rattler we would see in all the years we lived there.

Rattlesnakes seemed to turn up everywhere. George and I were once walking along side by side as I told him a story, and since I was usually trying to tell him a story, he was probably trying to concentrate on something else. His eyes flashed just as I was about to set my bare foot down, and he shoved me hard with both hands. I flew sideways several feet, fell down, and plowed into the ground. George pointed at a rattler, coiled right where I'd been about to step. The snake had been poised to strike my foot when he spotted it.

Both of our grandfathers were named George, so the first-born was naturally named after them. I always envied my brother for that name.

George was my big brother, and my hero. My mind's image is of a lean, muscular teenager, dusty cowboy hat, shirtless, darkly tanned from building barbwire fence in the blistering sun. Movements quick and sure, dark eyes thoughtful and distant.

He loved to read, and he loved the solitude of the prairie where he could ponder his own thoughts and dream his own dreams. If Mom didn't know where George was, she knew he'd be curled up with a book. He sometimes appeared to be a loner, but in reality he kept good company. He ran with the likes of Hemingway, Steinbeck, and Melville before others his age dared approach them. George discovered his love of classic literature and poetry as a teenager. Later in life he laughed and told me he'd done his best to keep it a secret from his friends at school. He'd been afraid they'd think he was just a bookworm and not really one of the boys.

George learned to swim before we moved to the ranch, so when I was six or seven he taught me in our favorite swimming hole on the creek. During one of the lessons, I slipped off into a deep hole and felt the water rushing in over my head as I sank to the bottom. When my feet touched bottom I pushed myself upward as hard as I could. I broke the surface and screamed "Help!" George quickly swam over, pulled me to shallow water, and walked me up on the bank.

We sat down in the sand while I coughed up water and regained my breath. "God, I was scared," I told him. "The water came in over my head, and I couldn't get back up."

He listened, nodded his head, and after a few minutes asked, "Wanta go back in and try a little more?"

I shook my head. "No, I don't want to go back in now."

"You've been doing really well," he said. "Let's just go back in for a little while and mess around in the shallow water." I felt reluctant, but I went back in. George paddled along with me and talked me into ducking my head under water several times before we left. I had no lingering fears of water from that experience and learned to swim after a few more lessons.

George and I slept outside most nights during the summer. It was the only air conditioning we had, as the prairie cools off at night even in the hot summertime. It was a great feeling to look up at the stars before you went to sleep and listen to the coyotes howling in the distance.

We were sleeping on the front porch one moonlit night on a heavy iron cot. The floor of the porch stood about three feet off the ground and had no railing around it; it was completely open on three sides.

Sometime after midnight the wind began to blow. We woke up and looked at each other in the moonlight. The night had been calm until now, but we knew what crazy things the wind could do. We lay on our backs and waited to see what developed. It began to blow a little harder and started to tug at our sheets and blankets. They began to billow in the breeze, so we tucked them under our feet and clenched them in our fists.

Soon the gusts became a gale, blowing harder and harder until loose ends of the bedcovers started getting away from us, flapping loudly in the wind as we held on tightly. We kept glancing at each other and gripping the covers tighter and tighter, wondering how far this was going to go. In a couple more minutes we were both pretty wild-eyed, desperately clutching the wildly flapping covers that threatened to jerk out of our grasp and fly away. Finally, as if on cue, we both jumped up and ran into the house, dragging the sheets and blankets behind us. We looked back just in time to see the wind blow that iron cot right off the porch. We slept inside the rest of the night.

George was an idea man. From as early as I can remember he'd get an idea about something and wonder if I could do it. He was either awfully convincing in the way he proposed his ideas to me, or I was just dumb enough to agree to them. One thing about his ideas puzzled me; they always seemed to come to him when Mom and Dad weren't around.

George and Larry once got hold of an old parachute someone had brought back from the war. When I was about five, they persuaded me to jump off the roof of the chicken house with it. The chicken house roof was ten or twelve feet high, and being a fairly inexperienced parachutist at age five, I had severe doubts that the plan would work. But they both assured me it would. It didn't occur to me to ask them how they happened to know so much about parachuting.

They helped me up onto the chicken house roof and somehow strapped me into the rigging. Then they kind of spread the parachute out behind me, so it would pick up and catch the air when I jumped. At least that's how they explained it to me. I guess in theory it might have worked, maybe if the straps from me to the parachute hadn't been longer than the distance from me to the ground.

I got real antsy about it right at the end, looking down off the chicken house roof. But, I supposed everyone felt that way on their first jump. George and Larry stood down on the ground near my proposed landing spot, urging me on with various sorts of encouragement—jeering at me, calling me chicken, etc. Anyway, they finally convinced me.

Off I went.

My flight was short and certainly less glorious than those two had predicted. The parachute was still up on the roof when my rear end bounced hard on the ground. I started howling, because it hurt.

George consoled me. I imagine he felt sympathy for somebody dumb enough to try such a thing in the first place. Through the pain I remember him advising me on one last detail. "Don't tell Mom." I didn't tell her either. He might not have let me in on any more keen ideas if I had.

In truth, I can't blame George for coming up with those ideas. With somebody like me around, the urge to see what I would attempt was probably irresistible.

Another great idea. We had a gentle old milk cow named Lucy. Lucy was tamer than most cows; she was even somewhat affectionate. She'd walk up to you and stand and let you pet her, and she didn't give us as much trouble as the others did at milking time. Lucy being so tame, I guess George's inquisitive mind got to wondering if she might let someone ride her. More specifically, he got to wondering if she'd let me ride her.

One day when I was five or six, George asked me matter-of-factly, "Think you could ride old Lucy?" Why, I could ride a horse well at that age, so of course I could ride Lucy. What made him think I couldn't?

"Mister, you're lookin' at one of the ridin'est guys you ever saw," I thought to myself. I hooked my thumbs over my belt, reared my shoulders back, and said, "Sure I can ride old Lucy."

Since it was his idea, and I was the rider, I stood by and watched him prepare my mount for me. George walked Lucy into the barn, put a halter on her, and tied her to a post. We were ready to start; at least George and I were. Looking back on it, I don't believe Lucy was.

George had left the barn door open. I guess the plan was for

Gary and George, 1944

me to first ride her out through the door and then ride her around in the corral for a while.

"Ya ready?" George asked. I nodded professionally, and he lifted me up and set me on Lucy's back. She didn't do much at first. I remember the skin on her back kind of shuddering as I eased down on it, but otherwise everything seemed fine. George slipped the halter off and turned her loose, so I could ride her outside. I did ride her outside too, about as fast as I ever rode anything, anywhere.

Lucy jerked her head out of the halter and headed for the barn door faster than I'd ever seen a cow move. Too late, I realized a bareback cow has nothing to hang onto. I stayed with her as we charged toward the door, then out through the door and into the corral. That only took a second. Things changed quickly once we got outside. Lucy bucked, one time, high and hard. The ride was over. I sailed high into the air, turned in a wide arc, and whumped down on my rear end. By now I was learning how to land pretty well.

George ran over to console me, which I naturally appreciated. After I settled down he suggested we not tell Mom. Somehow I'd already figured that was part of the deal.

George waited until he was well along in years before he took up smoking. He was about twelve. My curiosity peaked at a more reasonable age, six. We tried to smoke various things but discovered that many were impossible to smoke. Driftwood smoked tolerably well, but a piece of driftwood is a scarce commodity on the prairie. Coffee grounds made a fair smoke, and they were accessible as long as we didn't get caught, but they burned hot, they tasted awful, and they wouldn't stay lit.

We tried smoking several different kinds of native material, some best left unnamed. Surprisingly, the best smoke nature had to offer was the stem of a yucca plant. Yucca stems bear the seed pods. Growing straight up out of the center of the plant, they reach as high as three or four feet. The texture of the stem turns woody and pithy after they dry out and loose their seeds.

It took a little work, but with skillful carving we could make a short length of stem ready to smoke. We tapered one end so it would fit the mouth, and we poked a hole completely through it from one end to the other. Otherwise you couldn't draw air through it. With a length of yucca stem thus prepared, you had a good smoke.

It burned hot and fast, often with a flame on the end. This tended to burn the lips, tongue, and nose, but we dealt with that by taking short, quick puffs. It smelled bad, tasted pungent, and poured out smoke like a bonfire, but the availability was great. Yucca plants were everywhere. We could have a smoke anytime we wanted, if we had the patience to prepare it. We carried a knife to carve the ends, a sharp nail to poke a hole through it, and lots and lots of matches, because it was also hard to light.

We finally got around to tobacco. It was much harder to come by than yucca stems, of course, but we managed to find enough to satisfy our curiosity. First we tried Dad's cigars. They lit easily and drew well, but they had one annoying drawback. They made me so sick that I threw up.

George and I were smoking cigars one day when Mom and Dad had gone to town. In theory it seemed a good plan, but it began to go awry just when they were due to return home at any moment. I got sick. My head was pounding, I was reeling on my feet, and I couldn't stop throwing up.

George quickly took charge of the situation. He dragged me to the water barrel and pushed my head under. When I began to flail my arms wildly, he gave me a short respite. He'd let me up to gulp air for a few frantic seconds, then holler, "Hold your breath. Here we go again!" and under I'd go. Just seconds before I drowned each time, he'd let me up again.

Amazingly enough, it worked. I put on a hat to cover my wet hair, dried my face, and by the time Mom and Dad drove up I could hardly remember being sick. The memory of nearly drowning from George's remedy stuck in my mind, however.

After the cigar experience, George seemed to have had enough. I suppose that was understandable; he was older and wiser by that time, thirteen. I was seven myself by then, so I should have matured from the experience as well, especially since it was my head and stomach that had suffered the most.

Something bothered me though. We had left one area of smoking untested. We hadn't tried pipes.

Getting hold of a pipe and tobacco was a difficult order for a seven-year-old. After seeking counsel from George, however, I figured out how I could buy a corncob pipe and a can of Prince Albert. Sadly, the saga of the corncob pipe was short-lived.

George was milking a cow in the barn one brisk winter day. I was standing around chatting with him and felt like having a smoke. I lit up my pipe and began smoking away. I discovered that if I huffed and puffed in and out rapidly, I could make the pipe put out a tremendous amount of smoke. That was fun.

I was engaged in the huffing and puffing, and wreathed in a huge cloud of smoke when Mom walked in. She couldn't see what was going on at first. In that split second I missed my chance to escape behind the smoke screen. I hesitated though, and it cost me. When Mom began to see through the smoke, she didn't like what she saw. She said a strange thing to me. "You'd better get in the house and enjoy that thing while you can!" Pondering her unusual instructions, I walked to the house, puffing on my pipe.

Dad was out that morning, so I had the house to myself. I took off my coat, pulled my little rocking chair up close to the stove, sat down and began rocking and puffing on my pipe, cozy and relaxed.

In a few minutes I heard Mom come in and slam the door behind her. She walked in, stopped with her hands on her hips, and glared at me. Again she didn't like what she saw. I really didn't understand now; I was doing exactly what she'd told me to do. Had I possibly misinterpreted her instructions? The next few minutes confirmed that I had indeed and also clarified Mom's position on pipe smoking.

I walked back outside, drying my eyes and holding my overly warm behind. George asked me what had happened. "Mom told me to go to the house and enjoy my pipe while I could," I said. "So I did. I was sittin' in my rocker by the stove smokin' it when she came in. Then she really got mad and gave me a lickin'." George bent over laughing as if I'd told him the funniest joke he'd ever heard.

I once had a little red wagon, the kind all kids had at one time or another. The wagon had sat outside and gone to rust and ruin, but I decided to salvage the wheels and axles and use them to build another vehicle. The wheels were rusted worse than I realized, however, and I didn't yet understand the role that wheel bearings play in the world.

I took the wheels and axles off the old wagon and, using an excess of wire and nails, mounted them on a board. The board was about four feet long but only around six or seven inches wide. The old wheels were made of rusty tin and had no bearings left in them, only large holes where the bearings had been. I puzzled over a method to fasten them onto the axles; then with a bit of mechanical wizardry I solved the problem, or at least I thought so. I slid each sloppy-fitting wheel over the axle, followed it with a big washer, and fastened the washer on with a cotter pin I made from a bent nail.

The finished product was not exactly streamlined, but then I wasn't aiming for style. Unfortunately, it didn't prove very functional either.

My board wagon didn't have a tongue to pull it by, so I had to push it. It worked fairly well, just pushing it around trying to get unwilling cats, dogs, and chickens to ride on it. I noticed though, that all four wheels wobbled horribly. Each wheel wobbled and jumped independently, causing the thing to lope across the ground like a deranged grasshopper. Unbeknown to me, those rusty holes in the wheels were growing larger and larger with each turn, threatening to drop the wheels off over the washers that held them on.

George came riding up on Champ, stopped, and watched with interest as I pushed the board along, wobbling and hopping over the prairie grass. "Hey, want me to give ya a pull?" he asked, unrolling his lariat.

He was offering to pull me on the board. That sounded like more fun than pushing it. "Sure," I said. "Let's do it."

Tying the end of his rope to the saddle horn, George slid off Champ and fastened the loop around the front axle. I sat down on the board, facing forward, and stretched my legs straight out in front of me. I noticed then that a flat board has little to hang onto, but I didn't let it worry me. There were always these little details to contend with.

George climbed back on Champ and eased forward until the slack came out of the rope. He looked back and said, "Ya ready?"

I waved my arm. "Let 'er go!" I hollered. And George let 'er go.

Taking off from a dead stop, a horse can gain full speed in just a few feet. So can a board. In a matter of seconds we were traveling close to thirty miles an hour. The ride should have felt exhilarating, but I don't recall that sensation. The wobbly wheels went crazy, making the board jump and buck along like a ground-level bronc. I tried to hold onto the edges of the board, but that didn't help much. Seeing that this wasn't going to work, I started hollering at George to stop. "Hey! Hey!" I yelled.

Glad to hear me having so much fun, George joined in the hollering. "Yee-hah!" he yelled, and stretched Champ out in a full gallop.

As the board and I jumped, bucked, and hurtled across the prairie, something began to change. One front wheel came off. Then the other. Then both back wheels. Now I was really riding a board— just a board. With the board skidding across the prairie as fast as Champ could run, I couldn't hang onto the edges anymore. I tried to balance myself by sitting up straight, and I hollered as loud as I could. I couldn't outholler George, though. He knew I liked to have fun, and he could tell I was having the time of my life back there.

The board began to whipsaw back and forth in a wild, disjointed slalom. On about the third or fourth whip, it threw me. I kept up with the board for a while, rolling and tumbling along beside it like a rag doll shot from a cannon.

George felt the weight slacken on the rope when I flew off. Looking back, he noted that I was no longer on the board, but that I was still traveling nearly as fast anyway.

We all finally stopped—George, Champ, the board, even me.

George walked Champ back to where I lay, a few feet behind the dusty board. Dirty, disjointed, and dazed, I blinked up at him through dirt-filled eyes.

"Lose your wheels?" he inquired.

I don't remember learning to ride a horse. I remember being so little I had to stand on top of a board fence or the side of a water tank to climb onto a horse's back, but I can't remember learning to ride any more than I can remember learning to walk.

George and I had our own horses from the time we moved to the ranch. Dad saw to that. My first horse, Ginger, was an older, gentle pinto, a good horse for a little kid. Champ was George's horse, a younger, more spirited pinto. Dad's was a fiery sorrel named Tony.

Ginger grew too old to ride after a few years, about the same time Dad quit riding. We traded horses then. Champ became my horse, Tony became George's, and Ginger retired.

Of course Dad kept a team of workhorses too, a pair of huge draft horses named Jigs and Jim. Jigs and Jim were Belgians, a breed of large horses the size of Clydesdales. They weighed two thousand pounds each.

Dad's skill with workhorses was fascinating to watch. I've seen him steer a horse-drawn wagon backwards, through a gate, and park it against a stack of hay when he was eighty years old.

George also learned to work the team. He and Dad used a fresno to fill in creek crossings and washed-out spots in the roads. The team pulled a large wagon to haul feed to the cattle when the snow was too deep for the pickup. When the snow became too deep for the wagon, they pulled the cattle feed on a big sled. We even used them to pull the pickup out of the mud and snow when it was stuck, and Dad got it stuck often.

Jim was an ornery, uncooperative horse who didn't like people. He was troublesome and rebellious when Dad worked the team and required a great amount of discipline and threats to make him work. After putting up with Jim for several years, Dad traded him off for another big Belgian named Prince. Prince was a beautiful tan and silver horse, marked like a giant palomino. He was a hard worker and far more honest than Jim.

Dad would stand back and admire Jigs and Prince, smile, shake his head, and say, "Ain't they a pair of dandies?"

Jigs was a huge sorrel, and the greatest horse I'll ever know. He could single-handedly pull a pickup out of the mud that had sunk to its axles, muscles standing out like thick ropes as he squatted his powerful hindquarters and drove his body forward on pile-driving legs, a juggernaut who didn't know the meaning of giving up.

Jigs possessed that tremendous spirit, yet he was gentle as a house pet. From the time I was a little kid, he let me swing on his neck, stand up and ride on his back without even a bridle on, or do any other outrageous thing I wanted. I'd hang my head out the pickup window as we passed him far out in the pasture and holler, "Hey, Jigs." He never failed to raise his head and whinny back at me. He was my great friend, and my savior. I would one day owe my life to Jigs.

We had great fun riding our horses, but their real purpose was work. With two to three hundred head of range cattle spread over four thousand acres, we used saddle horses to round them up to go to market, to move them between pastures, to bring sick ones to the barn for treatment, and to round up the milk cows.

George and I rode bareback more often than we rode with saddles. There are only two things to remember when riding bareback: grip the horse's sides with your legs and lean into the turns.

Gripping the horse's sides with your legs is easy to learn, because if you don't you fall off. When that part becomes clear, it's easy to learn to lean into a turn. This is learned by not leaning into a turn. The first time you make a turn and don't lean into it, you go flying off the horse's back at around thirty miles an hour; after that it's easy to remember.

George and I rode bareback like the wind, as fast as our horses could fly and as sharp as they could turn. We could ride that way all day long.

Saddles became necessary when we worked cattle, however, especially if we were roping. I was very proud the day Dad bought me my first little saddle, when I was seven, but I still continued to ride bareback most of the time.

We rode our horses everywhere, to visit neighbors several miles away, to the creek to go fishing and swimming, and to chase jack rabbits and coyotes. That was great fun, and the horses really got into the spirit. Whenever we raced them or chased something, they always put out their best.

We also rode our horses to school. Our early years were spent in a one-room country schoolhouse that sat beside the highway three miles from our house. The people who owned the land next to the school let us to leave our horses in their corral during the day.

In the wintertime we usually rode double. George rode in front and I sat behind him, hanging on around his waist. He helped me stay warm that way. We had to cross Clay Creek on the way to school, at a ford where water ran most of the time. The water was usually only about a foot deep, so our horses could wade across easily. In the winter when the creek froze over, the horse had to cross the ice, but Ginger and Champ knew instinctively what to do. They didn't need any directions; they took charge of the situation themselves. The horse would walk up to the edge, pick up one front foot, slam it down on the ice several times, break it to pieces, and wade across as he normally did.

Sometimes we'd find the creek frozen solid, with ice too thick for the horse to break. He knew what to do in that situation too. He'd walk to the edge of the ice, stop, and slam it with his foot a few times to test it. If it didn't break, he knew it would support his weight. Then he'd slowly walk across the ice, carefully feeling his way with each step so he didn't slip and fall with us. When he made it across, we'd pat him on the neck and tell him what a good job he'd done.

We both rode our horses to school in warm weather. It was more fun than riding double, and faster. We had standing orders not to race them because of the danger that one might step in a

Gary, George, and Ginger ready for school, 1948

badger hole and fall down at high speed. I'm sure the coyotes and jack rabbits we chased wished we'd have complied with that rule more often than we did.

On our way to school one bright spring day, George on Champ and me on Ginger, we were riding along side by side at a slow trot, taking it easy, enjoying the morning. We each glanced casually at the other out of the corners of our eyes and began to pick up a little speed. We glanced back and forth again, and picked up a little more speed. The next glance we both grinned. Soon we were blazing along side by side as fast as the horses could go, their manes flying in the wind.

As we leaned forward over their necks, thundering along with big grins on our faces, Ginger stuck his right front foot in a badger hole.

Ginger was running so hard it flipped him end over end. With his front foot lodged in the hole, his rear end flew up and over his head in a perfect arc, catapulting me to the ground in front of him. I landed flat on my back, and Ginger came crashing down beside me on his back. His body slammed to the ground, and with a great gasp he rolled completely over the top of me. That mashed me into the dirt, squeezed all the wind out of me, and knocked me cold.

George jumped off Champ and ran over to where I lay, flat and motionless. The first thing I remember is him holding me up in a sitting position, checking me for broken bones and asking, "Are ya hurt?!" Not easily answered. I didn't even know where I was right then or who I was for that matter.

After I came around I felt stunned, dirty, and a little flatter than before, but to our amazement I wasn't hurt, not bad anyway. The next thing I remember is George's regular reminder, "Don't tell Mom." I didn't plan to tell her either. I didn't want to spoil our chances of having more fun like this in the future.

Also to our surprise, Ginger hadn't broken his leg. After he got to his feet, he seemed kind of jumpy, though, and didn't care for our company anymore. He ran away. It took a lot of chasing to catch him and a long, soothing talk to persuade him to let me climb back on him. We were late for school that day.

The little schoolhouse by the highway was named Sunny Slope School. One teacher taught all grades. I attended first and second grade there, while George finished the seventh and eighth. Very few kids attended the school; at one time George and I were the only two students.

Sunny Slope was a little one-room frame building with not a single tree to protect it from the elements. It had no electricity and was heated by a pot-bellied stove in the center of the room. The teacher sat next to the stove in the wintertime, and we all pulled our desks around it. Two old outhouses in back had served boys and girls since the 1800s. A hand-operated water pump stood on the school ground, but the well had gone dry. A little hand-rung bell called us in from recess and lunch hour, as the original school bell was long since gone. An old foot-operated pump organ sat in one corner, but nobody could play it.

The school was only a half mile from our favorite swimming hole on the creek. On warm days we could run to the creek and go for a swim during lunch hour; this was the physical education portion of our curriculum.

Our teacher when I was in second grade was a fine old gentleman named Mr. Preston. Mr. Preston was a slender, slow-moving man with only one hand, his left. A shotgun had exploded and blown the other hand off when he was young. He didn't have a college degree, but he'd been teaching most of his life. Mr. Preston was probably in his sixties at the time, and he was poor and not enjoying good health. He lived in the schoolhouse, sleeping on a canvas army cot and cooking on the pot-bellied stove by the light of a kerosene lamp.

Mr. Preston got sick that year. He lost weight and grew frail, finally becoming too weak to do anything but sit and read aloud to us. George and I still remember listening to him read Mark Twain the entire day. We were never told what was wrong with him, but he died before the school year ended.

Mr. Preston was a man of principle, and perhaps the greatest lesson he taught us was one of principle. Though he had lived a hard life and learned to rely on his own resources to survive, he was a polite, conscientious teacher and gentle with children. In spite of his age, his gentle ways, frailty, and a missing hand, we learned that Mr. Preston had the courage of his convictions.

There were three students in the school during the time Mr. Preston taught: George, me, and a huge bully of a kid named Luther.

Luther was a year or two older than George and considerably bigger. He was even bigger than Mr. Preston, probably outweighing him by forty or fifty pounds. Besides being big for his age, he was a loud, antisocial bully who directed derogatory remarks and insults at everyone around him, which was mainly George, me, and Mr. Preston.

Luther made snide comments to George and me regularly, but he was especially rude to Mr. Preston, often calling him a "one-armed old man." Mr. Preston was a gentleman, however, and hardly acknowledged Luther's insults.

Then one day Luther stepped over Mr. Preston's line. He directed a taunting, sarcastic remark at George and me concerning our religion, telling Mr. Preston that something we had done was probably "... because they're Catholics."

Mr. Preston wasn't a Catholic himself, and his reaction wasn't because the remark pertained to Catholics. Religion was a personal thing, and he simply wouldn't tolerate that sort of rudeness.

He tore into Luther with a fury, knocked him to the floor, jumped down on top of him, and started beating him. Luther was shocked at the attack, but he fought back with all his strength. George and I stood wide-eyed as they rolled all over the school room floor, slugging, scratching, and kicking each other viciously. Mr. Preston fought like a demon. He beat Luther with his good hand and his stump of a wrist until Luther's arms were bruised, his face was red, and his clothes were practically torn off.

I clung to George. This was the most violent thing I'd ever seen.

Luther began to holler. "Stop! I've had enough. I give up. Please stop," he cried. The old man stopped, pulled himself up off the floor and allowed Luther to get up. Then he looked him in the eye, pointed a finger from his single hand at him, and said, "Don't you ever let me hear any of that kind of talk again."

"Yes, sir," Luther replied. "I won't ever again, sir." And he never did.

A substitute teacher finished out the school year after Mr. Preston died. That was our last year at Sunny Slope. The following year we started riding a school bus to town, where I began third grade and George started high school. We still rode our horses to the highway to catch the school bus much of the time, but in bad weather Dad usually drove us in the pickup. On cold mornings Mr. and Mrs. Clark let us wait in the store until the bus came.

Going to school in town was certainly different from the country. The school was huge, with long, cavernous halls, larger than any building I'd ever been in. It was sparkling clean too, with bright pictures on the walls and electric lights—far brighter than old Sunny Slope had ever been. The conditions at Sunny Slope appeared harsh in comparison, and they were harsh as far as creature comforts such as decor, warmth, and light were concerned, but not in other ways. Being treated like a country bumpkin was a new and uncomfortable experience, even painful. It made me long for old Sunny Slope, where at least I had understood the reasons for the harshness.

There were more kids than I'd ever imagined too, having gone to a school with only three students the year before and one had been my brother. Town school was a lively environment, and I think it was supposed to be good for me, to learn how to make friends and get along with others. I remember being told that at the time anyway.

Chapter 6

DAD'S PLACE

Dad called George and me "Son" from the time I can remember. It made me proud every time he said it.

In the years before we all lived in the rock house, from the time I was four until I turned nine, I often stayed with him at his house, the place we called Dad's Place. He took me everywhere with him, he taught me things, and he let me help him with his work.

The door to Dad's little house opened into one side of the kitchen, a warm and friendly room. A large buffet stood to the left of the entrance, with a big battery radio sitting on top. A long, stout table extended from the far wall, and an old-fashioned coal and wood-burning cook stove sat on the right. On the immediate right, hidden behind the door as it opened, sat Dad's shaving stand. The shaving stand showed his preference for function when it came to house furnishings. It was a wooden orange crate, standing on end. A wash pan sat on the top end, while his razor, shaving mug, and other toiletries lay underneath on the natural shelf made by the crate's middle petition. It wasn't a stylish piece, but useful, tidy, and compact.

The bedroom, to the left of the kitchen, had a small closet, Dad's bed, a chair, and a bedside stand. The living room, to the right, held a kerosene heating stove, Dad's desk, assorted chairs, a rocking chair, and my bed.

We ate three meals a day together—breakfast, dinner, and supper, and his choice of foods didn't vary much. He regularly stated that all a person needed was "meat, bread, and potatoes. And a little coffee." And, "Well, sometimes a piece of pie or cake's pretty good too."

He fried nearly everything he cooked, and I loved most of it—but not his pancakes. Those thick, heavy trivets of unsweetened dough were just unbearable. Dad was hard to bargain with, but somehow we reached a truce, and I didn't have to eat them anymore. Cutting the deal turned out great for me. After that he cooked pork

Dad and Gary share a cigar, 1943

chops and fried potatoes for my breakfast instead of those awful pancakes.

Occasionally he even let me drink a cup of his coffee, though I couldn't stand it very often. He made the blackest of coffee by dumping seven heaping teaspoons of grounds directly into the water, then boiling the whole mess for exactly seven minutes. It would float a spoon.

We both liked canned chili, spicy hot, with lots of crackers. Dad once told me I should try a little extra chili powder in it. I did, and it tasted pretty hot, but good. He then proceeded to tell me a story about chili powder, how the natives in Africa ate a teaspoon of it every day when they were young, and it kept them in good health all their lives.

I decided to try this strategy for good health. Each day I'd get down the can of chili powder, dip out a level teaspoonful, and painstakingly eat the whole thing. The process took several minutes to accomplish and required a considerable amount of water. One day I caught Dad peeking around a corner watching me eat the chili powder, and grinning. That made me a little suspicious of the story about the natives and their health measures. It also made me wonder if Dad had been getting some of his ideas from George.

A little store sat on the highway near the turnoff to our place. Clay Creek Store was a combination gas station, grocery store, post office, and neighborhood gathering place. Old Mr. and Mrs. Clark, the kindly proprietors, lived in a house adjoining the store. Everyone within ten or fifteen miles picked up their mail there, as well as gasoline, tobacco, and many of their groceries. Neighbors would occasionally run into each other at the store and catch up on local gossip.

Dad went to the store every day about mid-morning to get mail and cigars, and most of the time he took me with him. The store was a wonderland of groceries, meats, gloves, hats, caps, fly swatters, toilet paper, lampshades, wicks, oil, gas, tobacco, candy, gum, and pop. I pumped up Mr. Clark's manual gas pumps if they needed it, pumping the long handle back and forth until the round glass at the top showed a full ten gallons. He rewarded me with a candy bar most of the time, or a pack of gum or a bottle of pop from the red cooler that said Coca Cola on the side. Dad bought me something if Mr. Clark didn't.

Every morning Mrs. Clark would hand a box of cigars to Dad so he could take out five, the number he smoked each day. He'd light one up on the way home, blow out a big mouthful of smoke, and sigh with pleasure.

Dad smelled like cigars, and his pickup did too. In the house he often asked me to carry a cigar butt to the ash bucket and extinguish it for him. I puffed on it all the way to the bucket as he tried to hide his grin.

Dad took me to town to see circuses and parades, and to see Santa Claus at Christmastime. On Saturdays I went to town with him and ate in a little diner across the street from the Elks Club. Dad nearly always had a chicken fried steak at the diner. I did too, because he did.

When we finished eating, shortly after noon, I went to a movie and Dad went to play poker at the Elks Club. He even gave me money to get popcorn and Coke at the movie. I didn't know any other kids to go to the movies with, but I don't remember caring either. To sit in the dark in that cavernous old theater, feast on popcorn and Coke, and become lost in those fantasies on the big screen was a thrill I looked forward to all week.

The Saturday matinees were always Westerns, always double features, and always had serials and cartoons with them. The good guys wore white hats, and the bad guys wore black ones. Everything was easy to keep track of that way—no gray hats to cloud the issue.

After Roy Rogers, Gene Autry, Tim Holt, and young John Wayne finished entertaining me, I put my own little cowboy hat back on and walked the one block to the Elks Club to meet Dad.

He had just bought the ranch a few years before and had to be conservative with his money, so while I enjoyed the movies those Saturday afternoons, Dad played poker with a plan.

Cottonseed meal, or "cake" as we called it, was our primary cattle feed in the winter, and a major expense in the operation of the ranch. Cake cost twenty dollars a ton, a cost equivalent to more than a hundred dollars a ton now. Dad knew if he played poker conservatively and didn't try anything fancy, he probably wouldn't win a lot, but he could almost always win twenty dollars.

After the movie I'd walk down into the big basement room of the Elks Club—a dim, smoky cave that smelled of cigars, cigarettes, spittoons, and pool chalk. Dad and four or five other grave-looking men would be sitting in a cloud of smoke around a worn poker table topped with faded green felt and dotted with years of tobacco burns. Dad was always in his regular chair, hunched forward with his hat pulled low on his forehead so that it nearly covered his eyes, his face thoughtful and expressionless as he looked at his hand, except for that cocky cigar jutting straight out the center of his mouth. He was usually about twenty dollars ahead.

When I walked in Dad's poker face would fade. He'd look up, smile, and say, "Hi, Son. How was the show?" His opponents grimaced a little as he folded his cards, stood up, and cashed in his chips.

We'd walk out to the pickup, Dad would grin at me, and drive directly to the feed store to buy a ton of cottonseed cake before we headed home.

The battery radio in Dad's kitchen was nearly as big as a portable TV set, a large amount of the inside space taken up by the battery compartment in the bottom. We didn't play it regularly since the battery was only good for a certain number of hours. The radio played when we wanted to hear a specific program, and then we sat and listened to it. We listened to Amos and Andy, The Hallmark Hall of Fame, Edgar Bergen and Charlie McCarthy, and Fibber McGee and Molly, the comedy couple whose famous overfilled closet spilled out the door in every single episode.

Friday nights were special. Dad and I sat by the radio and listened to professional boxing matches, the "Friday Night Fights." Boxing was the only sport that ever interested Dad, which seems to make perfect sense.

When "The Star-Spangled Banner" played, just before the fight started, we stood at rigid attention and held our hands over our hearts. Then the fight would begin. We'd listen closely as the announcer gave an exciting blow-by-blow account of the battle. Dad would grin and shake his head in wonder as giants like Joe Louis and Jersey Joe Walcott battered one another and strove to knock each other unconscious. During the intermissions between rounds, Dad would tell me stories of older boxers like heavyweight champion John L. Sullivan, who once fought seventy-five rounds in the hot sun with skin-tight gloves, or "Gentleman Jim" Corbett, who knocked out Sullivan to claim his title, and Bob Fitzsimmons, who in turn defeated Corbett. Dad said part of Fitzsimmons' boxing prowess was due to his arms being so long that his hands hung below his knees.

Despite his lack of formal education, Dad had somehow learned to read well. He read every evening, and his favorite reading material usually gave people a chuckle. He subscribed to a monthly publication called *Ranch Romances*.

Ranch Romances was a paperback book of love stories, all of which took place in some sort of Old Western setting. It was comical just to see one of them laying by his chair. Dad read *Ranch Romances* every evening and thought nothing of it. I guess love stories were all right as long as they took place on a ranch.

He also read to me when I stayed with him, though I don't think it was his favorite thing to do. He did like to read the newspaper comics to me, and he sometimes read children's books too if I coaxed him long enough. He couldn't see any sense in reading the same ones over and over, which is what I liked at that age. He probably thought I had some sort of problem with memory retention.

Dad had learned to write well too, and in fact had perfected a beautiful handwriting. He took pride in that skill and practiced regularly to keep it intact. He kept a supply of lined notebook paper in his desk, and about once a week he took out several sheets and practiced making various ovals, loops, and swirls.

He carried a bone-handled pocket knife and kept it razor sharp. When it would no longer shave the hair off his arm, it was time to sharpen it again. He used the knife for everything, from peeling apples to opening feed sacks to castrating calves. It had three blades, however, and he used different blades for different tasks. When I'd see him peeling an apple with it, I'd say, "Dad, isn't that the knife you castrate calves with?"

He'd grin and say, "Yeah, but it's clean now. I've peeled several apples with it since I castrated anything." I knew he'd say that; that's why I asked him.

I once dropped something at Dad's house, close to where his ax stood in a corner. As I reached down, I accidentally brushed the blade of the ax and cut a fine line in my finger as if I had touched a razor blade. I didn't know an ax could be that sharp. I picked it up and shaved the hair off my arm with it. His tools were dangerous instruments to have sitting around. He even sharpened his shovels.

Dad used various sayings and gestures regularly in certain situations. If he got his pickup stuck, had a flat tire, or anything of that nature, he'd get mad and holler, "We're blowed up!" Or when some plan didn't work out, he'd sigh and say, "Damn the luck."

I loved to ask him what time it was. He carried a pocket watch fastened to a belt loop of his Levis by a gold chain. When I asked him the time, he'd stop, lean back, pull it from his watch pocket, hold it way out in front of him, look at it with an air of exaggerated importance, and say, "Well sir, it's about two-thirty o'clock." Then he'd grin and slip it back in his pocket.

When some sort of mild frustration or snag baffled him, he'd shake his head and say, "Well, shit and two's eight." He didn't regularly cuss in front of me when I was little, but I'd heard him say that to himself several times. I thought it didn't sound like a nice thing to say, but he said it kind of lightheartedly and didn't stress it, so I wasn't sure. Besides, I couldn't figure out what it meant.

I decided to ask Mom. She was busy and not paying close attention when I asked her. "Mom, Dad says something every now and then, and I don't understand what it means."

"What's that?" she asked absently.

"Shit and two's eight."

She slowly turned her head and glared at me. "I think you and Dad both need your mouths washed out with soap." I still didn't know what it meant, but I did know better than to ask again.

I learned later it was part of an old saying. The whole thing went, "Shit and two's eight, five more's thirteen, and that's bad luck."

My cat once had a litter of kittens at Dad's Place, and after they grew big enough to run around he started letting me bring them in the house. His rule was that I could let in only one at a time, but sometimes I kind of lost count.

One day I was sitting at the kitchen table pasting cutout pictures into a scrapbook, using flour and water paste I'd mixed up in a little bowl. Dad went outside and left me working on my project. I decided to let one of the kittens in the house for a while, and somehow they all made it in.

While I was working on my scrapbook, one of the kittens jumped up on the table, stuck its head into the bowl, and began eating the paste. Seeing that he liked it so well, I set the bowl on the floor to see if the others liked it too. They loved it, so I decided to give them a feast. I scooped out more flour, poured water into it, and mixed up a large bowl of paste. Then I sat it down in front of them and let them have at it.

Those kittens dived in and ate until they were completely full of paste. When they finished they all stretched out on the floor, purred, mewed, and generally made happy sounds. Unfortunately, the paste did more than just make them happy. It acted as a laxative.

I was still sitting at the table pasting, and the kittens were purring, when Dad walked in. He scowled a bit at the sight of them all in the house, but he reached down, picked one up, and began to pet it. Suddenly he hollered "What the ...!" and dropped the kitten. I looked up and saw a streak running down the front of his shirt.

Dad's loud exclamation when he dropped the kitten excited the others. I saw one of them begin to experience the same problem on the floor. Dad saw it too and tried to grab it, but the kitten dodged him and took off across the house, leaving a trail behind it as it ran. Dad ran after it. That scared the rest, and they all began to run too, trying to dodge him. Unhappily, the excitement got them all going and leaving trails everywhere they ran.

Things were moving fast now. Dad ran, cussed, and knocked chairs over. The kittens were just a blur. I couldn't tell which one he was actually chasing; I don't think he knew. It didn't matter much though. He never caught a single one. That was probably a good thing, after the paste started affecting them all. Finally he opened the door, and with yet more cussing, shouting, and a couple more rounds through the house, managed to chase them all outside.

I was still sitting at the table, watching the eruption. Dad slammed the door, turned to me and sputtered, "What ya been feedin' them cats?!" I slowly began to tell him about the paste, how the kittens had liked it, and that I hadn't known what it would do to them.

He just shook his head. It took us quite a while to get the house back in order, and the one-kitten rule was strictly enforced after that. The kittens weren't very eager to come back in for a few days anyway.

Besides having cats and dogs, I tried to make a pet of every wild animal I could catch when I was a kid.

Dad once helped me catch a prairie dog in a live trap. It was a young male, and he quickly became very tame. I named him Paddy, after a prairie dog in one of my children's books. Paddy was soft and brown, about a foot long, and had lively, inquisitive eyes. He lived in a barrel, and appeared to like it fine. It must have seemed like a big prairie dog hole to him. He grew accustomed to being fed and petted, and he loved it when Dad or I would talk to him. When he heard my footsteps approaching, Paddy would sit up on his haunches and give a shrill two-syllable whistle. I'd lean over into the barrel, rub his head, and talk to him as he made a happy, cooing sound.

Paddy would eat almost anything, so naturally I began to experiment. It's amazing what he would eat. Fruits, vegetables, cottonseed cake, bread, desserts, corn on the cob—he liked everything. I guess when you live in a hole on the prairie you eat whatever you can get.

Dad had a favorite fruit, raw dates, a real luxury on the plains. He usually kept a small stash of dates and ate them sparingly because of their expense. He occasionally gave me one, and I loved to eat the tasty meat from around the long seed.

Who'd ever guess that a prairie dog would like dates? Paddy loved them. He'd sit up on his haunches and hold a date by each end, turn it as he ate, and strip the meat off the seed as if he were eating a miniature ear of corn. When he finished he'd drop the seed, look up at me, and whistle for another one.

I tried to see that Paddy ate dates sparingly too, as Dad didn't know he was eating them. He liked Paddy, but I figured he didn't like him well enough to share his dates with him, and I wasn't wrong there.

I was leaning over Paddy's barrel one day, feeding him dates and having a chat with him, when his eyes suddenly darted to the side. He looked past my head and saw something, or someone, behind me. There was only one other person on the place. I slowly turned around and came eye to eye with Dad. He'd just watched Paddy polish off one of his dates, and didn't seem amused.

"Ya feedin' that prairie dog my dates?" he asked incredulously. Given the situation, that question pretty well answered itself. I just shrugged my shoulders and didn't say anything. "Pretty damn expensive treats for a prairie dog!" he added, and stomped off.

A few days later I discovered he had moved his dates and hidden them in a place I never found. I later overheard him telling someone in town about Paddy eating his dates, however, and having a good laugh while he told it.

A horse turned Paddy's barrel over one night, and he escaped. I imagine he spent the rest of his life back in the prairie dog town trying to explain to the others what dates tasted like.

Dad let me sleep in later than usual one Saturday morning. When he woke me he said, "Come outside with me. I got somethin' to show ya." We walked out to a tree in front of his house. There hung a little swing, brand new, just my size. He'd spent the morning making it for me.

"Is it for me?!" I asked. He grinned and nodded. I about wore the tree limb out swinging on it.

One night he woke me up a couple of hours after I'd gone to sleep. He said he wanted to show me something in the sky. He took me outside and pointed to the north, near the horizon. Far in the northern sky I could see vertical streaks of light, with spots of light dancing through them like butterflies. Wide-eyed with wonder, I looked up at Dad. "That's the northern lights," he said. "Ya can't see 'em from here very often. They're also called the aurora borealis." I thought he must know everything.

Dad was a focused thinker. In a room with other people talking he would sometimes sit with a distant look in his eyes for several minutes while he figured something out. While he was working or walking from the house to the pickup, he'd often stop, look down, squint his eyes, and mull something over in his mind. And when he had something important on his mind everything became dead serious, no matter how old you were, or how young.

When I was six I gained more first-hand knowledge about the birds and the bees than I had ever dreamed existed.

Cows, like many other animals, occasionally have problems giving birth. When they do, they need assistance and fairly quickly. I know that now, but at the age of six no one had yet informed me.

I'm sure the cow didn't mean to shock me that night, but a little advanced information on the subject would certainly have helped.

It was a cold winter night, and Dad had been quiet all evening. I could tell he had something on his mind. After supper he put on his coat and told me he was going to the barn to check on something. Within a few minutes he came hurrying back through the door. "Get your coat on and come with me," he said. "I need ya to help me with somethin'." I put on my coat and hurried outside with him. We headed for the barn, and he was walking so fast I couldn't keep up with him, let alone find out what we were doing.

We walked into the barn, and there lay a cow on her side, with her head lying flat on the ground. She was either sick or hurt; I knew something was wrong anyway.

I had no idea what was happening, but the cow was undergoing a breached birth, trying to have a calf that was turned backward and coming out hind feet first. Without a word of explanation, Dad handed me the flashlight and told me to keep it trained on the cow. He then proceeded to pull the calf, a common procedure in a breached birth. The calf's hind feet protruded slightly from the cow, though I didn't have a clue what they were. Dad fastened a rope to the little feet, ran it through a set of pulleys, and began to pull the calf out of the cow. He had to coordinate the pulls with the cow's contractions, so the process took several minutes.

I stood holding the flashlight, trying to believe my eyes. I wouldn't have been more stunned if a spaceship had landed in the barn and some alien creature had walked out to greet us.

When the calf was completely out and lying on its side, it looked rather shapeless. I couldn't tell what it was at first, then Dad began to remove the placenta, and it took on a familiar shape. "Is that a calf?" I asked.

Dad answered, "Yes."

I've always been glad we had that long talk; it sure cleared things up for me. Later, after we returned to the house, we talked even more. "I thought the stork brought baby calves," I said.

"No, the stork doesn't bring calves," Dad replied.

To keep things from getting too serious, I did my best to brighten up Dad's life when he lived in his little house. He normally burned coal in the kitchen stove, but I'd heard somewhere that the early settlers had burned cow chips and buffalo chips when other fuel was scarce. It made good sense to me; a dry cow chip certainly looked like it would burn. What a saving that would be, since we had such a large supply of cow chips on the ranch.

It was easy to test.

Dad was sitting in the living room one afternoon reading *Ranch Romances*. The kitchen stove still had some glowing coals in it from the previous meal. I recognized an opportunity. I could test my idea and surprise Dad with a new and extremely cheap source of fuel. I went outside, gathered up a big bunch of dry cow chips, carried them into the house, and stuffed the firebox of the stove full of them.

I had planned to surprise Dad, and I did. The hot coals quickly ignited the cow chips, and I noticed the stove beginning to smoke a little. Then it smoked a little more, and a little more. Soon it was really smoking, a lot. I also began to notice something else, that cow chips don't smell like coal when they burn. These didn't smell a bit like coal. The best description I could give is that they smelled like burning cow chips.

The stove puffed like a steam engine. The kitchen was getting pretty smoky, but in the living room Dad hadn't noticed yet. I tried to fan the smoke away from the living room door, but it poured out of the stove too fast. As the room where he was reading began to fill with smoke that smelled like a barnyard, Dad took notice.

"What the hell!" he hollered, and came charging into the kitchen.

All I could do was stand there, looking at the smoke-belching stove. My experiment had worked; the cow chips were really burning now.

"What'd ya put in that stove?!" Dad asked, not in a calm voice.

"Cow chips," I muttered.

"Goddam!" he hollered, and ran for the door. He threw the doors and windows open, and we spent the next hour or so fanning the smoke out of the house. Then in a slightly calmer voice, yet still strained, Dad instructed me never to put cow chips in the stove again. He seemed quite adamant as I remember, but I also remember him laughing loudly when he told somebody about it later.

One moonlit night when my cousin Bill was visiting from Denver, he and I slept outside at Dad's Place. We were sleeping on a cot under one of his trees—anyway that's what Dad thought we were doing. What we were really doing was climbing up in the tree and jumping down onto the cot, using it as a trampoline.

We had spread several blankets out over the cot to soften our landing. Bill and I were having great fun taking turns jumping from a high limb while the other watched. We had both made several jumps without mishap and felt pretty good about it. Our success was short-lived, however; at least mine was.

We were jumping from a big limb high in the tree. The jeans I had on were too long for me, so I had rolled them up a couple of inches, making a deep cuff on each pants leg. As we jumped, our trajectory carried us past a little broken limb with a blunt end on it. In my final and most spectacular jump, as I flew outward from the big limb my pants cuff caught on the blunt end of that broken limb, spun me around, and hung me upside down. With my body pointing straight down, the pants leg then slipped off the limb and released me. I dropped straight to the ground, head first, and folded up in a pile—knocked cold.

Bill was watching from the far end of the cot. After he saw me take that unusual spin and my head dive straight for the ground like a pile driver, he wasn't surprised to find me lying unconscious at the base of the tree. I was unaware of it, but he somehow managed to get me to my feet and started walking me slowly toward Dad's house. I woke up walking. I remember Bill's voice as if coming from a distance, telling me to "Take another step, Gary."

Bill walked me to the house and knocked on the door to wake Dad. He was still holding me up when Dad came to the door. "Gary fell out of a tree on his head," Bill told him, "and knocked himself out."

Sounding somewhat disgusted, Dad looked at me and asked, "What were you doin' in a tree?" I was too woozy to talk. I just swayed around, smiled, and looked at him stupidly. Bill told him we'd been jumping out of the tree and how I had managed to knock myself out.

Dad parted my hair and looked at my head. Then he shook his head and said, "All right. You boys get back out there and get to bed, and don't be jumpin' outta any more damn trees."

I learned to drive a pickup when I was eleven, but I could steer one at a much younger age. When Dad and I went out to feed the range cattle, he taught me to steer the truck as we moved along slowly while he walked behind it and strung out the feed. I was six when I started doing that and could barely see over the steering wheel. The pickup had a standard, floor-shift transmission, and my legs were too short to reach the pedals. That didn't matter; I didn't know what the pedals were for anyway.

Dad had to get me started. I'd scoot over in the seat beside him, and he'd put the truck in low gear and just let it idle along on its own as slow as it would go. Then he'd step out and I'd slide under the wheel. I'd steer the pickup along while he strung the feed out on the ground. When he finished he'd run back up to the cab, jump in, and take over the wheel again with the truck still moving. I'd slide back over to the passenger side.

Of course I thought it was a big deal to drive Dad's pickup when I was only six years old. I was really proud of that. My enthusiastic approach wasn't all good, however, as my pride tended to make me a little overly zealous. This led to a couple of incidents that didn't make Dad especially proud.

My aunt Helen, who had become a nun, was visiting us one winter and asked to go out with Dad and me to feed the cattle one morning. With Helen riding on the passenger side and me in the middle, Dad and I did our driver-switching maneuver and he went back to throw out the feed. I was proud to be steering the pickup with Helen riding in it, and despite her nervous glances toward the front as I strained to see over the wheel, I explained to her how easy it was. While I was explaining and looking her direction, I ran into a cow and knocked her down.

The cow let out a beller, whumped down on her side, and all four legs went up under the front of the truck. The moving truck pinned the luckless cow under it and started trying to climb up over the top of her. That excited the cow. The only thing I knew how to do was steer, so I started turning the wheel rapidly back and forth. This resulted in bulldozing the cow along in a snakelike pattern. Her head and tail flopped up and down rapidly as she slid and bumped along, they being the only parts she could move. And she bellered, grunted, groaned, and made noises I'd never heard come out of a cow.

Aunt Helen got real excited. She started yelling, "Dad, there's a cow down in front of us!" Dad had already figured something was wrong. Anyone within a mile of that cow knew that. He came running up, jerked the door open, jumped in, and managed to stop the truck before it climbed over the cow.

We all jumped out to look at her. The cow lay pinned under the truck with the bumper extending partially over her, like a half-squashed bug protruding from under a shoe sole. She was looking pretty wild-eyed by now, but luckily she wasn't caught in the truck. She sure was stuck tight up under there though.

Dad jumped back in the truck, threw it in reverse, and backed off of her. The cow jumped up, let out a final beller, and ran off with her tail sticking straight in the air like an emergency flag. She actually looked pretty good, except for a big patch of hair missing from one side.

Helen wasn't quite so anxious to go with us to feed the cattle after that.

My next attack of exuberance occurred during a snowstorm. The problem began when Dad decided to have me steer down a little prairie road that ran beside a barbwire fence. This put the fence just a few feet from the right-hand side of the pickup. On the other side of the fence was the east road, a graded county road running along the east boundary of the ranch.

Dad stopped beside the fence, pointed at it sternly and said, "Now you be real careful, and watch out for that fence." Then he started the truck down the little road, slid out, and I took over the wheel.

As I steered along beside the fence, confidently and professionally, I thought of something Dad occasionally did when he was driving. He'd open the door as he drove, lean out, and spit. Well, here I was, driving the truck just like him, and in a snowstorm as well. Being a seasoned driver, I decided to open the door and spit.

I held onto the steering wheel with my right hand, opened the door with my left, turned my head, leaned out to spit, and steered the truck into the fence.

Sometimes it takes a minute to spit. I was leaning way out, trying to spit as far as Dad could, when I heard the barbed wires begin to scrape the other side of the cab. I looked over in time to see a taut wire snap against the passenger door window. The broken ends of the wire spiraled out through the air like party streamers. I pulled myself back up from spitting position and looked toward the front in time to see a fence post dead ahead. It didn't last long. The front bumper clipped it right off at ground level.

I knew I had a problem and badly wanted to correct it, but I was too flustered. I couldn't do anything. I just drove right down the center of the fence line, clipping off posts as I went. The rest of the wires snapped in two, flew through the air in great spirals, and rolled up on the ground like giant hair curlers.

All the noise and confusion scared the cattle, and they began to bawl and run in all directions. About half of them stampeded out through the ruptured fence and onto the east road.

Dad went insane. I heard him hollering and turned around to look at him helplessly through the back window. He was jumping around and yelling incoherently, waving his arms and wildly motioning me to steer it back out of the fence. For a brief moment he must have actually thought I could do it.

I saw him coming and scooted over to give him room. He charged up through the maze of broken posts, coiled wire, and confused cattle, jumped into the truck, and stopped it. Suddenly the whole world seemed to stop. Dad was breathing hard, and his face was red. He stared straight ahead.

I watched the snow fall lightly on the windshield and dreaded the inevitable question. Finally he looked over at me with narrowed eyes and asked, "Why'd ya open the door?"

Barely able to utter it, I said. "I was tryin' to spit."

"Jee-sus Christ!" he said. He opened the door, stepped out, slammed it shut, and stood and let the snow fall on him.

After a while he slowly looked around at the devastation. The pickup was sitting astride the fence line, four or five posts were broken off at the base, long coils of barbed wire lay everywhere, and half the herd was scattered up and down the east road.

He opened the door, sat back down in the truck, and moved it off to the side of the mess. Then he looked over at me and said, "Come on, we got a lot of work to do."

We managed to round up the escaped cattle on foot, and drove them back through the fence where they belonged. I guarded the hole in the fence to keep the cattle from going back through it while Dad drove to the house to get fence posts, wire, and tools.

We spent the rest of the day rebuilding the fence in the snow. It was a quiet day; we didn't talk much.

Jack Beatty often traveled in his sales work, and he stopped by to spend the night with Dad whenever he passed through southeast Colorado. Dad loved to see him come, and so did I. Jack made the evenings exciting, telling of his adventures on the road and reminiscing with Dad about their exploits in younger days. Dad laughed and talked and his eyes shone with pleasure when Jack was there.

Jack slept in my bed when he visited, and I slept with Dad. One night as we slept back to back, I felt a slight movement under the covers toward the foot of the bed. Then the movement stopped. In a moment I felt Dad reach over behind his back, between us, and grab something. He then jerked his arm out from under the covers and threw whatever it was against the wall. It hit the wall with a light thump and fell to the floor.

"What was that?" I asked.

"A mouse," he said. "I got 'im."

"Okay," I replied, and we went back to sleep.

The mouse had crawled into bed with us, ran up under the covers, and nestled against Dad's warm back. Dad simply grabbed him, squeezed him between his thumb and forefinger, and threw him against the wall. That's all it takes to get a mouse out of your bed.

Dad seldom went to town at night after he moved to the ranch, but one evening the Elks Club had something special going on, so he drove in to play poker. The game went well for him, and he won several hundred dollars. He left the club late, taking his cash with him, and headed home on the highway.

A mile out of town he looked in the rearview mirror and saw headlights approaching rapidly. The speeding car closed quickly and pulled up beside him. Dad could see the dark outline of two men inside it. As they drove down the highway side by side, the car suddenly swerved toward him. Dad jerked the wheel hard to dodge the aggressive move, stomped the accelerator, and shot out ahead of them. Then he quickly steered to the center of the highway and drove straight down the middle, as fast as his pickup would run.

He didn't know who they were, but the two men obviously knew where Dad had been and that he had all that cash on him. He couldn't outrun them, but he kept them from pulling up beside him again.

Dad had his .45 revolver in the glove compartment, loaded. As he sped down the highway in the glare of their headlights, he pulled the gun out and laid it in the seat beside him.

They chased him the full fourteen miles to our turnoff, trying to run him off the road all the way. Dad didn't stop when he reached the turnoff, however; he raced past it and swerved into the driveway of the store on the other side of the highway. He hit the gravel driveway at high speed, slid to a stop, ducked his head halfway behind the truck's window sill, and laid the barrel of his .45 on it. His pursuers followed him into the driveway. They slid to a stop beside him, and found themselves staring down the barrel of that big gun.

The wrong end of a .45 looks like a small cannon—worse if there's a bulldog looking down the barrel at you. The two men stared wide-eyed at Dad and the gun, then suddenly decided the whole thing wasn't worth it. They spun out of the driveway and took off as fast as they had come.

Dad loved to tell how that chase ended. "They come slidin' up there and they both started to jump out. Then they saw that pistol. They stopped dead still, starin' right down the barrel, and their eyes got about as big as silver dollars. Then they got the hell outta there."

I asked him if he had cocked the gun when he pointed it at them. "Ya damn right," he said.

Dad's self-assuredness could be contagious. When George was nine or ten he accompanied Dad to the office of a prominent lawyer and state senator, Wilkie Ham. Dad and George walked into Mr. Ham's spacious suite and sat down in front of his desk. Dad lit a cigar and began to talk with the lawyer, while George gawked around at the elaborate decor.

After they had talked awhile Dad leaned back and casually put his feet up on Mr. Ham's elegant desk, crossing one cowboy boot over the other. George looked at Dad, stood up, and pulled his chair closer to the desk so his short legs would reach. Then he sat back down, scooted way down in the chair, reached his legs up, and plopped his little cowboy boots on the desk beside Dad's.

Mr. Ham stopped momentarily and leaned over the desk to look at George. George looked up at him. He was practically lying on his back in the chair to reach the desk with his boots. The lawyer grinned at the display of inherited cockiness, then continued talking.

Most men his age had retired and stopped working, and many were collecting some sort of government compensation. Dad had no use for them. "Them old farts in town, sittin' around on the street corners drawin' the old age pension" were no cronies of his. He despised anything he saw as a government handout and anyone who accepted them.

He and I occasionally happened onto some of the old men at the blacksmith shop or the machine shop where they hung out. Dad was there to get something repaired, but they were just hanging around to pass the time and chat with customers. They would all stand up when Dad walked in. Those who knew him well enough would shake his hand. "Mr. George, how are you today? Ain't it a fine day, sir?" The ones who didn't know him well would only nod and not even look him in the eye.

One of the men he didn't know well once tried to start a conversation with him. "Well, seventy kicked me right in the ass the other day," he ventured.

"Hell, you're just a kid," Dad replied. The man sat down, and Dad went on about his business.

The men were often younger than him, and many had more education as well. Most of them were taller than him too, but they didn't appear so. He projected a presence that totally masked his size. His mental and emotional dominance intimidated the men, and they all knew that Mr. Blizzard was building himself a ranch out south of town.

As skilled as he was at driving a team of horses, Dad's ability to handle cars and trucks never reached the same level, not even close. He never acknowledged that point, however. In fact he didn't believe it. As far as he was concerned, he did a fine job of driving. I suppose in a sense he was right. His driving wasn't a problem to him. It was a problem to other people, those unlucky enough to be in the vicinity of his vehicle.

He drove forty-five miles an hour when he went to town, and he rode the left front wheel of his pickup right down the white line. This mechanized monster that he didn't understand was thus herded down the highway just to the right of center; parts of it even extended past center.

It was disconcerting to ride with him, even terrifying at times. The approach of every car looked like a sideswipe in the making. As his passengers clung to their seats and prayed that they might slide by the grim reaper one more time, Dad would clench his jaw and stare down the oncoming car as if defying it to invade his half of the highway. If you mentioned how close to the middle he was driving, he'd point at the white line and explain loudly, "Everything this side of that white line is mine!"

Listen to one of those explanations, and you knew you were destined to ride down that white line, perhaps to your doom.

Everyone knew to watch for Dad on the highway. As they passed by him, hugging the far shoulder and kicking up gravel, he'd give them a friendly wave from the center line.

Dad had never owned much before he bought the ranch. He'd been too poor most of his life to afford more than the bare necessities.

One day he went to town by himself, and when he returned that evening he came over to the rock house. He sat and talked with Mom and George for a few minutes, then looked at me and asked, "Wanta come over and stay with me?" Of course I did, so Mom gathered up some clothes for me and we went to his house.

Shortly after we walked in he said, "I've got somethin' to show ya. You wait here while I go get it." He went back outside while I waited. I couldn't imagine what it was.

He came back through the door carrying a rifle, a brand new Winchester lever-action .30-30.

"Whose is that?!" I asked.

"It's mine," he said proudly. "I wanted one all my life. Never could afford one till now."

I already knew what kind it was. A lever-action Winchester was a real cowboy rifle, the most cowboy kind of rifle you could get. I was born knowin' that.

"Can I hold it?" I asked.

"Sure," he said. "Sit down in the chair."

I sat down in a kitchen chair, and he sat in one facing me. He levered the rifle to ensure it wasn't loaded, then let the hammer down and handed it to me. I held it, aimed it, and rubbed my hands over it. The lamplight gleamed on the shiny new barrel and the polished walnut stock. He showed me how to work the lever, and he let me hold one of its powerful shells.

"Maybe someday you can shoot it," he said, "when ya get bigger." I couldn't imagine doing that. It was too big to imagine.

"Does anybody else know about it yet?" I asked.

"Nope," he said. "You're the first one I told."

"I'm the first one you showed it to?"

"Yep," he smiled. "You're the only one that's seen it."

My joy was complete.

The range cattle were often pretty wild, and in the winter when they were hungry and desperate for the feed in the pickup they became brave enough to get close to us. One morning when I was five I unknowingly walked between a wild cow and her calf. The cow snorted, bellowed, jumped stiff-legged in front of me, and threw her head down in a menacing stance. I froze with terror. Before the cow could ram me, Dad jumped between us, swept his hat off his head, and slapped her in the face with it. The loud slap startled her, and she whirled and ran away. I was so shaken that Dad had to walk me back to the truck.

While helping him feed the cattle another winter morning, I witnessed an amazing sight. Dad was standing beside the pickup bed throwing feed out on the ground as the cattle crowded around him. A desperate cow lunged forward, reared up, and landed beside him with both front feet in the bed of the truck. With her front feet in the truck bed, the wild-eyed cow was now standing nearly upright. Dad instantly reared back and slugged her in the jaw as hard as he could. The cow's head snapped over, she lost her balance, reeled sideways out of the truck, and fell to the ground on her side. That was an awesome sight to a little kid.

I'm sure the cow's precarious stance threw her off balance, and that's probably why she fell down when Dad hit her. But to me it looked like he had just slugged her and knocked her down like a prizefighter.

When we got back to the house I ran in and told Mom. "Dad slugged a cow in the jaw this morning and knocked her flat on the ground." She looked as if that didn't surprise her very much.

George says we grew up with John Wayne.

Dad at 75 on Tony

Chapter 7

RATTLERS

Rattlesnakes were the only thing that affected our daily lives as much as the weather. The damn things were everywhere. They roam the country all spring, summer, and fall. Only in the winter months could we stop worrying about them.

People who haven't lived with rattlers believe they always rattle to warn of their presence. Not so. In truth they only rattle a warning about half the time or less. The rest of the time they let you walk right up to them or lay your hand on them, and never make a sound before they strike.

Nothing in my memory is as sinister as a rattler. The sharp, menacing head, with its evil, foreboding face; the darting, probing tongue; the hateful gaze in those fierce, uncaring eyes; the sleek, fluid body of slithering muscle, its every move a deadly threat. That ominous rattle that sounds like nothing else on earth can chill your heart a hundred yards away.

Those devil serpents lurked everywhere, slithering behind every rock, yucca, bush, or gatepost, waiting in ambush to kill or maim. A rattler might be lying coiled anywhere you stepped or wherever you laid your hand, and we knew there would be no warning when the strike came.

A rattler's strike is lightning, a blur of movement. The snake first coils itself into a tight circle to wait for its prey. At a victim's approach the rattler's body tenses like spring steel, then leaps forward like a spring release, mouth wide open, fangs straight out like venomous daggers. The fangs pierce flesh and muscles squeeze sacs in each jaw, shooting venom through the hollow fangs into the victim.

Just as quickly the rattler draws back into a coil and tenses for a second strike. The entire action, strike and recoil, takes only a split second. Humans and most animals can't dodge it even if they see it coming.

The rattler's bite kills small prey such as rats and mice in a matter of seconds. Rabbit-sized animals take a bit longer, but it kills them just as surely. Large animals like horses and cows usually survive the venom but not without paying a high price. They undergo a tremendous amount of swelling and become deliriously sick and nauseous for days.

Mom, George, and I happened onto a rattler one afternoon as we walked through the pasture driving the milk cows to the house. Our cocker spaniel puppy had come along with us. He was running around sniffing everything in sight and having a grand time when we spotted the snake coiled in the grass. The puppy spotted it too. Before we could stop him, the pup walked up to the rattler and tried to sniff it. The snake remained perfectly still and never rattled. When the puppy came close enough the rattler struck, twice, hitting him rapid fire on both sides of the nose before he could back away.

The puppy jumped back, yelped, and pawed his nose at the pain, but in a few minutes it felt better and he started running around again. Halfway back to the house he dropped his head and began to stagger. A few more steps and he fell down. I picked the little guy up and carried him the rest of the way to the house, and made a soft bed for him in the barn.

I expected to find the puppy dead the next morning, but he wasn't. He probably wished he had died though. His head had swelled horribly, becoming bigger around than his body, and his floppy ears stuck straight out from his head. It would have appeared comical if he hadn't been so miserable.

The swelling lasted for several days, and the venom made him deathly sick. He occasionally stood up to drink a little water, but the rest of the time he lay on his side, barely able to breathe. Somehow he survived it.

The puppy knew about rattlers after that. If he saw one or even heard one rattling in the distance, he'd yelp and run for the house as fast as his little legs would carry him.

Our cats were too fast and too smart to get snakebit. Grown cats usually left snakes alone, but if a bunch of kittens found one they tormented it—darting in and out, nipping it, and beating it on the head with their paws. The bewildered snake would strike at them several times, but the kittens would keep him confused, and he could never bite them. So while they merrily pawed him, nipped him, and cuffed him around, he'd retreat as fast as possible. Kittens are hard on a snake's pride.

Occasionally a cow would try to sniff a coiled snake and usually get bit on the nose doing it. A snakebit cow was easy to spot in the herd; their head swelled up like a balloon. It made them so sick they couldn't eat for several days, but they usually recovered. A cow was never bitten twice. Like the puppy, she gave snakes a wide berth after that.

One of our cows did die from a rattlesnake bite. She was unlucky enough to get bit in the throat. The swelling closed off her windpipe and killed her before we found her.

Rattlers weren't a threat to every animal on the place though. Pigs didn't even watch for them. Their venom has little effect on pigs for some reason; consequently they aren't afraid of snakes. Pigs even eat snakes when they get the chance.

I once watched a big sow unknowingly walk up beside a rattler lying coiled in the grass. The rattler took her totally by surprise. It struck her squarely in the shoulder, then quickly recoiled. The startled sow grunted, whirled, stomped one front foot on the rattler, chomped down on it, ripped it to pieces, chewed it up, and swallowed it.

Not a trace of the rattler was left within a minute. The snake had taken its best shot and hadn't even fazed her. The sow licked her chops and calmly walked away.

Rattlers didn't just bite animals, of course; they regularly bit people too. Their venom can swell a forearm to three times its normal size. If unattended the arm will literally swell as big as the person's thigh. It also discolors the skin and destroys a great amount of tissue, often causing a finger, arm, or even a leg to turn black and burst open.

Many people lived even further from town than we did. It often took more than an hour to get a snakebite victim to a doctor. Valuable time was lost as the poison spread.

One of our neighbors, an old lady named Orrie, was working in her garden one day when a rattler hit her in the calf of the leg. She leaped back, and to her horror the snake came with her. Its fangs were caught in her stocking. Orrie panicked and ran screaming toward the house, the maddened snake writhing around her leg as she ran. She couldn't shake it off, but she regained her self control, stopped, and kicked it off with her other foot.

Orrie survived the bite, but she limped the rest of her life.

One man out there made a brave choice when a rattler bit him. He'd become engrossed in his work, let his guard down, and a rattler hit him on the left index finger as he reached for a tool.

The man was far from town and alone. He knew he'd likely lose the finger if the poison had time to spread, and could have lost his entire hand as well. He hesitated only a few moments, then made the choice. He picked up a hatchet in his right hand, laid his finger on a rock, and chopped it off. Considering that he avoided the terrible sickness as well, maybe that wasn't a bad choice to make. It certainly wasn't one for the faint-hearted.

Another neighbor, a little three-year-old girl, was happily walking along and stopped directly in front of a coiled rattler. She didn't see it, and it gave her no warning.

The rattler struck her in the leg. The little girl screamed, but she became too confused and terrified to move. As she stood screaming and crying, the rattler hit her again in the same leg. Still she stood and screamed, and the rattler struck again, sinking its fangs into the same little leg a third time. Finally she ran.

They lived too far from town. They rushed her to a doctor as fast as they could, but the three bites took their toll. The little girl lost her leg; it had to be amputated.

Stories of neighbors being snakebit as well as our own close calls kept an awareness of rattlers on our minds constantly. We habitually looked down to check every step we took, and watched where we placed our hands and what we touched. It became second nature, the only way we could survive.

Chapter 8

MY WONDERLAND

Clay Creek, a sinewy snake thirty miles long, drained a wide area of rolling prairie as it carved its way to the Arkansas River. Just a lazy trickle crawled along its bottom most of the time, and in places the water dried up to leave only patchy pools and short rivulets running. Big rains gave it the ambition to gush a few times a year, and occasionally a gully washer ran the creek bank full. Every two or three years though, the sky opened up and the trickle became a torrent of water a quarter of a mile wide, tearing up trees as it raged across the landscape and rolling boulders the size of a horse for miles along its track. In quiet times the boulders lay scattered over the creek's sandy plain, silent reminders of its dormant ferocity.

Most people saw the creek as just a quiet little stream that lolled across the prairie, occasionally roaring to life and isolating us for a while. But it was far more than that to me. It was a boy's dream—a wide, winding creek bed, lined with big trees and teeming with game, birds, and fish.

The creek was my wonderland, and I roamed it free.

I wandered every inch of the creek, and I knew it all: every tree, every rock and bush, every likely place to jump up a rabbit or a squirrel, every deep hole where I might catch a catfish or a perch. I knew where all the big birds of prey lived too. I watched every nest of owls, hawks, and eagles for miles along its course. Every year I watched a pair of golden eagles raise their young in a nest high in a big cottonwood tree. I got to know those eagles well as I grew up.

I lived to go to the creek. The kids in town had only television, sports, games, parties, and recreation centers. I had so much more. I had the creek.

The nearest bend of the creek was two and a half miles from our house. Sometimes I rode my horse, the fastest way to get there, but just as often I walked. I made six or seven miles walking to the creek and back, and in the summer I normally went barefooted. The soles of my feet were leather. When I walked I visited some of my favorite hunting spots along the way. I'd carry a gun or a bow and arrow and hunt two or three rocky bluffs on the way to the creek, and then hunt a few more on the way back. I knew all the rock outcrops by heart, and every place I might find game.

I went to the creek to hunt in the wintertime too, walking the same miles through the snow. Mom occasionally walked with me, both in winter and summer. We held long conversations about the wildlife and the countryside, the things that interested me. She even helped me carry the game I bagged.

Shooting guns and hunting was a way of life on the prairie, and kids learned about firearms at an early age. I started shooting a BB gun when I was seven, and a .22 rifle and a .410 shotgun when I was nine. I learned how to handle guns safely; if I hadn't I'd have lost the privilege of going hunting.

I developed another interest at a young age; I loved bows and arrows. My first memory of archery was a little hickory bow Dad made me when I was five. I loved that bow and shot it all the time, so when I was seven Dad made me another one, a little stronger than the first. It was a fine bow too, and that wide prairie was a perfect place to shoot it. I shot arrows in every direction, as far as I could see.

Dad gave me a lifelong love with those little bows he made. I never outgrew my fascination for watching the flight of an arrow.

I grew up loving nature, and learned that nature doesn't necessarily love you back. It doesn't hate you either; it simply doesn't care.

Nature's laws were readily apparent on the prairie; its lessons were everywhere. I once witnessed a duel to the death between a rattlesnake and a hawk, a fascinating combat that took place only thirty yards from me. As I walked along a rocky hillside on the way to the creek I spotted the rattler. I stopped and crouched down in the shade of a big rock to watch it. To my surprise, in less than a minute a hawk swooped down on the snake. I crouched low and watched the drama unfold.

The hawk descended like a helicopter. He came in slowly and precisely, landed a few yards from the rattler, and calmly folded his wings. The snake quickly drew into a defensive coil and faced its aggressor. The hawk eyed the snake coolly, strutted a few steps toward it, and began to hop from side to side. The sidewise hopping became an agile dance, a fluid movement that deftly carried him closer and closer to the coiled rattler.

The snake tensed for the strike, but the hawk paused in mid-step, danced backward, and appeared to stop. Then in a lightning blur he charged into striking range. The rattler shot forward, fangs straight out. Anticipating the strike, the hawk feinted back and dodged it with the agility of a ballerina.

Instantly the snake pulled back and coiled for the next shot. Out of range now, the hawk danced sideways again, strutting back and forth and darting his head in and out, taunting the rattler with every move. Then without warning he charged back in to tempt it again and danced back out in time to see it lunge and miss as before.

Again and again the hawk dared the snake, narrowly dodging the lethal fangs each time. The tireless bird danced, darted, and taunted until the rattler's fatigue began to show. Timing became its problem, split-second timing. Striking, missing, and flopping on the ground, the battle-worn snake took longer and longer to draw back into its coil.

The hawk picked up speed, charging in and out relentlessly, forcing the snake to strike more and more. Then it struck, missed, landed straight out, and the hawk pounced on the rattler's head with both feet and drove his talons through it.

As the snake writhed beneath him, its life ebbing away, the hawk stood up straight, defiant, proudly posing for the applause of an unseen audience.

I could easily applaud the bird in that drama. He appeared heroic, bravely risking his life to attack a deadly rattler.

Another hawk appeared less heroic, however, even cowardly. It flew over me one day with a baby jack rabbit locked in its talons, still alive. With easy swoops of its wings the indifferent bird carried its wailing catch off to some chosen dining spot. The little rabbit's helpless voice was haunting, echoing on a deaf landscape as it screamed its life away.

In time I realized that both hawks hunted for the same reason. The rattler was as much an innocent victim as the baby rabbit. Neither hawk acted bravely and neither acted cowardly; they both simply needed a meal.

For years I watched the golden eagles that nested on the creek. Huge, fascinating birds the size of bald eagles, they have the same physical appearance except for color. Instead of the white head and tail seen on bald eagles, golden eagles are dark gray to black over their entire body. And they are the fastest flying birds in North America. With its seven-foot wingspan, a golden eagle can fly seventy miles an hour on the level. In a dive it reaches even greater speeds.

Those majestic birds mate for life, the pair returning year after year to the same nest to raise their young. Every spring they add new material to the nest, making it grow larger and larger. Both mama and papa share the duties of caring for the baby eagles when they hatch.

I saw the eagles return to the big cottonwood tree every spring and watched their nest grow over the years. By the time I reached my teens, the nest was five feet high and six or seven feet across.

The baby eagles up there intrigued me. I wanted to see them. I'd wanted to see them for years, but I never had, because getting to the nest required climbing that big tree.

The nest sat on a large limb about sixty feet off the ground and twenty feet out from the trunk. When viewed from ground level the climb didn't look bad. I'd climbed lots of smaller trees; how much different could it be to climb a big one? After all, the same principles applied, just climb from one limb to another until you get there.

I did worry a little about my fear of heights. It certainly wouldn't help me when I was sixty feet off the ground, but I'd just have to deal with it if I was ever going to climb that tree. I looked the tree over many times, considered all the problems I could think of, and finally convinced myself I could do it. What I didn't consider, of course, were the problems I hadn't thought of.

One spring day I decided the time had come. I knew how long the eagles had been nesting and that the babies should have hatched by now. A slight wind was blowing, but it was still fairly calm for the prairie. I took a rifle with me and walked to the creek.

One of the eagles was sitting on the nest, glaring down at me as if I were an intruder. I guess I was. I looked around in the sky and couldn't see its mate anywhere. Aiming the rifle several inches over the bird's head, I fired a shot. At the sound of the shot it flew away.

I always climbed trees barefooted, so I leaned my rifle against another tree, took off my shoes, and began to climb. The tree had plenty of limbs to grasp, so the climb went pretty much as planned, until I reached the big limb the nest sat on. Sixty feet off the ground, I stopped, looked down, and began to feel a little queasy. The wind blew harder up here, I felt a thousand feet high, and the twenty feet out to the nest looked like a mile.

I sat on the limb for a while, clinging to the trunk, and tried to accustom myself to the height. The nest looked huge from where I sat, and after a few minutes I began to feel a little better. "Hey, things are going okay," I told myself. "And those baby eagles are only twenty feet away now."

The limb was over a foot thick. I lay my belly flat on it so I could hold on with my legs as well as my arms, and began to crawl toward the nest. I crawled only a few feet from the trunk and stopped; I could feel the limb swaying in the wind and me with it. It wasn't swaying too badly though, so I took a deep breath, held tighter to the limb, and began to inch forward.

I peeked around the limb once to look downward, and froze. Sixty feet feels really high looking straight down; I decided not to do that again. I began to think how great it would feel when this was all over and I was standing on the ground. Clearly the adventure was losing some of its romance.

All things considered, however, it went fairly well, until I got halfway to the nest. Ten feet from the nest I heard an ominous sound echoing in the distance, a shrill, chilling sound I'd heard before. The sound was a scream—an eagle's scream—once heard, never forgotten. I froze to the limb and turned my head to the right, the direction of the scream. An eagle came straight at me, screaming in at seventy miles an hour.

I turned my head away, closed my eyes, pushed my face into the limb, and hung on tight. The screaming came closer and closer, louder and louder, until it seemed to engulf me. At the last second the eagle pulled up and swooped over me, so close I felt its wind on the back of my neck.

I lay there hugging the limb for a long time, thinking I should probably get out of there. But then, look how far I'd come, and I was almost there. So, something unforeseen had happened, something I hadn't planned on. Was I to be so easily discouraged, turn tail at the first problem that came along? I looked up at the huge nest, so close now. No. No eagle could scare me off by just swooping down and screaming at me, not with only ten feet to go.

I raised my head and looked all around. Nothing in sight. Okay, here we go. I began to inch my way toward the nest again. Everything went fine for about five feet, then I heard a scream, another scream, and two screams together. I looked in the same direction as before. Both eagles came at me this time, diving straight in like black, screaming rockets. I turned away, grinding my face back into the limb.

They screamed in my ears as they blew by, inches over my back. This time they didn't leave. They slowly circled the tree, heads turned, watching me.

No more screaming now, only watching. This was it. Five feet from their babies was as close as I'd get. One more inch toward that nest and those eagles would send me to hell. I couldn't begin to fight them off if they attacked, certainly not up here. They'd knock me off this limb.

It all made sense when I thought about it. I shouldn't have been surprised to find they'd fight for their babies, and it would have helped if I'd figured that out before I got way up there too. I did figure out one thing though. It was time to get the hell out of there.

I started moving again, this time in reverse. I sure hoped the eagles could see I was going the other way. They continued to circle and watch me intently as I slowly crawled backwards to the trunk, and they stayed in close until I reached the ground.

As soon as I touched ground they both landed on the nest and began talking rapidly to their babies. I picked up my rifle and walked away. The eagles glared at me indignantly until I walked out of sight.

I became interested in yet another hunting weapon when I was a teenager, so I saved my money and bought a pellet rifle. The rifle shot lead pellets much like .22 caliber bullets, but fired them with compressed air instead of gunpowder. Pumping a lever beneath the barrel several times loaded it with compressed air. It shot considerably harder than my BB gun, which was also air-powered, so to me it seemed a very powerful weapon.

Dad warned me that my pellet rifle wasn't as powerful as I thought, but what did he know about guns? I didn't know as much as I thought I did, of course, and one day on the creek I received a lesson. A badger taught me.

Pound for pound the badger is the fiercest animal on the prairie. An adult weighs thirty-five to forty pounds, has a strong, stocky body, short legs with huge claws, a head like a small bear, powerful jaws, and vicious teeth. Couple all that with a fighting temperament, and this little powerhouse is a rough character. A dog twice its size usually won't mess with a badger. If it does and is lucky enough to live through the attack, the dog will never try it again.

I was exploring the creek on foot one summer day, carrying my pellet rifle with me. I stopped and peeked around a large cottonwood tree, and saw a rare sight coming down the creek bed: two badgers, trotting along single file, heading my direction. Being a brave and stalwart lad, and armed with a powerful weapon, I viewed the situation in much the same way a big game hunter in Africa might view the approach of a pair of lions, or maybe bull elephants.

The course the two badgers were on would bring them past my position behind the tree but out of range of my pellet rifle. I had to close with them. They would pass by me on an open stretch of sand a good way from the nearest cover. I waited until they reached that point, then I charged them. One peeled off and headed for the nearest brush, but the other took off running directly away from me, across the open creek bed. I chased after him and cornered him against a high bank. Now I had him where I wanted him, or at least it seemed that way at the moment.

The badger whirled, dropped into a crouch, bared his savage teeth, and uttered a low, vicious snarl. I stopped my charge, stood my ground, and took careful aim. I coolly shot him in the forehead with a pellet, and dropped him where he stood. He folded up and rolled over on his side, motionless. I had faced the beast bravely and brought him down.

I laid down my gun, ran over to the badger, grabbed hold of his hind feet, and picked him up. I wanted to get a close look at him. He was sleek and heavy, and had a beautiful coat. Grasping those huge back claws in my hands, I held him up at eye level to look at his head. I turned him around to get a good look at his face.

I looked at his face, and looked at his forehead where I'd shot him. I looked at my pellet—hanging from the hair on his forehead. The pellet hadn't penetrated his skull; it had hardly broken the skin. Then, a terrible realization. The badger was breathing. The pellet had merely knocked him unconscious.

The badger, that I now held inches from my face, was alive!

I screamed, dropped the badger, and tore off across the creek bed as hard as I could run. I ran several hundred yards before I lost my breath and had to stop and sit down. As I sat gasping for air and marveling at what a close call I'd had, I remembered Dad's warning about overestimating my weapon. I never told him about shooting that badger, and I never messed with one again either.

Four ponds lay near our house, all strung out in a line along the bottom of the draw. Each was about thirty feet across by sixty or seventy feet long, and only three or four feet deep. The ponds were normally dry, with clay bottoms as hard as cement. It took a gully washer to fill them, and gully washers only happened once or twice a year. When the ponds did get filled, the water only stayed in them for about three weeks, then dried up again.

An amazing thing happened when the ponds filled with water. They quickly filled with life: garter snakes, insects, all kinds of little swimming creatures, and strangely enough, frogs. The ponds could lay bone dry for a year, and when a flood came they would instantly fill with frogs. In fact, when a gully washer made the draw run in the middle of the night, along with the roar of the water we would hear the croaking of thousands of frogs. When the water stopped running, the ponds teemed with them.

I swam in the ponds with all those mud-loving creatures. I caught them, studied them through a magnifying glass, and learned all I could about them. The sudden appearance of the frogs mystified me. Where did full-grown frogs come from on the dry prairie?

As soon as a gully washer brought the frogs out, they laid thousands of eggs. The eggs hatched in just a few days, so within a week or so the ponds would fill with tadpoles. The tadpoles quickly matured and turned into baby frogs. The ponds then dried up, and the frogs disappeared until the next gully washer came.

A simple experiment explained where the frogs came from when it rained and how they disappeared when the ponds dried up. I filled a big bucket with damp dirt and put several in it. As the dirt began to dry out, I watched the frogs dig down into it and bury themselves. They used their hind legs to dig in backwards, burying themselves upright so they could come out quickly when the water again softened the hard earth above them.

The prairie harbors millions of those frogs. They hibernate under the dry washes and come out for only short periods of time, just long enough to reproduce. I figured they must really look forward to those times. Mom laughed when I told her that.

Life blood of the prairie

Duststorm approaching the Rock House

Chapter 9

WORK, WINDMILLS, and WEATHER

A major change took place about the time Dad moved to the rock house, one I could have done without. I became old enough to start working regularly. George had been working every day for several years, however, so I didn't have much room to complain.

Dad was always the boss when you worked for him. He ran the show, and he had an uncanny quality, a mystique, that made everyone want to please him. This instinctive ability to lead others operated like a sixth sense. Everyone around him—family, friends, and those who worked for him—strove for his approval, and most of their efforts went unacknowledged. What little emotional reward one might receive from time to time was hard won. Dad had spent a lifetime working rough men under rugged conditions, and he seldom extended a compliment, a pat on the back, or a "job well done."

Although he offered few compliments, what he didn't say was important. He referred to kids who lived in town as "town kids," and he didn't care for town kids, unless they were willing to work hard. That wasn't surprising; he didn't have much use for anyone who didn't work hard, kids or grownups. George and I didn't get many direct compliments, but we knew we weren't town kids.

When we had a job to do, that's what Dad wanted done. "Now listen," he'd tell us. "At the end of the day I wanta hear that a job's done, not a buncha damn excuses why it ain't."

Being the oldest, George had worked harder than me from the time we moved to the ranch. While I'd spent most of my younger years playing, he'd been off building barbwire fence or driving the tractor in one of Dad's vain attempts to farm that dryland soil. The work was hard labor, and George worked hard.

Farm laborers work long, strenuous hours in the sun, and they pay a high price for it. Their work is extremely tiring, and anyone who has lived around them knows their routine when they wake up in the morning. They don't get right out of bed when they first wake, nor do they lie there for awhile savoring the moment as some of us do. Soon after they wake, they sit up on the side of the bed, lean forward, rest their arms on their legs, and hang their head down. They stay in that position a while before they do anything else.

All the farm laborers I've ever seen followed this same routine when they woke. They did it for two reasons: because even after a night's sleep they were still bone tired, and because they had to go out and do it again. Those few minutes were needed to gather determination before they forced themselves to their feet, stretched their tired muscles, and faced another hard day.

Every laborer I ever saw sitting that way was a young man or a middle-aged man. All except one, that is, George. George did it when he was a teenager. He'd wake up, sit on the side of the bed, and hang his head—bone tired, working up the fortitude to face another day. Then after a few minutes he'd slowly stand up with quiet resolve in his eyes, and go do it again.

In an effort to save the cost of winter cattle feed, Dad tried his hand at farming, God help us. There was nothing wrong with the idea; it simply didn't work most of the time.

He tried various grain crops, his goal being just to raise enough to feed the cattle through the winter instead of having to buy it. This dryland farming was a risky endeavor at best. Our sad attempts proved either that Dad was no good at farming or that the land wasn't suitable for it. I believe we proved both those things.

Dad didn't know much about farming, but he knew we needed a tractor. So he went to town and bought a little tractor, a very little tractor, and with it we set about to farm five hundred acres. The tractor had no cab to fend off the blowing dust or the blistering sun, a seat that felt like a rock, and not enough power to cultivate a respectable garden. It struggled across the field like a dying tortoise crawling to its doom.

The little tractor could plant only two rows at a time and was a miserable thing to drive. Hot, dusty, and loud, it crawled along so damn slow that an entire day's planting looked like you hadn't covered any ground at all. George and I knew there were plenty of tractors on the market with more power. We complained about it as much as we dared, but Dad always had the same old-fashioned argument, "It runs faster than a horse can walk." True enough, but the logic escaped us.

Our farming attempts were largely failures, and I suspect ultimately cost more money than they made. Dad didn't give up easily though. Year after year we crawled the fields on the little tractor.

George and I learned to despise that tractor, but driving it did have one benefit; we were paid for it. Normal chores such as taking care of the livestock were everyday responsibilities for all of us, but for tasks such as driving the tractor or building fence, Dad paid us a daily wage. It wasn't a great amount, and considering the hours we put in it wasn't even minimum wage, but it was more than most of our neighbors' kids made for working at home. Most of them made nothing.

George and I had our own cattle too, usually three or four cows apiece, and we each had our own brand registered in our name. The calves our cows produced each year belonged to us, as well as the money they brought when they grew big enough to go to market.

We had plenty of spending money, and we had earned it.

Several chores had to be done before we left for school in the morning, and the same ones again in the evening.

During the winter we were up at 4:30 in the morning in order to finish the chores in time to catch the school bus. Four-thirty sounded awfully early then; it still does. Our chores included milking the cows, feeding the pigs, and helping Dad load the cattle feed on the truck. With the truck loaded he could feed the range cattle by himself after we left for school.

Mom got up earlier than we did. She woke us with a pleasant word and a touch, then gave us some hot cocoa while we pulled on heavy coats, caps, gloves, and overshoes. We lit a kerosene lantern, gathered up the flashlight and two or three milk buckets, and headed for the barn.

It was dark at that time of morning and the coldest it had been all night. Calm mornings were frosty and still, and kind of pretty. We could just see the outlines of the windmill and the barn against the dawning sky. Our breath blew steam in the crispy air, and frost glistened in the lantern light.

Windy mornings weren't so pleasant. The wind gave the cold a harsher bite, and blowing snow and ice seared our faces and burned our eyes. If it had snowed the night before, or if snow was still falling, we had to set the lantern down and shovel the drifts away from the barn doors and corral gates before we could open them. We shoveled snow like tornadoes on those mornings.

First we milked the cows, a job neither George nor I particularly enjoyed. I think the cows did. Milk cows are the most cantankerous animals on earth under the best of conditions, and at 4:30 A.M. in the middle of winter they're at their worst.

We usually had between two and four cows to milk, which was more than enough. We milked them in a corner of the barn petitioned off just for that, the part we lovingly called the "milk barn." The milk barn had four stalls, or stanchions, attached to a manger. Each stanchion consisted of two vertical boards, separated by enough space for a cow to put her head through and eat grain from the manger. One of the boards was hinged at the bottom so the top could be moved back and forth, and also locked in place. When the cow stuck her head through we pushed the board against her neck and locked it, fastening her into the stanchion. The stanchion held the cow's head securely but loose enough to allow her to stand comfortably and eat from the manger while we milked her.

Before we went out to bring the cows in from the corral, we prepared the milk barn perfectly for their entrance. First we hung the lantern from a nail on an overhead rafter to light up the place, then we poured grain into each of their stalls. With that done we walked out into the corral with the flashlight, found the cows in the darkness, and drove them to the milk barn. With the grain already waiting in their stalls, they could walk right in, put their heads through the stanchions, and begin eating. We could then fasten them in and begin milking.

That's how it should have worked anyway; in theory it sounds simple and efficient. In practice, however, it didn't come close to working that way.

The fun began before the cows even got to the milk barn. As we drove them through the dark corral with the flashlight, herding them toward the lantern-lit doorway, they'd all try to veer off and make a run for it. We anticipated that and usually headed them off successfully and forced them through the door.

The milk barn wasn't a large space. It was only wide enough for four cows, and barely deep enough for us to walk behind them as they stood locked in the stanchions. The cows really put on a show when they got in there. Each one had her own stall from which she ate twice a day, and each stall had grain in it. They all knew which one was theirs, so all they had to do was walk to their stall, put their head in, and begin eating. They didn't do that. Instead they all tried to rob grain from another cow's stall, while at the same time trying to protect their own by swinging their rear ends over the opening. This resulted in several impossible skirmishes going on simultaneously. The milk barn wasn't big enough for that kind of chaos. The cows knew that.

We always had to plunge in and break up the fights, and try to get the cows started toward their own stalls. When we'd get one to her stall, she wouldn't just put her head through and begin to eat as you might hope, instead she'd poke her head in quickly, grab a mouthful, and jerk it back out while one of us tried to trap her by diving for the stanchion lock.

All this was just the prelude. When we finally outflanked them and actually got them all fastened into their stanchions, the part the cows enjoyed the most was about to begin.

Milking a cow is a simple thing, or at least it should be. It's a matter of sitting on a stool, placing a bucket under the cow's bag, and methodically squeezing the milk from her teats into the bucket. Again the procedure sounds simple, but it doesn't play out that way at all.

Milk cows hold their bladders in check for hours, refraining from relieving themselves until just the right moment. They hold it until they get into the milk barn, and until the milker sits down and starts milking them. Then without fail, they let go. All milk cows know that trick, and all of them do it. It disrupts the milker—their only goal in life.

Another favorite milk cow trick is kicking. They love to kick the milker. To prevent this we used "kicker chains," small chains that wrap around the cow's back legs and fasten them tightly together. With her legs fastened together, it becomes impossible for the cow to kick with one foot. Sometimes though, as you're milking away, a particularly ambitious cow will attempt a mighty kick even with the chains on. This throws both back legs from under the cow, and causes her to fall down on her side. This too is fairly disruptive to the milking process.

Some cows don't kick, but it's only a ploy. They do it so you won't bother to put the chains on them. Then when you're halfway through the milking, they pick up one foot and stick it down in the milk bucket.

Milk cows are resourceful. They even know how to make the best use of their tail. A cow will wait until you're well into the milking, then casually, so as not to draw your attention, she'll swing her tail far to the other side, tense it up like a spring, and snap it back into your face like a bullwhip.

If one has never had the experience of milking a cow, it's difficult to appreciate what a combination of skill, dexterity, cunning, and blind luck it takes to actually finish the drama and emerge with a bucket of milk and your life.

After we finished the milking, the rest of the morning chores were pure delight. Back at the house we ate a quick breakfast and changed clothes. Mom handed us our lunches and told us goodbye as we jumped on our horses to ride to the highway to catch the school bus. Mom waved to us until we rode out of sight.

After school we rode back to the house and changed clothes. Mom was there to greet us and ask how our day had gone, then it was time to start the chores again. The milk cows were glad to see us, having spent all day restraining themselves in preparation for the evening performance.

When we finished outside we had one last chore in the house—turning the cream separator. The cream separator was a hand-turned device that separated the cream from the milk. The separator stood about four feet off the kitchen floor and worked like a centrifuge. It had a crank that George and I turned by hand for about twenty minutes each evening. The separator was where Mom got the cream to sell to her customers in town, where the pigs got the skim milk that made up part of their daily diet, and where George and I got a workout turning the damn thing.

I once became forgetful about a daily chore. I had a hard time remembering one thing, but Mom helped me. She gave me a memory lesson, the best one I ever had.

Mom normally gave spankings with a board. It wasn't a big board, but adequate. She didn't generally give hard spankings either, just adequate. Some were harder than others though; she varied them as the violation warranted and according to whether or not she was dealing with a repeat offense.

One summer I fell into the habit of leaving a cow's head locked in the stanchion after I finished the morning milking. After a couple of hours of trying to pull her head out, the cow would really get desperate. Mom had found her locked in there several times, thrashing around wildly and trying to force her head out.

She had told me several times I'd better quit forgetting to unlock the cow's head, and the last warning had been a stern one.

I was sitting in the outhouse one sunny morning, in a dreamy mood, at peace with the world. My pants hung comfortably around my ankles. Life was good. Suddenly the pastoral scene was shattered. The outhouse door flew open and Mom came boiling through it, a board in her hand and fire in her eyes. I didn't know what was going on, but from where I sat it looked pretty serious.

She didn't say a word. She grabbed me up by the back of the neck with her left hand and laid the board across my behind with her right. With my pants down around my ankles, the only way I could move was to jump flat-footed with both feet. The first swat and the first jump propelled me out through the door. Another swat followed, and another jump. That board landing on my bare bottom gave me the idea to pull my pants up the first chance I got. Not only would the swats feel a little less raw, I could also make better headway than I could hopping along with my pants down. I still didn't know what this was all about, but wherever we were going I wanted to get there as fast as we could.

In between a couple of hops, I reached down and took hold of my pants, but the board landed again before I could pull them up. Now I was hopping along bent over, trying not to lose the grip on my pants. I managed to yank them up a little more with each jump, and somehow got them up around my waist and buttoned. Now we could make some headway.

The swats did feel slightly less rude with my pants on, and I could make better time, but I couldn't outdistance Mom and that board. She still hadn't said a word, and I still didn't know where we were going, but it didn't seem prudent to stop and inquire.

I tried to get a bearing on our direction, and it began to look like we were heading for the barn. I steered myself, Mom, and the board in that direction as best I could, trying to make it as straight a shot as possible. I headed for the nearest barn door, but Mom propelled me around to the back side toward the door to the milk barn. The light began to dawn. I opened the door and saw the answer.

There stood the cow, her head locked in the stanchion. Mom looked me hard in the eye, laid that board on one more time, and walked away without comment. No comment was needed; she had communicated perfectly.

Occasionally a range cow would reject her calf. For unknown reasons she wouldn't claim it, nor would she let it nurse. One winter Dad and I noticed a little heifer calf trying to nurse a few days after she was born. She was following her mother along, but the cow kicked her away whenever she came close. We roped the calf and took her home to care for her in the barn.

The little heifer had her own pen inside the barn, and it became my job to feed her each day. I started out feeding her milk from a bottle, then slowly she graduated to drinking it from a bucket, and finally to eating solid food. I played with her from the time we brought her in, and she became a pet. Head butting was her favorite game. I'd get down on my hands and knees and lower my head in a mock fighting stance. She'd put her head against mine and we'd both push each other back and forth across the pen, pawing the dirt and acting as if we were fighting in earnest. She loved it, and she knew it was only a game, never trying to butt me hard or ram me unexpectedly. She just pushed with her forehead and pawed the dirt like I did.

After a few months the little heifer grew big enough to fend for herself and went back to the herd. I missed playing with her, but now she was just another range cow. I could recognize her in the herd all her life, however.

Dad and I were out feeding the cattle one morning the second winter after we had rescued her. She was a grown cow by then. I was driving the pickup as Dad walked behind stringing out the cottonseed cake. Suddenly I heard him holler, "What the hell!" I looked back and there was the playful cow with her forehead against his side, pushing him and pawing the dirt. Dad thought he was being attacked. "What the hell's wrong with this cow?" he hollered at me, as if I might know.

I stopped the truck, walked back, and pushed her away. I also gave her a couple of pats that Dad didn't see as she walked away. He didn't recognize her as the heifer we'd rescued; he just looked confused. "Wonder what's wrong with her?" he said. "First I thought she was tryin' to butt me, but all she did was just push and shove. I never seen a cow act like that before."

"Me neither," I said, shrugging my shoulders. He looked a little suspicious as I turned and walked back to the cab.

The most exciting day of the year came in the spring. Branding day, the day we branded all the calves born in the past year. We also dehorned them, castrated the males, and vaccinated them against hoof and mouth disease, all at the same time. It was an exciting day for the calves too.

Displaying a registered brand on cattle was the only way to prove ownership in case they strayed onto someone else's land or were stolen, the brand filling much the same role as an automobile registration. Before cattle could be sold at an auction yard their brands were inspected closely by a state inspector to ensure that they hadn't been altered.

A calf would generally stay with its mother until close to a year old, and was fairly safe from straying off alone until then. After that age we had to brand them to prevent their possible loss and to sell them.

The perfectionist in Dad demanded that everything be done exactly right, so he prepared long and hard for branding day, and underwent a lot of anxiety in the process. He planned so long and worried so much that by the time branding day arrived he was a nervous wreck, and so were we.

A wood fire heated the branding irons, and as Dad did much of the branding himself, he was especially particular about the firewood. Each year we cut every single piece of firewood to an exact length, and stacked it neatly on the very same spot as the year before.

One year when I was ten, on the day before branding day, the whole thing got the best of him. I was riding in the pickup with Dad as he drove around checking and rechecking everything in preparation for the big day. He was very intense, so we weren't talking much. Though we'd already done it several times, he decided to drive up by the branding chute and check his firewood, one more time. We went careening up to the branding chute, Dad slid the truck to a stop, jumped out, and took off practically running toward the stack of firewood. I stayed in the truck.

Suddenly he tripped over his own feet and fell down, flat on his side. He hit the ground with a loud whump and lay still. It worried me to see him fall like that, but I sat still and watched him for a minute. It was a good idea to give him plenty of room at times like this.

He fell hard on his left side and lay with his left arm pinned under his body. His hat was still on his head. After he fell he didn't move; he didn't even twitch. He lay with his back to me, so I couldn't see his face from where I sat in the truck. As he continued to lay in that position, perfectly still, I became frightened. Afraid he might be badly hurt, I leaped out of the truck and started running toward him.

I ran around in front of him, close enough to see his face, and stopped short. His eyes were open, and seething like a volcano. He was just lying there in a rage because he'd fallen down.

I backed off, slow and easy, walked around a little, looked all around, and watched him warily out of the corner of my eye. He still didn't move.

Then he began to move his right arm. Still lying perfectly still, he slowly reached up toward his head, took hold of his hat brim, and hollered.

"Goddammit to hell!" he bellowed. He lunged to his feet, threw his hat on the ground, and began cussing and dancing around wildly and stomping and kicking his hat.

He danced, cussed, kicked, raved, and stirred up a big cloud of dust. I leaned on the fence and watched. After a while he began to wind down, and the dust started to settle. He finally stopped, reached down, picked up his hat, dusted it off, and put it back on his head.

We both walked to the truck, stepped in, and drove away without a word.

Dad may have approached branding day with anxiety, but George and I looked forward to it. It was rough, hard, and exhilarating, a real cowboy kind of day. We had to get up extra early that morning so we could finish the chores and start rounding up the herd. When the chores were done we hurriedly saddled our horses and headed for the distant corners of the south pasture. Dawn was just breaking as we galloped through the cool wind.

Branding was more than we could handle by ourselves, so our good neighbors and friends, the Eddlemans, always helped us. They were hard workers, and they respected Dad and what he was trying to do. Ernest Eddleman, his two sons, and his daughter came to help, and sometimes other members of the family as well. They all knew how to work cattle, and Mr. Eddleman's daughter, Ethel, could ride and rope with the best of them.

We did all the branding at Dad's Place. The Eddlemans arrived early with their saddle horses in trailers, and while Ernest helped Dad start the branding iron fire and other last minute chores, the others unloaded their horses and headed out to the pasture to help George and me. As we were rounding up the cattle, the Eddlemans would come charging over the hill like a band of wild buckaroos,

Branding day, Gary on right "helping"

and soon we'd have the whole herd heading for the corrals at Dad's Place.

After we drove the cattle into the corrals, we separated out the young ones, those born in the past year. Their ages varied from baby calves to yearlings, but the youngest ones got a respite; we let them go back with their mothers and wait until the following year. When the larger calves and yearlings had all been separated, we turned the cows, bulls, and little ones back out to pasture. Then we tied our horses to fence posts, and the real work began.

The yearlings went into the "crowding pen," a small pen from which we funneled them into the branding chute. The branding chute was a large device that locked one in and held it stationary while we branded, dehorned, and vaccinated it. The entire process took only a couple of minutes after we fastened a yearling in the chute.

The branding chute would hold only yearlings and full-grown cattle, and wouldn't accommodate the smaller ones. We roped the smaller calves and held them down to work on them. It took two people sitting on the ground to hold a calf down, one to hold the head and front legs, and the other to hold the back legs.

Dad and Mr. Eddleman did most of the branding, while others worked the branding chute, roped, dehorned, vaccinated, or held calves down. The work-charged atmosphere was intense, fast-paced, and fun. Cedar smoke from the branding iron fire mixed with clouds of kicked-up dust as folks chased bawling calves around the corral, whirled lariat loops through the air, ran sideways to dodge the occasional charge of a mad yearling, hollered back and forth at one another, cussed loudly, and laughed heartily.

One year when I was sitting on the ground holding a calf's back legs, it kicked loose and threw me off balance just as Dad was about to brand it. My left leg flew upward, and hit the red hot branding iron in Dad's hands. Before he could pull it back he branded me, right on the shin bone. My leg still carries Dad's brand.

Branding day was a long one for Mom. She cooked the biggest dinner of the year, because she knew eight or ten hungry people would converge on her at noon. Since she normally didn't like to cook for just four people, she certainly didn't enjoy cooking for that many. But she gave it her best anyway and made great meals on branding day.

When we finished late in the afternoon, and the Eddlemans went home, we unsaddled the horses and did the evening chores as quickly as possible. Then we headed for the Eddleman's place to share a big supper and celebrate another successful branding day. Everyone except Dad, that is. Dad was too tired and emotionally drained from all the anxiety he'd put himself through in anticipation of the event. He was older than the rest of us too, thirty years older than even Mr. Eddleman. He went to bed early and got a good night's sleep.

Another exciting time occurred each year when we sent cattle to auction. George and I rounded up the herd early in the morning similar to branding day, then we corralled them and separated out the ones to go to market. An eighteen-wheel cattle truck came and backed up to the loading chute. The big trucks and their tough drivers always fascinated me.

Part of the truck driver's job was to help us separate the cattle in the corrals and drive them through the loading chute onto the truck. It was hot, dusty work, in a corral full of milling cattle and an overly excited Dad.

A particularly surly truck driver came one year when I was ten or eleven. He glared at me as he worked, obviously disapproving of the way I drove the cattle around the corral. He thought I was a little overly exuberant, and I probably was. Finally he got mad enough to start hollering and shouting orders at me. Dad was working on the far side of the corral, but he overheard him. "Hey, who do you think you're talkin' to?" he hollered at the driver.

"That kid's too full of piss and vinegar," the man hollered back at him.

Dad flared. He pointed at the cattle with a jabbing gesture and shouted, "You take care of these goddam cattle! I'll worry about the kid."

That really miffed the truck driver. He glared at me as I smirked and went on doing the same thing, only with added gusto. He didn't say any more though, he just fumed.

The driver really disliked me by the time he left. I waved goodbye to him as he drove away. He didn't smile.

The infernal wind blows too much on the prairie, but the wind was a blessing we couldn't have lived without. A herd of cattle drinks a large amount of water every day, and because Clay Creek didn't cross our land, we were totally dependent on the wind.

Five windmills supplied our water. They were spaced fairly evenly over the ranch, all pumping from aquifers one to two hundred feet deep. Tanks of metal or cement sat beside them to catch drinking water for the cattle.

Windmills and their underground equipment are mechanical devices, and though most of the components are durable, all are subject to wearing out or breaking. With five of them running almost constantly, at least one usually needed repair at any given time; sometimes more than one did. George and I learned more than we ever wanted to know about windmills. We could fix anything from the top of the derrick to the bottom of the well.

Our windmill derricks stood thirty feet high from the ground to the walkway, and depending on its diameter, the wheel added another six or eight feet. The derricks were made of stout timbers and anchored by four large cedar posts buried six feet in the ground. A ladder ran straight up one side for climbing to the top.

Atop the windmill sits the wheel, tail, and gearbox. The wind turns the wheel, rotating a shaft that extends into the gearbox. The gearbox converts the rotary motion of the wheel into a vertical, reciprocating motion that pumps the water from the ground.

The tail positions the wheel, keeping it pointed into the wind as it changes direction. Like a high-flying flag, the flat, vertical tail points in the direction the wind is blowing. The tail intersects the wheel at nearly a right angle, keeping the wheel facing directly into the wind. The tail isn't rigidly held at that angle, however; a spring holds it in position. The spring allows the windmill to be turned off. This is accomplished by pulling a shutoff wire that extends from the top down along one of the corner timbers of the derrick. The shutoff wire pulls the wheel around parallel to the tail, taking it out of the wind stream, and also sets a brake to prevent its turning.

Extremely high winds can turn the wheel too fast and tear it apart, and may damage other equipment as well. The windmill has an automatic shutoff in case the wind gets too high, but the shutoff doesn't always work properly. It's best to turn the windmill off before hard winds hit if possible.

The manufacturer's name is normally imprinted on the tail, and that name was usually Chicago Aermotor in our part of the country. Chicago Aermotor made a large percentage of the windmills used in the West. The tail always had another distinctive mark as well—bullet holes. It had long been a Western tradition to shoot bullet holes through windmill tails, most commonly with .22 rifles. The holes didn't hinder the windmill's function, nor did they help it. They simply documented the fact that it had been standing longer than two or three days.

The gearbox on top transfers the vertical motion to a set of long rods, or "sucker rods," that move up and down and pump the water. The sucker rods run down through the derrick and into a standpipe extending three or four feet above ground between the legs. Both the pipe and sucker rods run completely to the bottom of the well and several feet below the water table, usually somewhere between one and two hundred feet deep.

The individual sucker rods are wooden, about an inch in diameter, and fifteen to twenty feet long. Heavy iron connections with threads on them are attached to each end of the rods. These connections allow the rods to be screwed together into a continuous string. As the wheel turns at the top, the rods move up and down inside the pipe in approximately a ten-inch stroke.

At the bottom of the well, below the water level, is a simple pump consisting of a one-way valve. It opens on the downstroke to allow water to enter the pipe, and closes on the upstroke to trap the water and move it upward. Thus with each stroke the amount of water trapped at the bottom is pumped out at the surface.

So—the wind blows, the wheel turns, the sucker rods move up and down, and water flows up the pipe and into the tank. The windmill is a wonderful thing.

Though our windmills ran almost constantly, the wheel, tail, and gears at the top were surprisingly the most durable parts and required the least maintenance and repair. That was good for me, as I never liked climbing on the derricks very well anyway. The little walkway at the top was only about a foot and a half wide, and nobody ever used safety belts when they worked up there. It always took me a few minutes to get used to the height again if I hadn't been to the top of a windmill for a while. I could adjust to it and do the job, but I still didn't like it.

Working on top of windmills was considered a real cowboy thing to do. Being a good "windmill man" boosted a cowboy's qualifications for a ranch job. I guess I wasn't a real windmill man at heart; I always felt better standing at the bottom of a derrick than perched on top of it.

Most of our problems with wells occurred when the pipes froze in the wintertime. Water would freeze solid in the standpipe above ground and shut down the well. A simple device should have prevented its freezing, but sometimes it didn't work well on the coldest nights.

All through the winter the ground stays several degrees warmer a few feet below the surface. The standpipe had a small hole in it below the surface, designed to take advantage of that warmer ground and prevent its freezing. The pencil-sized "freeze hole" allowed the water to drain back to the warmer level when the well wasn't pumping. That worked fine if the windmill stopped running, but if it continued to pump through a cold night, the water near the surface began to freeze inside the pipe in spite of the drain hole. The ice continued to build up as the well pumped, until the pipe was frozen solid.

Every winter morning we had to drive around and check all the wells to see if any had frozen overnight. If we saw ice sticking up out of the pipe as we approached, Dad would shake his head and say, "Froze up." Our hearts sank a little as we got out to check it. If the pipe had just frozen and stopped the windmill without breaking anything, we were ecstatic. In that case we simply wrapped the pipe with burlap sacks, doused them with kerosene, and set them on fire. This quickly melted the ice inside the pipe and put the well back in operation.

Freezing could sometimes seriously damage a well, however. The ice would either burst the frozen pipe or seize the sucker rod and cause it to pull in two, or it could do both. We shuddered when we saw that. George and I would look at Dad with a silent plea, "Please tell us we don't have to fix this today." But we knew better.

With snow covering the ground as far as you could see, and long icicles hanging from the windmill derrick, Dad would stand there in his old Stetson and long sheepskin coat, his breath blowing steam in the frigid air, and look over the frozen, damaged well. He'd gaze at it with tired disgust, shake his head, and mutter, "Damn the luck." Then he'd set his jaw, look at us with that hard resolve in his eyes, and say, "Well, we gotta pull it."

We knew we had a long, cold job ahead of us, pulling out the pipe, the sucker rods, or both, and replacing the broken ones. First we had to go to Dad's Place to get a block and tackle, several large pipe wrenches, and replacement parts. Then back at the well we thawed out the pipe with burning burlap sacks, and went to work. Either George or I climbed up high inside the derrick to hang the block and tackle while Dad fastened a pull chain around the damaged pipe. We broke the pipe loose with the big wrenches, and the three of us hauled it out of the well with the block and tackle.

Repairs of this sort took most of the day. The temperature might be fifteen degrees above zero, it might be zero, or it might be fifteen below, but the well was repaired. Dad did his share of the work, and more. All through his seventies he bent down and strained on those big wrenches to break the frozen pipe connections, grunting, "Break, damn ya. Break!" He hauled on the ropes from the block and tackle to pull the pipes and rods out of the well too. We were all miserably cold and tired, and sometimes Dad stumbled, but he never fell.

Our stock tanks froze over every winter night too, as well as the water barrel at the house. The ice on the tanks would often be six to eight inches thick in the morning and as much as a foot thick on the barrel. Every day we had to break it up to make the water accessible to the cattle and us. We could break the ice with shovels when it was less than about three inches thick, but any thicker required hand axes. Chopping all that ice made for many a fun winter morning. No wonder we thought the prairie looked so beautiful when spring finally came.

Cottonseed cake came in one hundred-pound burlap bags called gunny sacks. We stored the cake at Dad's Place in an old building originally used to house wagons and buggies, a building we called the "garage."

The feed stores in town paid a good refund for each gunny sack returned in usable condition. Since we fed hundreds of sacks of cake each winter, George and I stacked all the gunny sacks in a corner of the garage and saved them until spring. In the spring Dad helped us tie them into bales, took them to town, and sold them for us. The gunny sack money belonged to George and me.

When the ground was covered with snow, we had to supplement the herd's diet with more than just cottonseed cake. Along with the cake we fed them baled hay and "bundles." Bundles were stalks of feed cut from various grain crops and tied together with heavy twine. We stored the hay and bundles at Dad's Place too, stacked in a feedlot specially built for that purpose. With all the cattle feed stored there, we had to go to Dad's Place every morning to load the truck before we could feed the herd.

The workhorses were kept at Dad's Place too, along with the wagon and the big sled in case we had to use them to feed the cattle in deep snow.

Dad's impatience wasn't suited for winter. It wasn't suited for any time of year for that matter, but winter taxed it the most. Never able to sit back and accept life as it came, he raged at whatever held up the show, and winter weather often held up the show.

If it happened to snow all day and prevent his getting out and completing some task, he would curse the snow as if it were a living thing, an enemy that existed solely to frustrate his efforts.

The wind nearly always accompanies snow on the prairie, blowing it in all directions as it falls, sometimes piling it up in large drifts and other times only small ones. The wind can turn a snowstorm into a full-blown blizzard, or it may just blow it around lightly. But whatever the case, a little snow invariably blows along close to the ground as it falls.

This snow moving along the ground was a common occurrence each winter, but it always disgusted Dad. On those snowy, windy days when he couldn't get out, he'd sit and read for as long as he could stand it, then he'd look narrowly at the window, stand up, and walk over to it. He'd stand and stare out the window, scowl at the blowing snow, and mutter in a low, caustic voice, "Look at it, siftin' along out there." He had to make sure the snow knew how much he hated it for keeping him from his work.

A three-foot snow fell one winter, the deepest we ever had. Most of it fell in a single night. It had been snowing a little at bedtime the evening before, but so lightly that we hadn't even bothered to put the pickup in the barn.

The world was an amazing sight the next morning. Snow reached nearly to the windows in the house and was still falling, and in places the drifts covered the fences over. We noticed a particularly high drift out by the water tank. At first we couldn't understand it, then we remembered. That's where we had left the pickup. It was completely buried now; not a square inch of it showed through the snow.

The snow stopped by mid-morning, and the sun came out. The new-fallen snow sparkling in the sunlight was beautiful, but its other qualities made it less enjoyable. We had to get to Dad's Place to feed the cattle and workhorses. The pickup being buried in the drift didn't matter; the snow was too deep to drive it anyway. Not even the tractor could have made it through that much snow.

The temperature stayed below the freezing point all day, but for once the wind wasn't blowing so it didn't feel particularly cold. And as it hadn't yet begun to melt, the snow remained soft and powdery.

The saddle horses were in the barn. Mom helped us bundle up, fretted over our safety, and saw us out the door. The three of us walked together, pushing hard against the snow, and plowed our way to the barn. Dad saddled Tony while George and I saddled Champ and Ginger.

The horses didn't like the idea, as the snow was nearly too deep for them to negotiate. Ginger was the oldest, and he particularly balked at going. Dad and George were out in front when I hollered, "Ginger doesn't want to go."

"Well, he's gonna have to," Dad hollered back. "Kick 'im in the ribs and get 'im goin'."

We headed for Dad's Place despite the horses' reluctance. They managed fairly well between the drifts, but they had to break their way through the deepest snow by lunging at it in great leaps. Their chests threw it in the air like snowplows, covering them and us with white powder as they plunged. We looked like moving ice sculptures. The horses had to stop and rest several times to make the mile to Dad's Place, but we finally made it.

The cattle had all reached shelter and were huddled up safely under the sheds. They just needed to be fed. We tied the horses to fence posts and plowed through the snow on foot to feed the cattle. Then we fed the workhorses, Jigs and Jim, and broke the ice on the water tanks. When we finished we sat down in the barn to let the saddle horses rest a while longer before starting back. The horses didn't like the idea of plowing through all that snow again, but they did it. The return trip wasn't quite so hard on them though, as we rode back in the same tracks we had come in.

The deep snow lay on the ground for several weeks that winter, but we never once missed feeding the cattle.

After a big snowstorm the temperature usually stayed below freezing for a while, sometimes for only a day and other times much longer. Eventually the days turned warmer, however, and the melting began. That made conditions interesting for feeding the cattle. During the day the melting snow turned the ground into a river of mud. At night the temperature dropped again and froze everything solid. The running water froze into ice and the mud into frozen ground as hard as ice. The mud and water stayed frozen until around 9:00 in the morning, when it all thawed out and began to melt again.

The combination of mud and melting snow turned the ground into a soft, gooey mess and made driving conditions worse than before the melting began. That slickest of mud not only made driving difficult, it was also easy to get stuck in. Since Dad was known for getting stuck in far better conditions, we had to figure a way to deal with the melting periods.

At only one time of the day could we drive the pickup—early in the morning before it began to melt. Old tire tracks were usually left in the mud, and at night they froze into a hellishly rough surface. Driving on the frozen ground felt like bouncing across a pile of rocks, but that was the only time we could feed the cattle without getting stuck.

We had to leave the house early enough to get the truck loaded, feed the cattle, and make it back before the mud thawed. Sometimes the ground was beginning to feel mushy as we dashed for the house, but we usually made it.

Thunderstorms brought their own special danger—lightning. Lightning was particularly perilous to cattle and horses on the prairie, especially the ones caught out in the open when a thunderstorm hit.

After a storm we had to look over the entire ranch to see if lightning had killed any stock. We drove over it unless the ground was too muddy for driving, then we rode horses. All the pastures had to be checked, as well as every mile of barbwire fence on the place.

Lightning often hits barbwire fences. The electrical shock travels down the wire for hundreds of yards in both directions, jumping off and electrocuting whatever is near the fence. Our fence lines all had cow trails alongside them, and if a cow had been walking down one of the trails when the lightning hit, we'd find her dead beside the fence.

Cattle often walked single file down the trails in groups, all of them practically touching the fence. Our biggest fear was that lightning would hit a fence and kill a large number of them at one time. We had neighbors who suffered such losses, but we were lucky. Altogether we probably had twenty-five head of cattle killed by lightning on fence lines over the years, but we were thankful they were all single strikes, taking one animal at a time.

Lightning hits cattle on the open prairie too; single animals or groups are vulnerable. Lone cows were killed in our pastures fairly often, and a few times we had several killed by a single bolt. Our greatest loss at one time was five; three cows and two calves huddled together in a storm died from one lightning bolt. Another group of three died together. They'd been walking single file about twenty yards apart when a bolt dropped them all.

None of our horses were ever struck by lightning; they were usually inside the barns when the storms hit and relatively safe.

Droughts are another common plague in that arid land. Farmers and ranchers can spend months on end waiting for rain while their grass and crops dry up and die. Some years the buffalo grass hardly came up in the spring, and the prairie didn't turn green all summer long. In those years it was necessary to feed the cattle through the summer months as well as the winter.

Whatever the weather has to offer, the wind nearly always plays a role. The combination of drought and wind spawns one of nature's real oddities, the duststorm. Huge duststorms occurred during dry periods—monsters unbelievable in their size, power, and destructiveness. Droughts in western Oklahoma, Kansas, the Texas panhandle, and eastern Colorado created parts of what became known as the "Dust Bowl" in the 1930s, a period commonly referred to as the "Dirty '30s."

Droughts in the late 1940s and early 1950s brought a return of the Dust Bowl days. A government program called the "Soil Bank" added to the problem. The Soil Bank program supplemented farmers during drought years by paying them a certain amount per acre for not planting crops in their fields. Its purpose was to help sustain farmers who otherwise might have gone broke trying to raise crops. Although Dad's operation wasn't primarily farming, and what farming he attempted usually failed, he and everyone else with acreage designated as farmland were paid by the Soil Bank program for not farming it.

But the program had a catch. For the landowners to qualify for Soil Bank money, the government somewhat naively required them to plow the designated farmland each year. They couldn't plant it, but they had to plow it. Of course everyone would rather collect Soil Bank money than plant crops destined to fail, so they all plowed their fields.

The High Plains soil has the consistency of a very fine silt. In a severe drought the dry soil would have remained more stable had it been left untouched, unplowed. The plowing program decreed by the government broke the soil down into the finest particles of silt. The wind could then lift it as much as a half mile high and carry it great distances, building volume as it moved across the land.

Dad once drove to town during a duststorm and took the county commissioner for a ride to show him how the plowed fields were fueling the storms. The commissioner could easily see that the fields were blowing away, but he was powerless to affect the Soil Bank program.

In all fairness, however, if the government hadn't required the farmers to plow the Soil Bank land, some could have been tempted to try to collect payments on acreage that wasn't farmland at all.

On a calm day a duststorm would advance toward us like any other storm. A thin line first appeared on the horizon, the upper edge of a brown cloud far in the distance. Then the cloud would roll up over the horizon and grow to a tremendous height. The term "dust cloud" is very descriptive, though it isn't a cloud at all; it only looks like one. It is simply tons of dirt suspended in the air and carried by the wind. And this storm cloud is connected to the ground. In fact, a duststorm's greatest intensity is concentrated near the ground.

The first to spot a dust cloud rolling over the horizon ran to tell the others, then we all flew into action. One of us jumped in the pickup and went charging across the prairie to try to shut off all the windmills before it hit. This was a round trip of several miles, and we drove like mad with a duststorm bearing down on us.

Most of the livestock took cover, smart enough to realize a storm was coming. But the chickens would go happily about their business, unaware of a thing until the storm hit. So the first thing we did was round up all the chickens that time allowed and fasten them inside. We also grabbed up every loose thing in sight and threw it into one of the outbuildings so it wouldn't blow away. As the storm bore down on us, we retreated to the house.

Inside the house we ran around plugging the bottoms of the doors and windows with towels, rags, and anything else we could find. Mom became frightened, as she usually did when a storm was imminent, walking through the house nervously peering out the windows to watch the storm's approach.

The air remained strangely calm until it hit, but the menacing storm front looked anything but calm. Relentlessly closing the distance, the boiling wall of the dust cloud marched across the prairie. We watched and listened, and waited.

We could hear it just before it hit, a low, ominous howl. Then it would hit—a dirty, boiling, wall of wind—a dirt blizzard. The huge mass of howling dirt blocked out the sun and pounded sand against the windows.

Nothing could keep the dirt out. The dust filtered under the doors and windows in spite of our makeshift plugs. Within minutes the inside of the house would fill with fine dust, visibly moving through the air and coating every surface.

The unlucky chickens that we hadn't gotten inside didn't fare well when the storm hit. The dirt-filled wind swept them fifteen to twenty feet in the air and sent them tumbling like feather dusters in a hurricane. Most of them found some kind of shelter before the wind carried them completely away, but a few didn't. Occasionally a chicken would come wandering back from somewhere on the prairie after the storm passed, but others blew away and never returned.

The duststorm might be over in an hour, or it might last several hours. If we could, we stayed inside until it subsided, though sometimes it caught us in the pasture still driving around madly trying to get to all the windmills.

Visibility often became so limited in duststorms that cars on the highway were forced to pull off to the side until it cleared. On the way home from town one afternoon, a blinding duststorm hit our school bus and forced the driver to slow down to five miles per hour. As we crept down the highway the back of another school bus suddenly loomed only five or six feet ahead, traveling even slower than we were. We hit the other bus before our driver could react, but neither vehicle was really damaged with both of them moving so slowly.

Duststorms are nature's sandblasters. During the worst of the Dust Bowl days, cars traveling between Lamar and Springfield, a town forty-six miles to the south, reportedly lost all the paint off one side. The finish was sandblasted down to clean metal as they crept down the highway. The blowing sand also clips off grass as efficiently as a lawnmower. Of course, during the drought years when the duststorms were the worst, the prairie grass wasn't very high anyway.

The blowing dirt moved across the ground much like snow, and piled up like a snowdrift against obstacles such as buildings and fences. But unlike snow, when the weather changed the dirt didn't melt; it stayed there permanently unless we removed it. Occasionally the blow dirt drifted so high against barn doors and corral gates that we had to shovel it away. We shoveled it out and spread it over the ground so the next time the wind came up it would carry it away and pile it up somewhere else.

When the dirt blew against our stock tanks, it deflected up and over the top, fell into the water, and settled to the bottom. Water tanks on the open prairie always gather a little dust, and usually have a thin layer of mud on the bottom as a result, but during the Dust Bowl the storms filled our tanks to the rim with mud.

The mud in the tanks was totally waterlogged and very heavy. The only way to remove it was to shovel it out by hand. We shoveled tons of mud during those years, as we had to clean seven water tanks continuously to stay ahead of the duststorms. George and I shoveled that damn mud with blisters on our hands, but it was hard to complain with Dad shoveling right along beside us. He grunted and groaned, and his hands got sore and blistered too, but he shoveled mud out of those tanks for all the years the duststorms prevailed.

One sweltering summer day Dad and I were shoveling mud from a tank on a high point in the south pasture, a spot that afforded a distant view in all directions. Dad stopped working for a minute, leaned on his shovel, and gazed around at the sultry landscape. The sun blazed down like a torch, distant whirlwinds kicked up dust and dry weeds, and heat waves shimmered along the horizon.

He pulled off his hat, wiped his leather glove across his sweating forehead, and spat in the dirt. "Hot, dry, son of a bitch!" he said, then put his hat back on, picked up his shovel, and sunk it in the mud.

Mom shoveled mud along with us during the worst days of the Dust Bowl. When we were getting ready to go shovel one of the tanks, she'd get her own shovel and throw it in the back of the pickup with ours, then sit in the cab and wait for us. Dad would come out and tell her, "Now Lois, you don't need to be doin' this."

"Yes I do," she'd reply. "You guys need the help."

One of the most amazing results of the big duststorms was their ultimate effect on barbwire fences. As impossible as it may seem, the blow dirt covered the fences over completely, and made it virtually impossible to uncover them by any means.

For blowing dirt or snow to form a drift, it first needs a windbreak. The drift begins to pile up in the relatively calm area on the lee side of the windbreak. Naturally, the larger the windbreak is, the larger the drift becomes. Barbwire fences provide practically no windbreak at all, so how did blow dirt manage to cover them up? With the help of an accomplice, the tumbleweed.

Tumbleweeds are ball-shaped dried thistles, varying in diameter from approximately one to three feet. Their tough, woody texture makes them resistant to breakage. With a shape that catches the wind and allows them to roll, and a toughness that protects them from damage, they can tumble along the ground for miles. The early settlers saw the wind rolling them across the prairie and called them "tumbleweeds." They're always on the go on that windy prairie, until they run into an obstruction such as a house or a barn, or a barbwire fence.

Barbwire fences normally have three or four strands of wire spaced a foot or so apart. The wires are fastened to posts fifteen to twenty feet apart. When a tumbleweed blew against a fence the wire stopped it, and as more and more blew in they piled up on each other, soon making a stack of weeds as high as the fence. The weeds began to stack outward as well; in time the stack extended five or ten feet out from the fence.

The tumbleweeds became intertwined with the wire and with each other, and began to form a resistive framework. When a duststorm hit, this tumbleweed obstruction acted as a partial windbreak. The blowing dirt began to settle behind the windbreak and inside it, and collected there. After the storm subsided, the dirt continued to settle and became firm. Then when the next duststorm hit it was an even better windbreak and piled up yet more dirt. If a little rain happened to soak this pile of dirt between duststorms it compacted even more.

The wind blew from various directions at different times, causing the pile of tumbleweeds and blow dirt to build upward and outward on both sides of the fence. It finally became a pile of tightly compacted soil as high as the fence and ten to fifteen feet wide. The tumbleweeds that caused the pile to form now served as a framework inside it, holding it together and making it virtually impossible to remove. The tumbleweed framework was so tough and resilient that if we attempted to force a shovel into it the shovel would just bounce back without cutting it.

The final result—the covered fence lines became smoothly rounded ridges about five feet high, shaped like endless loaves of French bread extending across the countryside for miles. In places the tops of the old fence posts could be seen poking up out of the ridges; in others they were buried completely.

At this stage the cattle could simply walk up over the ridges.

This forced us to build new fences, straight down the tops of them. Miles and miles of those elevated fences stretched all over that country, running along the ridges formed by the duststorms, with a little help from the tumbleweeds.

Chapter 10

NEIGHBORS

Mr. and Mrs. Clark sold Clay Creek Store when I was ten or eleven, and moved to town. What a surprise that was to me. They'd always been part of my world, and at that age I thought familiar things like the Clarks and the store went on forever. Mrs. Clark nearly did. He died a few years after they moved to town, but she lived to be nearly a hundred.

The Lamborn family bought the store and moved into the Clark's old house adjoining it. They continued to run the store in much the same way the Clarks had and soon became just as popular. The Lamborns had several kids near my age too, which I was glad to see. They rode the school bus with George and me every day, and as we waited for the bus in their store on cold mornings, we quickly became friends.

The store continued to carry Dad's favorite cigars too, and he got along well with the Lamborns. After their first meeting, however, I was surprised it worked out that way.

The Lamborns had several Chihuahuas, nervous little short-haired dogs with high-pitched barks. The dogs barked a lot too, especially at strangers. The first morning after the Lamborns took over the store, Dad and I went to get the mail and cigars as usual. He pulled up and parked under the trees, and we started walking toward the store. Suddenly two of their little Chihuahuas came charging out and started jumping around in front of Dad and yapping at him. They stopped directly in front of him, darting in and out and threatening to bite him on the shins. Dad glanced down at them with disgust and continued walking. That infuriated one of the dogs, prompting it to yap more aggressively and jump even closer to him. In one smooth, unbroken motion, Dad pulled back his boot and kicked it as he walked. His boot toe went under the dog's belly, picked it up, and lofted it ten feet in the air.

The kick didn't hurt the dog, but the flight sure took the meanness out of it. The little dog thumped down on its side near the other one, let out a yelp, and they both ran howling to

Mrs. Lamborn. She quickly shooed them inside and shut them in the house. As we walked into the store and introduced ourselves, I wondered how this would play out after Dad's little episode with the dogs, but Mrs. Lamborn didn't mention it. She graciously introduced herself and all the family to us, but not the dogs. They never came close to Dad again.

Mrs. Lamborn was a serious lady, hard-working and God-fearing. She moved her stout frame about the store with ease, greeting folks amiably, waiting on them politely, sharing a little neighborhood gossip, and occasionally lending a bit of good advice. Mr. Lamborn was a perpetual motion machine, a wiry guy who raced his skinny body around the store like a flash, his friendly face eager to help as he leaned forward and half-walked, half-ran waiting on folks and threatening to trip over the toes of his cowboy boots with every quick step he took. Their quiet, polite children stood around and grinned at them with a loving tolerance.

The Lamborns and others like them embodied the essence of that hard land. Their spirit proved the prairie's worth, and the prairie proved theirs.

People like Mr. and Mrs. Clark. During their years at Clay Creek Store they provided not only the necessities of life for us, but a central gathering spot, a loose sense of community for widely-separated folks who otherwise had little contact.

The Clarks were spirited people, and their hearts were always young. Mr. Clark caught Mrs. Clark bent over one morning and, thinking himself cute, shot her in her ample behind with a BB gun. Immediately after firing the historic shot, he sensed she didn't consider it quite so cute. He prudently ran away and hid out the rest of the day. Hours later, under cover of darkness, he slipped back in the door. He wasn't stealthy enough. Mrs. Clark lay in wait behind the door he crept in and ambushed him with a broom.

Mr. and Mrs. Silvey. Old Mr. Silvey walked out to the barn in a blizzard one evening to check the livestock. As he headed back to the house he became disoriented, lost his way in the storm, and wandered out into an open field. Feeling his body beginning to freeze, he took refuge in a shallow plow rut, the only windbreak he could find. The rut was less than a foot deep, but he lay down and stretched out in it so the freezing wind would blow over him.

All night long he lay there with the blizzard howling over his head, while Mrs. Silvey sat up by the light of a kerosene lamp waiting for him. They had a telephone by then, and though the line was usually troublesome in bad weather, sometime during the night she reached the operator. The operator alerted the Colorado National Guard.

They found the old man the next morning, nearly frozen, but still alive. He survived the ordeal, and the two of them lived to endure several more winters out there.

Clarence and Opal Smith. Great big Clarence and little bitty Opal, but she was big enough to handle him and all those kids.

Clarence was a big, likable galoot who loved to dance. He'd scoot across the floor perpetually grinning and totally enveloping Opal in his gangly arms, shuffling his big cowboy boots along in a complete nonrhythm as he counted aloud to keep time—one, two, three; one, two, three—all the while seesawing her outstretched arm up and down and bending his waist back and forth in a sidewise motion that spawned a name for itself, the Pump Handle Pete.

Clarence was the essence of a good neighbor, and he loved his horses so much that Opal put photographs of them on his gravestone.

Opal, tiny but mighty, kept a pack of wild kids in tow and swept a rattlesnake off her own front step with a broom. Opal rescued her baby daughter in the front yard, rocking in her little rocker and singing to a rattler as it raised up and swung to and fro in her smiling face, its deadly head swaying with the rhythm of the rocker. The mesmerized rattler danced its last as Opal whacked it away from her baby's face.

Opal, now in her nineties, recently told me she still has some more "battles to fight."

And Annie Claybrook, an energetic, outspoken lady who lived life with gusto. Annie was as tough as the land. Ross, her slow-talking, easy-going husband, tended to take life as it came. Not Annie. She worked, hollered, cussed, and fought everything in her way, and most things were.

Ross made the mistake of riling her one day when the two of them were working outside. With hell in her mouth and fire in her eyes, Annie ran him in the house with a horsewhip. A little fire flashed in her eyes every time Ross told that story on her too, which he never failed to do.

Annie wasn't subtle about anything. If she didn't like you, you knew it. If she did, you knew that too. But even if she didn't like you, if she liked your wife or your kids you were still welcome in her house. She'd treat you politely too; no sidewise glances from Annie, no venom in the air. The person she didn't like was always aware of it, and that arrangement worked fine.

Ross died several years before Annie, and after all her kids were grown and gone, but she didn't change her life a bit. She stayed in her little rock house and went right on raising cattle and gardens by herself.

Mom stopped by to visit Annie one day and found her in overalls, a work shirt, and leather gloves, hauling some large rocks to decorate her flower beds. While she and Mom chatted, Annie inquired about the health of a mutual friend of theirs. Mom told her their friend had been having trouble with adhesions. "Hah," Annie grunted. "He oughta be out here haulin' some of these goddam rocks. That'd take care of his adhesions!"

Annie died the way she lived, in high gear. It happened in town one day on a shopping spree with her daughter, something she loved to do. As she hustled down the sidewalk, talking fast and walking faster, she suddenly grasped her chest and said, "My God, I'm dyin'!" and fell dead. Annie was worthy of a death like that.

The last time I saw Annie was several years after I'd moved away from Colorado. During a visit back home, I walked into a supermarket and saw her halfway across the store at a checkout counter. She had on a great long winter coat, unbuttoned down the front, and was talking loudly to somebody and busily picking up two sacks of groceries.

She turned around with her groceries and spotted me. "Gary, Gary!" she hollered. "My little Gary!" She dropped both sacks of groceries and charged across the store at me with arms wide open, long coat tails flying behind her. Somehow I managed to keep her from knocking me off my feet, and hugged her tough old neck as she danced around me and hugged mine.

Those hearty people all lived much the same as we did. Some lived closer to the highway and didn't get quite so isolated by winter storms and gully washers, but they had no more luxuries than us. While everyone in town had television, we were all still listening to battery radios. We all carried water to the house in buckets, we all used outhouses, and we watched the horizon constantly for storm clouds. Most of their houses were like ours too, rugged and poorly lit. Many were even smaller than ours.

Though Dad wasn't very particular about furnishings for the house, he liked to keep everything in good repair. The floors in the rock house were creaky old planks covered with ancient linoleum. I don't remember anyone complaining about them, but Dad announced one day that we were getting new floors.

When Dad invested in something, he liked to get quality for his money, so he usually bought the best. The installers came out from town, ripped up the old wood and linoleum, and replaced them with shining oak floors. I suppose it looked a little strange when someone walked into the old house and saw those glistening new floors, but we loved them.

Dad surprised Mom another time, probably even more than he did with the new floors. He came home from town, walked into the kitchen with a half-embarrassed grin on his face, held a fancy wooden box out to her, and opened the lid. It was a new set of sterling silverware. Mom looked at it in disbelief; she'd never had many nice things in her life. She took the box, carried it into the living room, and sat down at the table. There she just sat and stared at the silverware, as if it might vanish before her eyes.

Company seldom stopped by our place. People living next to the highway had neighbors stop to see them fairly often, but casual visitors had to go far out of their way to get to our house. It happened once in a while though, and when the Smiths, the Claybrooks, or other neighbors dropped in it practically called for celebration. It certainly did for Mom anyway; she was elated to see anyone come over the hill.

We did have company come to stay with us from time to time. Jack Beatty's overnight visits were always a treat, and when Dad's brother, my great uncle Sam, came from Missouri we had great fun.

Aunt Ruby, Uncle Sam's quiet, polite little wife, whom he indelicately called "Rube," would step down off the train, grin shyly, and hug us all. Sam would step off behind her, ruffle my hair, and say, "Damn if you ain't gettin' big, boy. What the hell they feedin' ya, anyhow? You're shootin' up like a goddam weed." I didn't hear a single cuss word he said. I just knew Uncle Sam was going to be around telling funny stories for a while and keeping Dad's spirits high.

Sam was a natural performer, and he loved the role of family storyteller. When he finished supper in the evening, Sam would slowly stand up and walk around the room. Everyone else sat at the table and listened. He wouldn't say anything for a minute or so, then a slight grin would cross his face, a faraway grin of reminiscence as some old memory came through. Then slowly he'd begin talking and start to build a story. As the story took shape he'd change his tone of voice to mimic his father or another ancestor, loudly emphasize something for dramatic effect, gesture wildly to drive home some outrageous point, and pause in perfect comedic timing. Dad would watch him with a widening grin and slowly begin to laugh.

Within minutes Sam would be so wound up and his audience so involved that the dining room felt like a dinner theater. Dad would rock back and forth and howl with uncontrollable laughter, nearly falling out of his chair as tears poured down his cheeks.

I think Sam told the same stories every time he came, but they always had the same effect on Dad. If Dad hadn't laughed so hard at Sam, I would never have known he could.

The way we lived was certainly old-fashioned for the 1950s, but a family to the south of us, the Greens, made us look modern. The floor in their house was a bare cement slab, and their table legs rested in tin cans, an 1800s remedy for keeping mice off the table. When telephones and electricity became available, the Greens didn't participate. As Abner Green told Dad, "Never needed them things before; don't need 'em now."

The Greens didn't go to town very often, or even to Clay Creek Store, so we seldom had any dealings with Abner. Dad figured that was probably best anyway. A coincidence once forced us to deal with him, however, in an exchange that turned out to be nearly as strange as the incident itself.

One summer the tortoises dug several holes up under one of our water tanks by the windmill in the draw. The metal tank was round, two feet deep, and eight feet in diameter. The turtles scooped most of the dirt from under the north side of the tank, leaving a gaping hole six or eight inches high and three or four feet wide.

A terrific wind blew in from the north one night when the tank sat empty. The wind had died down by the next morning when Dad and I drove up the draw to check the windmill. As we approached it something looked strange to me, or maybe out of place. "Dad, something doesn't look right about that well," I said.

As we drew nearer Dad said, "Hell, one of the tanks is gone!" Indeed the tank was gone. We figured out pretty quickly what had happened. The wind had blown up under the tank through the turtle holes, picked it up, and carried it away. It had to have gone south, as the wind had been blowing that direction the night before. From where we stood by the windmill, we could see a mile and a half to the south, and the tank was nowhere in sight.

We set out to track down our runaway water tank. The tank had metal beads around the top and bottom edges, and we soon found the faint double tracks the beads had left as it rolled across the prairie. As we expected, the tracks ran up the long hill to the south. The tank had traveled upright, rolled on its edge like a giant pie plate. I rode on the front fender of the pickup and watched for the narrow tracks while Dad drove.

We followed the tracks for two and a half miles, up and over the hill to where they intersected the barbwire fence that bordered our place on the south. The tracks indicated the tank had hit the fence and jumped over it, only loosening two wires in the process. It jumped the fence and landed on the other side without even falling over.

That tank rolled on its edge all the way, never once falling over, and probably traveled faster than any water tank had ever gone before.

The tracks continued on south after they jumped the fence and headed in the direction of the Green's place. We followed them another couple of miles until the Green's house came into sight and finally lost the tracks a few hundred yards from their place.

As we pulled up in front of the Green's house we saw wide-eyed kids running everywhere, darting between dilapidated buildings to dodge out of sight. Mrs. Green peeked out the kitchen window at us, then quickly ducked back. Then with kids peeking around the corners of buildings and out the windows of the primitive house, Abner ambled out to greet us.

He had a ragged black cap pulled down around his ears, a gray, scraggly beard covering his gaunt face, and a dark, tattered coat that had neither buttons nor a zipper to hold it together. The coat was fastened by a length of yellow binder twine wrapped around his waist and tied in front with a big bow knot. His weathered face framed a suspicious grin and wary eyes.

As Abner walked up with his hands poked into the front pockets of the old coat, Dad nodded and said, "Mornin' Abner." He smiled slightly and nodded back. Dad asked matter-of-factly, "Haven't seen a water tank of ours around here, have ya?"

Abner pivoted a little and pointed toward the corral with his pocketed hands. "Yeah, it's layin' out there in the corral," he replied coolly. "Blowed in last night, I guess." He sounded as if a water tank blew in every now and then.

Dad and I walked toward the corral with Abner, while a whole bunch of curious kids fell in behind us. As we walked along Abner said, "That tank tore the side outta my barn when it come through." He established that point early on. Abner understood negotiating.

There it was, our stray water tank, sitting on its bottom in the middle of Abner's corral. It had rolled and bounced five miles across the prairie and hardly had a dent to show for it. Abner's "barn" that the tank had allegedly damaged, wasn't a barn at all. It had no roof, and its sides were only a line of vertical boards haphazardly nailed together to form a crude fence. The boards hung loosely on rusty nails, and weren't even all the same length. They varied from around eight to ten feet long, their tops forming a jagged outline against the sky.

The "barn" was simply a high, rickety old fence, and an uneven one at that. We could see a sizable gap in the weathered boards on the north side of it, however. Dad pointed at the gap and asked Abner, "Is that where the tank came through?"

Abner nodded grimly, "Yep, that's where it come through. Tore all them boards outta there."

I saw amusement in Dad's eyes.

The water tank was several years old and had already had some rusty spots before it blew away. The jarring five-mile trip across the prairie had shaken the rust loose, and now several visible holes appeared in the bottom.

Dad looked at the old tank, and Abner looked at his old barn. The kids and I looked at each other. Dad finally broke the silence. "Think you could get any use outta this old tank?"

Abner jumped at it. "Yeah, it's got them holes in it, but I could probably bank dirt up around it and get it to hold water."

"Then how about you keep it to pay for your barn, and we'll just call it even?" Dad offered. Abner looked thoughtful for a moment, then nodded. That was exactly the deal he'd wanted.

Dad shook Abner's hand before we left, and the crowd of kids stood and watched us until we drove out of sight. Dad began to laugh. "That's quite a 'barn' Abner's got, ain't it?" he said. "I knew he wanted that old tank before we even got out there to it."

A modern convenience came into our lives when I was ten, a telephone. Actually it was only semi-modern, and it didn't work all the time, but just having a phone made Mom feel less isolated.

The antiquated telephone system that came to the neighborhood was a party line. Ten or twelve families hooked up to it, nearly everyone in that part of the country. The main telephone line ran along the highway, with individual lines branching off to the houses. The main line, from town to about eighteen miles south, ran on poles approximately fifteen feet high. The branch lines were strung on about everything. Some ran neatly on a set of poles similar to those on the main line, some zigzagged up and down across the pastures on a haphazard collection of poles of different heights, and some were strung on fence posts.

Our phone line ran along the top of a barbwire fence. Insulator brackets pointed upward from the posts to keep the phone wire elevated above the barbed wire and out of the reach of cattle. This strangest of telephone lines spanned the three miles from the highway to our house.

The telephones themselves were old-fashioned even for those times. They were the antique wooden kind that hung on the wall.

The caller had to stand and talk into a mouthpiece on the front of the phone while holding a separate earpiece to his head. Outgoing calls were made by turning a crank on the right-hand side of the wooden body. With the crank you could either call one of your neighbors or ring the operator. A neighbor could be rung directly, but to talk to someone in town or make a long-distance call required ringing the operator for assistance.

All the phones on the line rang when someone received a call, so everyone heard it. Because of this, everyone had their own individual ring to distinguish it from the others. To call the operator you just turned the crank and made one continuous ring, then waited for her to answer. Someone else on the party line could be called by simply ringing their particular ring. One person's would be three short rings, another's would be two long rings followed by one short, and so on. Ours was two longs and three shorts.

Anyone who picked up the phone could listen in on their neighbors' conversations. With around a dozen families there was little privacy on the line. When the phone rang everyone listened to the number of short and long rings to see if it was theirs. The person being called always picked up the phone wondering how many others were picking up theirs to listen. At times you could even hear someone pick up their phone or accidentally make a noise that interrupted your conversation. This led to some memorable incidents. Mom once said something funny to a friend she was talking to, and Mrs. Silvey laughed out loud on the phone. That started Mom laughing, which made Mrs. Silvey laugh even harder. Then she hung up, still laughing.

Occasionally someone would make a snide comment about the person they suspected of listening. Sometimes when you made one of those comments you could hear the eavesdropper hang up. You knew you'd guessed their identity correctly.

The telephone system was a little private company made up of all the people on the party line. The system suffered a great many problems due to the weather, the curious ways the phone lines were strung, and the ancient equipment. As a result the line would often go dead, especially in bad weather.

The president of the little phone company was an old guy named Mr. Hopworth. Mr. Hopworth was elected president simply because he was the only one who knew anything about telephones. He only knew the old-fashioned kind, however, which is why everybody had them. And, as he delighted in pointing out, he was also the only one who knew anything about electricity. I never understood the significance of that, as no one had electricity anyway.

Mr. Hopworth wasn't as old as Dad, but he seemed much older to me. He let his quiet, old wife drive the tractor in the field while he complained of aches and pains that prevented such activity. Hopelessly rotund and dumpy, his ample belly hung far out over the baggy pants he left unbuttoned at the top to accommodate his bulge. His round, puffy face perfectly matched his girth. A misshapen little narrow-brimmed hat teetered precariously atop his wide head, white hair poking from under it in all directions. He'd long since given up on belts and surrendered to wide suspenders that he loved to hook his thumbs in and stretch out in front of him while sharing his immense knowledge with the ignorant and uninformed. Dad called him a "shiftless old fart."

Though he was paid nothing for being the phone company president, Mr. Hopworth loved the job. He spent much of the time driving around in his ancient, dilapidated car, swelled with importance as he checked out the lines. He also liked to sit around Clay Creek Store and talk. Dad and I walked into the store one morning when he had several people cornered, suspenders stretched out in front of his belly as he leaned back and held forth on the mysteries of the phone system. He stopped his lecture when Dad walked in, turned, and with a patronizing, self-important air, called out loudly, "Mornin' there, Mr. Blizzard. How are you today, sir?"

Dad looked narrowly in his direction and neither spoke nor nodded, only stared at him with disdain. Dad then turned and spoke amiably to Mrs. Lamborn as she handed him the cigar box. Mr. Hopworth didn't talk much until we walked back out the door, then we heard him start up again.

On the way home Dad said, "Ol' Pus Gut sure was wound up this mornin' wasn't he?" The name Pus Gut caught me by surprise. Dad's regular name for him was the "chickenshit electrician."

Our telephone was slightly newer than the others. It was a transitional model, halfway between the old ones everyone else out there had and the modern kind that people in town used. Modern models were equipped with hand-held receivers like the phones of today and sat on the table. Ours had a wooden body, a hand crank, and hung on the wall the same as the old phones, but also had a one-piece receiver on a cord like the modern ones. That made it handier, as it wasn't necessary to stand up to talk into it.

Dad bought our phone from a friend in town and not through Mr. Hopworth as everyone else had. He also had his friend install it in our house, string the wire on the fence posts, and hook it to the main line without Mr. Hopworth's authorization.

Mr. Hopworth didn't understand our "new-fangled" phone, and was suspicious of it. What really bothered him was that Dad had bought it and hooked it up without consulting the president.

Every time the system developed a problem, Mr. Hopworth blamed it on our phone. He'd show up at our place, knock on the door, and Mom would bring him into the dining room where our phone hung on the wall. With eyeglasses perched far down on his nose and his belly practically touching the wall, he'd look it over critically, thump his finger on the box, tap the receiver, shake it, listen to it, and ask Mom questions about it.

If Dad was in the house when Mr. Hopworth came, he never said a word, totally ignoring him though the phone hung only three or four feet from his easy chair. I remember Mr. Hopworth coming into the room with Mom one day while Dad was sitting in his chair reading. He tapped on the phone, looked inside it, shook the receiver, and asked Mom questions while Dad sat two feet away, engulfing him in cigar smoke. He never looked up to acknowledge Mr. Hopworth's presence all the time he was there.

Of course, all this finally came to a head one day. Mom tried to make a phone call early one morning and found the line dead. The weather was sunny, so the phone should have been working.

Later that morning Mr. Hopworth drove up to the house and came to the back door. Mom showed him in, while Dad sat in the dining room reading *Ranch Romances*. He gave Mom a grand, presidential greeting and sat down in a kitchen chair. "Something's wrong with our phone," she told him. "The line's dead."

With a knowing, indulgent smile, Mr. Hopworth nodded and replied, "Yeah, I know. I cut it off over at the highway. I'm tryin' to find a problem on the line and thought it might be your phone."

Dad overheard him from the dining room, stood up, walked into his bedroom, put on his hat, and came back out carrying his .30-30. He walked into the kitchen with the rifle in his hand, his hat cocked to one side, and his eyes seething like live coals. He stomped past Mr. Hopworth without even looking his direction, loudly muttering something about "chickenshit electricians."

That got the man's attention. With fear and concern in his eyes, he sat up in the chair and said, "Oh, I'm gonna hook it back up. I was just tryin' to find the problem."

Dad stopped, turned around, and stared at him as if he might be a bug in need of extermination. "You'd better not," he spat out. "I'll get somebody from town to come out and hook it back up. And I'd better never catch anybody up on that pole messin' with our phone line again!" Then he turned and stomped out, rifle in hand, slamming the door behind him.

I was standing in the kitchen watching the show. Mr. Hopworth slumped in the chair, his face drained of color. After a moment he stood up, visibly shaken, and looked at Mom. "I'm sorry," he stammered, and started for the door.

Dad hadn't reached his pickup yet. "You probably ought to wait in here until he leaves," Mom said. Mr. Hopworth stopped abruptly and stood nervously by the kitchen door until he heard Dad drive away.

Dad drove to the store and used their phone to call to town. The friend who had installed our phone line drove out and hooked it back up.

That was the last time Mr. Hopworth ever came to our house, and he never touched our phone line again.

Mr. Hopworth wasn't the only person to misjudge Dad.

We once kept a hired man working on a fairly regular basis for several months. Cecil was around forty, trim, muscular, and a hard worker. He was a friendly, confident, fun-loving guy with a shock of curly hair and lively, devil-may-care eyes that added up to rugged good looks. Cecil seemed exciting to George and me, grinning and joking with us as we watched his agile, muscular body accomplish any task he set out to do.

Cecil had been married several times and was known as a womanizer. He was a fighter too, always talking about "whuppin" somebody. He liked to party more than Dad cared for, but he was a skilled and efficient worker, and stayed on the job.

One day when Dad was gone from the house, Cecil insulted Mom. In a fury, she told him to get out. He took off in a hurry, leaving several personal belongings behind. I was never told the nature of the insult, but when Dad returned and heard what had happened, his eyes ignited. "Wonder if the bastard'll come back for his stuff?" he growled.

A few days later Cecil did come back. We were all in the house when he drove up with two other men in his car. He parked just outside the yard fence. They all stepped out of the car, casually folded their arms across their chests, and leaned back on it like gangsters. Cecil wore dark sunglasses and scanned around as if he owned the place.

Dad gathered up Cecil's belongings in his arms and stomped out through the yard. Mom followed behind him as George and I watched from an open window in the house. Cecil moved a few steps toward Dad as he approached, and they stopped face to face. Dad threw his things on the ground between them, bent forward in a menacing stance, and spat out something George and I couldn't hear. From his attitude, however, we knew it was a challenge.

The other men apparently hadn't expected such a reaction. They both looked at the ground uncomfortably, then got back in the car. Cecil tried to act nonchalant. He reached up and removed his sunglasses, as if preparing for a fight. Dad stepped forward like a coiled spring and poked his face directly into Cecil's. Now we could hear him—he practically screamed his rage. "Come on!" he yelled in Cecil's face. "Come on, you cur!"

Dad rocked back and forth like an enraged rooster, a seventy-five-year-old rooster, the likes of which Cecil had never seen. The smirk left his face as Cecil bent down carefully, picked up his belongings, and got back into the car. Dad followed him, yelling in his face through the side window, "Go on, get the hell outta here, you cur. You yellow cur!"

Cecil avoided Dad's eyes as he backed up, turned, and drove away.

Dad and Mom walked back to the house, and we all sat down. We didn't say anything for a while, as Dad was still seething. Then after a few minutes we began to chuckle. Mom said, "I didn't expect you to call him a cur. I looked for you to call him a son of a bitch."

"No, I know his mother," Dad said. "I never liked to call a man a son of a bitch if I knew his mother."

Gary on Champ, backwards

Chapter 11

COMPANIONS

I gained a lifelong love for animals while I was growing up. They weren't just pets on the prairie, they were my companions and buddies.

One spring morning as I headed for the creek on foot, a little white kitten followed me. She was young, only about eight weeks old, but seemed determined to go with me. I'd never seen a kitten do that before, so I let her come along. She made it all right for three-quarters of a mile, then she began to tire. She lagged far behind, finally sitting down and meowing pathetically at me. We were setting out on a six to seven-mile sojourn, so something had to change. I walked back, picked her up, and began carrying her.

That was what she wanted. She talked to me as we walked along, and gazed around at the scenery. If I needed to sit down for a while or stop to take a shot, I'd set her on the ground. She'd wait patiently until I was ready, then I'd pick her up and away we'd go again. We did that for the entire trip, and it worked out fine.

The kitten went to the creek with me many times after that. She loved to go, as long as I carried her most of the way.

The Western movies I saw when I went to town with Dad were great for gathering ideas. It occurred to me that the creek was the perfect place to try something I'd seen in numerous Westerns. Movie cowboys were always riding their horses off into rivers, raging rivers of course, usually to head off a stampede.

Some things about the movies puzzled me, though. First, having dealt with livestock all my life, I couldn't understand why the cattle stampeded so often. And it puzzled me even more that the stampedes usually ended up in the water. I suppose that should have given me a clue; maybe everything on the silver screen didn't necessarily reflect real life.

I didn't have a raging river at my disposal, but I had the creek.

Champ was my horse by then, and remembering George's roping antics, he probably hoped I had less taste for adventure. It's a good thing he didn't know what I had in mind the day we headed for the creek, or his worst fears would have been confirmed.

It was going to be glorious. Champ and I would leap off a high bank and plunge into the water, I'd lean forward on his back like a movie cowboy as he swam across the creek, and we'd climb out victoriously on the far bank.

Our swimming hole was the deepest spot in the creek, with a steep bank on one side that rose straight up out of the water five or six feet. It was the ideal place for our big plunge.

When we reached the swimming hole, I rode Champ to the edge of the steep bank to look at the layout. He didn't even like walking close to it. We looked the situation over though, and I patted him on the neck and told him everything would be all right. Then I walked him back about thirty yards so we could get a good run at the bank and jumped down from his back to take off my pants.

Champ didn't really know what I had in mind yet, but even so he seemed a little apprehensive as I climbed back on. I turned him toward the creek, leaned forward a little, and made ready to charge off the bank. Then I closed my eyes, and for a long, quiet moment Champ and I stood still, mentally preparing ourselves for the challenge. I felt prepared, but somehow I don't believe Champ did.

I let out some sort of Indian war whoop, and we raced for the creek bank as hard as Champ could go. Everything went fine until he figured out what I was up to; then he threw on the brakes, hard, and I nearly flew off over his head. We stopped several feet short of the bank, and Champ whirled and charged off in the opposite direction. Maybe it would have helped if he'd seen the movies too.

When he whirled and ran away I grabbed around his neck with both arms and somehow managed to stay on his back. Then I pulled him up short, jumped off, stood in front of him with my hands on my hips, and told him sternly that we were going through with this thing, and that it sure wasn't going to work out very well unless he put his heart into it.

He didn't want to go, but I led him to the same place we'd launched from before. I talked to him a little more, climbed back on, patted him encouragingly, and prepared to try it again.

"Yee-hah!" I yelled, and off we charged toward the bank a second time. Champ took off fast. I was impressed. I thought he really had his heart in it this time. He galloped like a charger, pounding toward the creek with everything he had, but halfway to the bank he tried to veer off to the right and avoid it again. I vetoed that idea; jerking hard on the reins and pulling him back to the left, I forced him toward the bank. Seeing that it was inevitable, Champ poured on a burst of speed. We hit the edge of the bank, I leaned low over his shoulders, and Champ leaped far out over the water.

I raised my left arm and whirled it in the air, whooping loudly as I imagined a movie cowboy might do. Everything went according to plan as we glided through the air, for about two seconds. Then we hit the creek. A huge fountain of water shot skyward, and Champ and I submerged. We sunk to the bottom of the swimming hole, and I got kind of confused. I'd never been underwater with a horse before. I couldn't begin to stay on his back underwater, and barely managed to hold onto the reins. We came fighting back to the surface, and sure enough Champ headed for the far bank, swimming as hard as he could, but it didn't remind me of any movie I'd ever seen.

I didn't have to swim. I had such a tight grip on the reins that Champ pulled me through the water by my outstretched arms, rolling me around and around like a fishing plug. I thought I was going to drown.

When we reached the far bank, Champ struggled up on the sand, dragging me like a drowned log. He'd have run off if I hadn't had a death grip on the reins. I'm sure he didn't stay around because he enjoyed my company at that particular time.

As I lay on the sand coughing up the gallon of water I'd swallowed, Champ turned and faced me. For a while he just stood there hanging his head, then slowly he raised up and looked me in the eye. I'd never heard a horse talk before, but Champ's message couldn't have been more clear. Tired, disgusted, and with a slight tone of sarcasm, he said, "I tried to tell you it wasn't going to work out."

I acknowledged his point and told him we'd never try anything like that again. I don't think he believed me.

I began to research the problem to find why our plunge into the creek hadn't work out as planned. I learned that a horse doesn't swim very well with someone on his back. I guess I already knew that; I'd learned it right after Champ and I hit the water. The rider was supposed to dismount, and swim alongside the horse while holding onto the saddle horn. Since I normally rode bareback I figured I could hold onto his mane instead of a saddle horn. Also, maybe it would work better if we didn't jump off a bank; that's where the plan had really fallen apart.

I knew the creek wasn't a good place to try it again. Champ would never fall for that twice. It was hard to even get him close to the creek for a long time. We'd do it in a pond on our neighbor's land, a deep pond fed by a windmill. This time would be less spectacular but a well-thought-out plan based on experience.

One sunny day Champ and I headed for the pond. We were both in good spirits until we approached the water, then Champ got antsy. He began to hold back as we neared the pond, so I jumped down and led him to the edge. The pond was big, about thirty yards across, and had an easier access than the creek. I pointed out to Champ how the bank sloped gently down to the water's edge. He wanted to leave.

I talked to him at length and told him I understood how he felt after the way things had gone the first time. But being the leader of the operation, I was obligated to continue the quest until we got it right. This time I had a sure-fire plan. He still wanted to leave.

I held the reins tightly while I took my pants off, because Champ knew what I was up to for sure this time. I climbed back on him, patted him on the neck, and tried again to reassure him.

He certainly didn't want to, but I managed to get him started into the water. When the water reached his shoulder I slid off beside him, holding the reins in one hand and his mane in the other. We moved slowly into deeper water and both began to swim. Champ seemed calm. It was working this time.

About the time we started swimming, I began to feel a strange sensation. Something in the water brushed against me, something slimy. We weren't alone in the pond. It didn't feel like just one thing either. Hundreds of slimy things brushed me—my arms, my legs, all over my body. The things felt slick, rubbery, and slimy, slimy, slimy.

Champ felt them too. He rolled his head around and looked at me, the fear in his eyes bordering on panic. I patted his neck and, in the most soothing voice I could muster, told him everything was all right. All the while I'm thinking to myself, "Sure it's all right. The water's full of slimy things, and you don't know what the hell's going on!"

Champ rolled his eyes at me several times, but considering the situation he stayed fairly calm and kept swimming. Thousands of those slimy things brushed us before we reached shallow water. We gratefully felt the mud under our feet and hurried up onto the bank.

I turned and looked back at the water.

Salamanders. The pond was infested with them. They hadn't been visible before we stirred them up, but now the water teemed with them. Thousands of salamanders poked their noses to the surface, then dove back down into the crowded water in a continuous rotation. Each was about a foot long, with several tentacle-like appendages protruding from the sides of its neck. Big, green, and ugly. No wonder they'd felt slimy. I began to feel slimy all over again just watching them.

Champ just stood and hung his head. He didn't say a thing. He didn't need to.

Evidently I had a lot to learn about horseback swimming, and I don't think Champ even cared to know. Oh well, deep water was scarce on the prairie anyway, so maybe I didn't need to learn how to do that after all. Besides, I was pretty sure Champ would buck me off if I ever tried it again.

My closest pal was a dog named Sandy. Sandy was the size of a collie, brown, short-haired, and of no particular pedigree. He was lean and fast, and he loved to chase things. Sandy chased everything that walked or ran, and some that flew. He even chased low-flying birds, and though his futile efforts seemed to frustrate him, he never gave up trying.

Sandy's lifelong goal was to catch a jack rabbit, but even he wasn't that fast. I explained to him that greyhounds were the only dogs I knew of faster than a jack rabbit, but it didn't bother him. He never gave up his quest. He chased hundreds of them and never caught a single one.

I was nine when Sandy came along, and he was young himself, just barely full grown. We needed him for a special reason. Our barn had become infested with rats, and though we tried every poison on the market, none fazed them. I learned to shoot a .22 rifle that year, and I loved to shoot rats with it. I also shot them with BB guns, arrows, and slingshots. I killed quite a few, and had a lot of fun, but I didn't thin the rat population much; there were thousands of them.

We asked everyone we saw at the store for advice on how to exterminate the rats, but none of their suggestions worked. Then one day Mr. Clark said some people who lived fifteen miles further south had a young dog that loved to chase everything, including rats. He had told them about our problem, and they offered to let us have the dog.

Mom and I drove to their place, where we met a lean, brown, short-haired mutt with a slurpy tongue and an upturned tail that wagged habitually. Sandy—friendly, lovable, wildly energetic, and convinced he was a greyhound.

Sandy and I hit it off immediately. I think he'd have been disappointed if we hadn't taken him home with us. I certainly would have. He rode beside me in the pickup seat all the way home, and practically beat me to death with his tail.

Sandy leaped out of the truck at our house and looked all around. About that time a flock of pigeons flew over him. They were flying low, just going from one rooftop to another, so Sandy took off after them, barking and jumping as high as he could in a vain attempt to reach them. The crazy dog was indeed a chaser of things.

That evening I took a flashlight and quietly walked Sandy to the barn to show him the rats. When I opened the barn door, his reaction was amazing. He tore into them like a wild animal, running, jumping, growling, and killing rats. He'd chase down a rat, grab it, kill it, and tear off after another in a blur of motion. I'd never seen anything like it.

Sandy and I made rat hunting a nightly game. After the sun went down I'd walk outside with a flashlight and tell him we were going to get the rats. I didn't have to say any more; he knew the game. My weapon was a short baseball bat. Sandy had his teeth. We'd walk to the barn quietly with the light off so the rats couldn't see or hear us coming. Sandy would walk silently along beside me to the barn door, where we'd stop and prepare for the attack. Holding my bat in one hand and the flashlight in the other, I'd squat down beside him and whisper, "Ready?"

Sandy would crouch and tense up when he heard that, ready to spring when I opened the door. I'd switch on the flashlight and throw open the barn door in one motion. The inside of the barn exploded with rats. Rats ran everywhere, squeaking and scurrying across the floor, running up walls, along the tops of petitions, and jumping across rafters. Sandy dove into the barn like a demon, jumping, growling, and grabbing rats. He'd grab one in his mouth, kill it with a quick snap of his head, throw it down, and grab another.

I ran in after him, swinging my bat. The melee lasted only a couple of minutes before the rats all made it to their holes—the ones Sandy and I didn't get, that is. I could nail a number of them in that short time, but I couldn't come close to Sandy. I might get five or six rats on a good night, but Sandy could get a dozen.

When it was all over, Sandy would look up at me and wag his tail with pleasure. That was his favorite time of day.

When we finally found a new brand of rat poison that worked, Sandy and I were kind of sad to see them go.

Sandy was full of surprises. A short while after he arrived, Mom and I walked up on a coiled rattler. We spotted the snake hiding under a weed a few feet away, and stopped. It started rattling at us as we backed away.

While retreating from that deadly buzz we heard a distant growl behind us, moving rapidly in our direction. We looked around and here came Sandy, stretched out in a dead run, a low growl rolling from his throat. He ran past us, his eyes fixed on the rattler. We hollered, "Sandy, no!" but our yells didn't slow him. He bounded in close to the snake, stopped short, jumped sideways, and barked in its face. He kept jumping sideways until the rattler moved, then he leaped in, grabbed it in his mouth, and shook it violently.

Mom and I backed further away when that started. Sandy snapped the snake back and forth several times, then lost his grip on it. It flew out of his mouth and came whirling through the air toward us. Mom screamed, and we ran in opposite directions. No matter though, the snake was stone dead. It hit the ground with a dull thud, and Sandy went over and sniffed it to make sure it was dead. Then he walked back to us and rubbed his head against our legs.

Mom and I were flabbergasted. We hadn't known he could kill rattlesnakes, nor had we ever witnessed such a spectacle before. We looked at each other, looked at Sandy, and started petting him and praising what he'd done. He liked that; he was proud of himself.

Sandy hunted rattlesnakes. We never knew why, but he hated them, and he hunted them with a vengeance. He ranged over the countryside for miles, hunting them on rocky slopes, under ledges, around buildings, or anywhere else one might be lurking. He looked for them, listened for them, and sniffed them out. The hair would stand up on his back when he heard one rattle, and he'd lower his head and start growling as he searched for it.

When he found the snake, watching him do combat with it was truly fascinating. In a partial crouch, Sandy would face the coiled rattler with his head low, and always that low growl rolling from his throat. He'd begin a delicate dance around the rattler, circling it and darting in and out as he circled, forcing it to turn around and around as it followed his motion. While the snake kept turning to follow his movement, it had to keep its coil intact so it could strike if Sandy came close enough.

Sandy would pick up speed and make more noise. He'd begin circling faster and faster, feinting in and out, jumping back and forth, barking, growling, snapping, making it harder and harder for the snake to keep track of him and remain coiled. The rattler kept turning around and around while holding its head up several inches above the coil to watch Sandy, its savage buzz underscoring the battle. In the heat of the fierce noise and movement, Sandy would dive in without warning, grab the rattler in his mouth, and shake it violently. He'd snap his head wildly back and forth, breaking the snake's spine in a dozen places.

When the rattler was dead, Sandy would stop and stand with its body hanging limp in his mouth. Then with a last growl of contempt, he'd dash it to the ground like a piece of garbage.

Sometimes he'd shake one so hard that it came apart in his mouth, and pieces of snake would go flying everywhere. Spectators cleared the area fast when that started.

Sandy was snakebit many times in his life. The first bites were tough on him, but over time he built up an immunity to the venom. He would only swell a slight amount and get sick for a couple of days. He'd just stop eating and lie on the porch while he recuperated, then he'd be off again to find more rattlers.

If he found a rattler under a rock ledge he'd spend hours digging it out. The snake would try to get away from him by squeezing itself into a tight space far up under the ledge, but Sandy would dig it out, no matter how long it took. Working very carefully, he'd never give it an opportunity to bite him. He'd start by pawing dirt away several feet in front of the snake, then he'd steadily move toward it, removing dirt from under it as he went, undermining its perch. When the perch began to crumble, and the snake slid off, Sandy would either grab it or force it out into the open where he could overcome it with his dance.

If the rattler was under a ledge and lying on hard rock that Sandy couldn't dig, and he found he couldn't reach it any other way, he'd just dive straight in, grab it, and drag it out. The snake would bite him on the nose if he had to resort to that, but if that's what it took, that's what he did. He would never let one get away.

Sandy knew instinctively that rattlers could harm people, and he was very protective of us. He wouldn't risk letting us get snakebit. If one of us accidentally wandered close to a rattler, he'd dive straight in and grab it with no hesitation and usually get bit in the process. Whenever we saw one we tried to back away from it as quickly as possible, so Sandy would take his time and avoid getting bit.

Mom and I went for a walk on the prairie one day, and Sandy came with us. We saw a big clump of yuccas in bloom and stopped to look at the flowers. Sandy wasn't close at the time; he was running around trying to sniff out a rabbit or whatever else he might chase.

The clump of yuccas was large and thick with brush, so we couldn't see down inside it very well. As we stood there admiring the blooms, a big rattler suddenly rose up in the middle of the yuccas and started buzzing at us. Sandy heard it from a distance and came charging between us, growling viciously and ramming himself straight into the yuccas. He forced his way in, grabbed the rattler, backed out with it writhing in his mouth, and began to shake it furiously. Mom and I cleared out fast, as pieces of snake flew in all directions.

When Sandy finished with it and dropped the last piece from his mouth, we walked over to him. The rattler had struck him as he dived in after it; we could see the fang marks on his nose. Both of us

156 Rivers of WIND

hugged him, patted him on the head, and thanked him. Then we started walking him back to the house, because he was going to be sick for a while. We treated him like a hero when he saved us from rattlers, because he was.

Sandy was everyone's favorite, including Mom's, except for the day she sat several pies out on the back porch to cool, and he ate the centers out of every one of them. I pleaded his case hard, but he had to pay considerable penance for that one.

He was affectionate, protective, and a great friend, but Sandy had a mind of his own, and something in him was untamed. He had a wild nature, and he was born to roam that prairie free. After he'd been with us five or six years he began to stay away from home for several days at a time. He'd show up and stay around for a while, and then leave again. One day I saw a pack of coyotes in the distance, and noticed that one of them was dark brown and looked larger than the rest. Then I saw it was Sandy, standing among them. I called to him, "Sandy, come here, boy." He left the coyotes and came to me. He trotted up and greeted me, then turned and looked back at the coyotes for a long time. They stood and looked at him.

Dogs and coyotes are usually bitter enemies and will fight each other to the death. I'd never heard of a dog running with coyotes, but Sandy acted like he was one of them. The coyotes acted like he was too.

The most fascinating animal I ever had was a bobcat. He was a homeless baby when I first met him. A group of boys on a field trip had found him in the wild several miles south of our place and decided to take him home with them. They should have left him where they found him, but they figured that out too late. The boys were halfway back to town when they began to wonder what they were going to do with a bobcat.

At Clay Creek Store they asked the Lamborns if they would take the little cat. The Lamborns saw the little guy's plight and took him in, hoping to find someone to care for him permanently. When Dad and I went to the store the next morning, I picked the little bobcat up and started petting him. He quickly began to purr, and the Lamborns asked me if I wanted him.

I looked at Dad, and with some misgivings he said, "Oh, okay." The little bobcat purred all the way home on my lap.

He was healthy and fat, so he surely hadn't been lost from his mother when the boys found him. Though he was just a soft, furry kitten, he was as big as a full-grown house cat, and a fat one at that. He loved to be held and petted, the same as any kitten, and his purr resounded throughout the house. He was feisty and loved to play with the other cats, but along with the playfulness of a kitten he had the strength of a bobcat, so the others soon became leery of him. He'd run up and give another cat a playful swat, and knock it rolling end over end. When the cat jumped up and ran off screeching, he'd look hurt and confused.

The little bobcat wasn't afraid of a thing, especially dogs. If a dog ever came close to him, it never did it again. He had teeth like needles, and claws to match. He'd jump onto a dog's back, lock on with all four feet, and sink those sharp teeth into the back of its neck. One lesson per dog is all it took. They all looked at him warily when they saw him outside, and went far out of their way to avoid crossing his path. The little bobcat just pranced along merrily, daring them to try something.

I didn't have to give him a name. His name was Bobcat. Bobcat took to domestic life easily, probably because he was so young. He spent most of his time in the house, lying on the couch, following Mom around, trying to get someone to pet him, or playing with invisible things on the floor that only he could see. He was a kitten, and the house belonged to him.

I played with him every day, and he grew attached to me. He liked Mom too, and would tolerate anything from her. She could shoo him out of the kitchen, scold him, or shake her finger in his face, and he'd just sit and gaze at her pleasantly as if he enjoyed the attention. That was a comical sight, especially after Bobcat became full grown.

Bobcat was a wild animal, however, and intolerant of anything or anybody he didn't care for. He couldn't stand to be teased; in fact he hated it. Dad couldn't resist teasing him when he was little, and Bobcat never forgave him for it. Dad didn't understand what a grudge Bobcat held until one day when he sat down on the couch beside him and started reading. He quickly became lost in his reading and wasn't even thinking about Bobcat, sitting just a couple of feet away. A few minutes later Dad glanced over and saw Bobcat crouched beside him, glaring up at him with his teeth bared and his ears laid back.

"Goddam!" Dad said. He jumped up and changed seats, never to sit near Bobcat again. Wild animals don't know about forgiving and forgetting.

Bobcat followed me everywhere until he was half grown, then I couldn't let him run loose anymore. He was tame and didn't even care to run away, but he never took his eyes off the chickens. Chickens are irresistible to a bobcat. I started putting a small dog harness on him and walking him around with it.

Bobcat grew to be a big bobcat, and I adjusted his harness to fit him. But one day he'd had enough of that harness and refused to let me put it on him again. I insisted that he wear it, but after enduring all the bites and scratches I could stand, I took the hint. We still got along after our tussle, but now I understood his feelings about the harness quite well.

He was fully grown now, nearly forty pounds of bobcat. Because he'd gotten so big and wouldn't wear the harness anymore, Bobcat was no longer welcome in the house. He had to move out and live in an old empty shed. I put his food and water bowls in the shed, and made him a bed. He seemed fairly content with the accommodations, but I'm sure he still considered himself a house bobcat.

Since I couldn't take him outside in the harness anymore, I sometimes carried him around in my arms. He seemed to enjoy the ride, though he did sorely want to get down every time we walked close to a chicken. The jealous dogs resented me carrying him, but they kept their complaints to themselves.

Unfortunately the old shed was in bad shape and couldn't contain him for long. One night the inevitable happened. Bobcat escaped. It was easy to tell he'd gotten out; dead chickens lay everywhere the next morning. The chickens hadn't been eaten, just killed. Bobcat was fulfilling his dream.

Mom saw the dead chickens, stomped back into the house, and hollered at me, "You'd better go catch that ... bobcat, and quick!" I went looking for him. He was easy to track; I just followed the trail of chicken carcasses. I soon found him, happily stalking another one, and walked over and picked him up. He just looked at me like he'd been having a wonderful time, and from the looks of the blood on his face and the feathers in his mouth he certainly had.

I was barely able to talk Mom into giving Bobcat another chance. He was fortunate that she liked him, though she wasn't particularly fond of his habits. I did my best to repair the shed and make it escape proof.

Everything returned to normal, but stayed that way only a few days. One morning Mom walked out to the barnyard and found several dead chickens. Bobcat had struck again. Steaming mad, she started looking all over the place for him. Frustrated in her search, she stopped in the middle of the barn and stood there with her hands on her hips. Suddenly she felt eyes on her, looked around, and saw him a few yards away looking at her. Mom got goose bumps then, realizing that a full-grown bobcat had walked up on her while she was looking for him.

The surprise didn't slow her down much. Mom stomped over and grabbed him by the scruff of the neck, picked him up, and headed back to the shed with him.

I was still in the house, unaware that Bobcat was loose again. I happened to look out a window just as Mom was heading toward the shed with him and witnessed an unforgettable scene. Mom was stomping along, mad as hell, holding a full-grown bobcat at arm's length. Bobcat looked quite at ease. He hung limp from her hand, all three feet of him hanging straight down as she bore him along. He was almost smiling. He'd had his fun.

Mom put him back in the shed, came in the house, and told me what he'd done. My heart sank. I knew I had to do something about the problem.

I'd like to have taken him somewhere and turned him loose to live in the wild, but Bobcat was tame and wouldn't have stayed in the wild. He'd have gone to someone's place and started killing chickens. And when they chased him and tried to kill him, he wouldn't have even understood what was going on.

I went to the shed, sat down beside him, and talked to him for a long time. He was happy; he'd had a good time with the chickens. I rubbed his belly and scratched his ears. He pawed me affectionately and purred loudly. He was just a big, lovable guy who didn't even know he was a bobcat, or that it mattered.

I knew what I had to do, but I didn't want him to be afraid, or to have an unhappy moment. He hadn't done anything wrong. He was just a bobcat.

Mom looked at me sorrowfully as I loaded my rifle and slowly walked out of the house. She'd have spared me such pain if she could have.

I walked back to the shed, rubbed his ears until he purred, and threw the door wide open. His eyes lit up, he walked out, turned and looked back at me for a moment, then headed for the chickens. I raised the rifle.

Mom told me she was sorry, hugged me, and we both cried. He was just a bobcat.

Chapter 12

CHANGES

Dad didn't generally discuss money with us, and consequently we didn't know much about his business or finances. He sometimes complained about the high prices he had to pay for feed or the low prices he got for beef, and I'm sure he worried about finances; but he worried alone.

He kept his financial records in a handful of ledgers and checkbooks neatly fastened together with rubber bands and stacked in a drawer in his bedroom. We knew he sometimes took his records to town to talk with the bankers, but he went by himself. I've always assumed the bank had to bear with him through the drought years when he had to buy cattle feed all through the summer, but I don't know that for certain.

We ate well, had good clothes to wear to school, and spending money that we had earned. I never thought we had a great amount of money, nor did I feel like we were poor. I didn't feel any need to worry about it at all.

As far as we knew Dad just worked hard and raged at the weather, and anything else that needed raging at from time to time. We left the finances, and the raging, to him. He seemed good at both.

Dad had never been able to afford a new car in his life, but he had dreamed of owning a Packard since they first came out in the early 1900s. For years Packards had been considered fine automobiles, even luxury cars, and they were still luxury cars in the 1950s.

Dad's finances must have been doing well in 1950. He bought himself a brand new Packard, and a big expensive one at that. He went first-class when he did it.

He put on his khaki dress pants one day, his best cowboy boots, and his going-to-town Stetson, and asked Mom to ride to town with him. She asked him where they were going. "Aw, goin' to look at a car," he said matter-of-factly.

He drove straight to the Packard dealership, walked into the showroom, and started looking at the fanciest, most expensive model the dealer had. It was sitting on display in the front window, its deep maroon finish glistening in the showroom lights. A gleaming four-door, it had big whitewall tires, fender skirts, extra chrome, and a luxury interior. Dad looked all around the big car and under it, opened the doors, sat down in it, and asked the dealer everything about it.

Then he started talking price and negotiated at length. When he and the dealer finally agreed, Dad wrote him a check for the full amount. He paid cash for the finest car the town had to offer that day, and drove his Packard off the showroom floor with his big Stetson on and a cigar sticking straight out the center of his mouth.

He loved to drive that Packard, and he drove it fast. In his words, it was "built to run." He only drove his pickup forty-five miles an hour on the highway, but Dad set the Packard on a full fifty, and held it there. As far as he was concerned, fifty miles an hour was flying low. When he passed oncoming cars with the left front wheel of that big Packard straddling the white line, he probably looked like he was flying low, and also flying close.

Driving on the prairie didn't work out any better for Dad than driving on the highway. Whenever the ground was even a little bit muddy, either from rain or melting snow, Dad got stuck. If there was just one spot of soggy ground on the whole ranch, when he drove away from the house we knew he'd be stuck in it before the day ended. He carried shovels, pry bars, and boards in his pickup, and anything else that might help him get it out of the mud. Those things usually didn't help much though, because when Dad got stuck, he really got stuck.

One year he decided the reason he got stuck so often was his old pickup. It didn't have enough power, and it didn't have four-wheel drive. He bought a rugged four-wheel drive Jeep pickup to replace it, with big mud and snow tires on all four wheels. He knew that would keep him from getting stuck. It didn't. The Jeep was far more powerful than a conventional truck, and its four-wheel drive certainly gave it a better grip in muddy conditions, but it didn't hinder his ability to get stuck at all.

Because of its greater power and grip, Dad thought the Jeep would go anywhere. It was a good truck, but not invincible as he seemed to believe it should be. He'd plunge it off into places he wouldn't have even tried with his old truck. And to his utter surprise, he could get stuck worse in the Jeep than in the old one.

When the wheels of an automobile first sink into the mud and begin to spin, it's usually best to stop, get out, and assess the situation before it gets any worse. Then you can decide the best plan of action. This calm, methodical approach wasn't Dad's way. When the wheels started to spin, he'd clench his jaw, stomp on the accelerator, race the engine, and dig all four of them into the mud. He didn't give up easily either; he'd continue to dig the truck in until he buried it up to both axles.

Dad would really be mad by then, so after he finished digging the truck into the mud he'd holler, "We're blowed up!" and try to cuss it back out. That didn't work either, but it wasn't due to lack of effort.

Dad often got stuck when he was driving by himself. From the house we'd hear his pickup, the engine roaring and wheels spinning as much as a mile away. We knew what that sound meant. George and I would load some heavy chains on the tractor and head the direction of the sound. If he got stuck so far from the house that we couldn't hear his engine, we'd look off across the pasture and see a dot moving in the distance. It was Dad walking to the house. That called for the same procedure. Grab the chains and head for him on the tractor, and quickly, because the further he had to walk the madder he'd be when we got there.

We even got the tractor stuck a few times while trying to pull the pickup out with it. With the pickup and tractor both stuck, there was nothing left to do but walk to Dad's Place and get Jigs. We'd harness Jigs, climb on his back, and ride him back to the vehicles, where he would pull them both out.

Dad had a strange habit that sometimes affected his driving. He daydreamed. He could get so completely lost in thought that he no longer knew where he was or what was going on around him. You could see it in his face when it happened; his eyes would go out of focus and his head would drop slightly as if he was looking at the dashboard. Sometimes he'd have a pleasant, dreamy look on his face, and maybe a faint smile. Other times he'd clench his jaw and scowl as he relived some past battle. His lips might even move as he silently dressed down some enemy from days gone by.

If Dad was sitting in the house when he started daydreaming it didn't cause a problem, but if he went into one of his reveries while he was driving, then it could get pretty crazy. He always started speeding when it happened and never realized he was doing it.

If George and I were riding with him, we'd first notice that he wasn't saying anything and that we were picking up speed. We'd look at him to see if his eyes were glazed over, or if he was smiling or scowling, or maybe moving his lips in that silent mutter. For a short while it was amusing. We'd poke each other, grin, and try not to giggle, until the speed began to scare us.

Left alone in his fantasy, Dad would get to going forty-five or fifty miles an hour across the prairie. When George and I couldn't stand it any longer, we'd brace our arms on the dashboard and one of us would say, "Dad, you're goin' a little fast, aren't you?" He'd open his eyes wide and look kind of addled for a moment, then he'd notice the landscape flying by, look down at the speedometer, and slam on the brakes. He always hit the brakes when he discovered how fast he was going; that's why we braced ourselves before we broke in on him.

Dad's daydreaming caused an unforgettable incident one day involving me, one of the Lamborn boys, and a pickup load of sucker rods.

Our water well in the far south pasture had run dry, and we had drilled another a mile away to replace it. Dad hired Albert Lamborn, a boy twelve or thirteen like myself, to help salvage the underground equipment from the old well to use in the new one.

We pulled about a dozen wooden sucker rods from the old well, each fifteen feet long with iron connections attached to both ends, and stacked them in the back of Dad's pickup to haul them to the new well. The pickup bed was only six feet long, so the rods extended from the front of the bed up over the tailgate, and hung out nine or ten feet behind the truck. Because they were flexible and had those heavy metal connections on the ends, the rods bent down over the tailgate so far they nearly touched the ground. They needed extra weight on the front end to keep them from falling out or dragging the ground as we hauled them across the prairie.

Dad told Albert and me to ride in the pickup bed and sit on the front ends of the sucker rods to weight them down. They made a precarious seat, but we figured we'd be all right as long as Dad drove slow and didn't hit any big bumps.

Albert and I climbed into the front of the pickup bed and sat down on those hard connections. As Dad instructed us, we sat crosswise facing each other so we could hold down all twelve rods with our legs and rear ends. He cautioned us to hold on tight and to keep the rods from flopping around too much. Then he got into the cab and started off, slowly and carefully.

There was no road to the new well, so Dad drove straight across the prairie. The rods bounced up and down a little as we rode along, but as long as he went slow they didn't bounce badly.

Everything went fine for a while, then the rods started to bounce up and down a little harder. Albert and I began to get a strange sensation—speed—we were picking up speed. We began to go faster and faster, and the rods bounced up and down harder and harder.

Soon we were charging across the prairie about fifty miles an hour, and I knew Dad was no longer with us. He was off in some reverie of bygone years, and Albert and I, trapped in the present, had a problem. The rods bounced up and down so hard they began to hurl us completely off the pickup bed, those iron connections pounding our behinds like hammers. The back ends of the rods flopped up and down and around and around like paper streamers trailing in the wind. Albert looked wild-eyed when his face bounced past mine.

I tried to holler at Dad as we thundered along, but he had the windows rolled up and couldn't hear me. Suddenly everything changed, drastically. Dad hit a huge hole with his left front wheel. The front end of the pickup made a tremendous bang, bounced two feet off the ground, and crashed back down as if dropped from a crane.

That brought Dad back to the present. It also threw Albert, me, and all those rods out of the pickup. Albert and I bounced ten feet high, came back down in a flurry of flailing arms and legs, hit the ground at fifty miles an hour, and rolled and tumbled across the prairie like rag dolls. The sucker rods bounced high in the air, bending back and forth like vaulting poles as they flew, and rained down on top of us.

Dad slammed on the brakes and skidded to a stop. He jumped out in a panic, hollered, "We're blowed up!" and ran around to the front of the pickup. There he dropped down on his stomach and looked up under the front end. At first I couldn't tell what he was doing, then, incredibly, I realized he was looking to see if his pickup was damaged.

He quickly checked out the front end, jumped to his feet, looked back at Albert and me, and hollered, "That coulda cost me five hundred dollars!" As he stood there hollering and jumping around, it finally dawned on him that we were lying on our backs thirty yards behind the truck with sucker rods piled all over us. He suddenly looked startled and came charging back toward us, still hollering, "Either of you boys get hurt?"

We looked at each other in amazement and shook our heads. Neither of us had a scratch.

We stood up, looked around at the mess, and started gathering up the rods and stacking them back in the truck. Albert looked puzzled. He couldn't understand why Dad had been driving so fast, and he didn't look very willing to climb back in and sit down on those rods again either. I nodded confidently, trying to reassure him that we'd be all right. He looked awfully skeptical, but we climbed in the truck and sat down on the rods again.

As we rode along I explained to Albert what had happened, that Dad had simply been daydreaming and checked out on us for a while. That didn't do much to settle his anxiety. He kept glancing nervously at Dad through the back window for the rest of the trip.

George and I enjoyed watching rodeos, but neither of us ever participated in them. There was no reason to; I felt like we were living in some kind of rodeo anyway. One memorable day, however, we decided to try our hand at bull riding. Actually, we decided to try my hand at bull riding. A half-grown bull calf just happened to be hanging around close to the barn at the time; that's probably the only reason the subject came up in the first place.

We'd tried similar experiments in the past without success, such as the riding incident with Lucy the milk cow, but that had been six or seven years before, when I was young. I was older now, and knew how to think these things through.

George reminded me what a good rider I was, and brave. And of course he was right. Why should I be afraid to ride a stupid calf? It looked easy. It should be noted, however, that my assessment of these situations wasn't always flawless.

The setup was simple. A corral fence ran parallel to the side of the barn about fifteen feet from it, forming a narrow lane between the fence and the barn wall. The lane was closed off near the back of the barn but open at the front. The opening was clear except for a rock about two feet high that leaned against the corner of the barn.

Our plan was to drive the little bull into the open end of the lane, run him to the back, and corner him. There I'd jump on him and ride him back down the lane like a rodeo cowboy, gloriously busting out the front into open pasture.

How could anything go wrong with a plan like that?

We herded the little bull into the lane. As he neared the back end, we rushed him and trapped him against the fence. I quickly hopped on his back and hollered, "Let 'im go!" and George let him go. The calf whirled and galloped back down the lane as hard as he could run. Surprisingly, he didn't try to buck me off, not yet anyway. He was eyeing that open pasture just beyond the big rock by the barn wall.

I stayed with him as we thundered toward the opening, the calf bawling and me hollering "Yahoo!" and waving my arms in the air. When we reached the opening the little bull decided I'd gone far enough. He dropped his head, jumped sideways, kicked up his heels, and lofted me high into the air. Sailing gracefully, my arms straight out like a glider, I turned in a wide arc toward the barn and came down on my head, squarely on that rock.

The lights went out—knocked cold.

When I woke up George was holding my head and nearly in tears. I'm sure he'd wondered if I'd ever open my eyes again. It took me a while to figure out where I was, then I realized that my head felt like it was split in half.

"I'm sorry, Brother," George said. "I didn't mean for you to get hurt."

"That's okay," I told him. "It wasn't your fault."

It wasn't George's fault either. Hell, I had scars all over me from my own doing. I'd thought riding the little bull was a fine idea myself. The ride was admittedly short-lived, but I'd done pretty well for as long as it lasted. We just hadn't taken the rock into account in the planning, and as always, it was the landing that got me.

Our lives changed considerably in 1953, when I was twelve. George left home to join the navy, and the Rural Electrification Administration (REA) reached the High Plains.

We could track the approach of electricity as the line of tall poles marched across the landscape and the heavy power lines followed. In anticipation we had our old rock house wired for it. An 1800s homestead house made of sandstone blocks wasn't designed for electricity, but Dad hired a man with enough perseverance to wire it, and the house was ready the day the magic stuff came down the lines.

Electricity made an unbelievable difference in our lives. The most amazing change was simply light. Our old house lit up like we'd never dreamed. The moment the main breaker was closed, I ran from one end of the house to the other, throwing on the light switch in every room as I went.

The light was overwhelming. Now we could sit in the evenings and see each other clearly from across the room. Instead of having to hold a book directly under the kerosene lamp at night, we could read anywhere in the house. Mom could leave the radio on all day long if she wanted to and listen to music while she worked. It was wonderful.

Besides lighting up the house, electricity made a few of our jobs easier as well. Mom had the old gasoline engine taken off the washing machine right away. That noisy, cantankerous, smoke-spewing beast was replaced by a little electric motor that just purred on washday. She got an electric refrigerator too, one she didn't have to kick to keep it running. And the cream separator, the monster that George and I had to crank every night was also fitted with a little motor that happily turned it with no effort at all on our part.

A big yard light allowed us to see our way to the water barrel to fill the buckets after dark, to walk to the barn easily, and to make a straight shot to the toilet at critical times. Dad could even see the light from way up the draw at night when he drove out to check the windmills, except during duststorms.

Life was good.

Living on the ranch with Mom and Dad was the only life I knew or cared to know. The rest of the world didn't concern me much. George had a more studious, poetic nature, however, and being older than me, remembered a life before the ranch. Constantly expanding his knowledge through reading as he grew up, he longed to see the world he studied in books, to explore horizons beyond the ranch.

For years George had dreamed of going to sea when he finished high school and planned to join the navy the summer after he graduated. Dad didn't want him to go, however; telling him how badly he was needed there on the ranch, he pressured him with guilt.

George talked to Mom about it that summer. He badly wanted to see the world, but it would leave only Dad, Mom, and me to run the ranch. He knew it would be hard on us if he left.

Mom knew the needs of the ranch, but she also knew George and his needs. To her everlasting credit, she told him he had a life of his own to lead and that the ranch imposed no obligations on him, regardless of what Dad said. She told him to go find what he wanted in life.

It was a proper decision on Mom's part and a bold stand for her to take. I'm sure she felt some pangs of conscience for Dad having provided a home for us for many years, but mostly it was bold because it flew in the face of his wishes. It took courage to buck Dad's authority, but she did it, and stuck with her decision.

George left for the navy that fall, his eyes shining with excitement as he went off to Denver to join.

The difference in our ages as well as personalities somewhat separated George and me as we grew up, but we were brothers, and in our hearts we'd always been best friends. I missed him from the moment he left.

Dad thinking

Dad and Gary with the new Packard

Chapter 13

TEAMWORK

I started seventh grade the fall after George left, my first year of junior high school. One evening while I was doing homework, Dad picked up my arithmetic book and started looking through it. He browsed it for several minutes, then laid it down and turned back to his reading. A few minutes later he stopped reading, and just sat in his chair thinking. Then he looked at me and asked, "Could you get me a book like that?"

"Sure," I said, surprised at the request. "I can buy you one at the school bookstore." He gave me the money, and I brought the textbook to him the next evening. He opened it and wrote "Geo. Blizzard" inside the front cover.

He started studying seventh grade mathematics every evening. At first he was reluctant to ask me about a problem or calculation he didn't understand, but when he hinted at something I'd offer to help. With his reading glasses riding low on his nose, he'd sit next to me and we'd discuss it until he understood.

He studied hard, and we worked through many problems together. He learned what he wanted to know about mathematics from that book, and I began to understand how someone with a third grade education had learned to read and write so well.

I didn't ride my horse to meet the school bus very often after George left. Dad usually drove me to the highway and picked me up again in the evening. The same routine of chores still took place each morning, including the wild cow milking of course. After I milked the cows and fed the pigs, I ate a quick breakfast, changed clothes, and Dad and I headed for the highway to meet the school bus. On the way we passed by Dad's Place and loaded the cattle feed on the pickup. Dad fed the cattle by himself after I left for school.

Each morning we loaded whatever roughage we were feeding, baled hay or bundles, plus three or four sacks of cottonseed cake. We backed the pickup to the door of the old garage building and loaded the one hundred-pound sacks of cake onto it. I was twelve then, and Dad was seventy-eight. We each took one end of a sack and loaded it onto the truck together.

We faced a different problem in the winter when the snow was deep. The drifts wouldn't allow us to back up close to the garage, forcing us to carry the sacks of cake fifty yards through the snow to the pickup. First we had to hoist the hundred-pound sacks onto our backs, then carry them through the snow. I was strong enough to carry one on my back, but not strong enough to hoist it up there. Dad could lift one by himself, so we solved the problem together. Dad would help me hoist one onto my back, then he'd hoist one onto his, and away we'd go.

We had to reverse roles the following winter. Dad was still strong enough to carry a sack of cake, but he could no longer lift one up to his back. I grew strong enough to lift one by myself that year, so now I helped Dad hoist a sack onto his back, and then I lifted one onto mine.

We were a team. One growing up, and one growing old.

One hot summer day Dad and I decided to salvage some floorboards from an old building on an abandoned homestead. The place had stood alone on a hill for sixty or seventy years and long since gone to ruin. The walls of the old building had fallen and rotted away, but a few of the floorboards were still good enough to be used elsewhere.

Some boards in the old floor were broken, leaving large cracks between them. I was standing near one end of the floor with a crowbar in my hand, while Dad worked ten or twelve feet away near the other end. I happened to glance his direction and saw a rattlesnake poke its head up between the boards, just inches from his leg. Dad didn't see it. The rattler was concentrating on his leg and positioning itself to strike as soon as it could wriggle enough of its body up through the crack in the floor.

"Look out!" I shouted, pointing at the snake with my left hand and swinging the crowbar with my right. Dad looked down and saw the rattler just as I threw the crowbar at his feet. He jumped straight in the air as the crowbar passed under him, caught the snake six inches behind the head, and broke its back.

The snake was already out of commission when Dad's boots touched the floor. He stumbled around a little when he landed, but didn't fall. When he regained his balance the rattler was writhing in its death throes at his feet. Dad quickly stepped back from it, took off his hat, and looked first at the snake and then at the crowbar. Then he looked over at me, shook his head, and said, "Hell of a throw, Son. Hell of a throw."

Being a perfectionist at everything he did, Dad turned ordinary projects into works of art. Most people's barbwire fences didn't run exactly straight, nor were the wires that tightly stretched. Dad built fences that ran straight as a ruler for miles, and he stretched them so tight the wires hummed in the wind.

Building fence with Dad was an experience in precision. It started with the very first step, digging the postholes. Each hole had to be exactly the same depth, two feet. Dad carved a mark on the posthole diggers to ensure that every hole reached that depth, and not an inch deeper or shallower. Each hole had to line up perfectly with all the previous ones. After we dug fifteen or twenty holes exactly two feet deep and chalk-line straight, we set the posts in the ground in the same meticulous manner.

First we drove along and dropped the posts out of the truck into the holes. Then using the blunt end of a shovel handle, we tamped the dirt in around their bases to hold them solidly in the ground. This should have been a simple procedure, but Dad didn't do things that way. As I tamped the dirt around the base of one, he'd stand at the far end of the line of posts, close one eye, and sight down their tops. Then he'd motion for me to move the top of the post one way or the other as I tamped it in. After we had painstakingly built a half mile or a mile of fence, you could stand at one end and sight down the straightest line of posts that ever stood on the prairie.

Dad sighted down those posts too, many times. He'd often return days after a fence was finished just to look down it again and see if he could spot a post slightly out of line. If he did he'd stand there and keep it in view while he motioned to me to walk down the fence line and find it. I would then walk hundreds of yards down the fence trying to locate the errant post. Each time I put my hand on one, Dad would wave his arms or his hat to let me know whether or not it was the crooked one.

This procedure for locating out-of-line posts may sound simple, but it wasn't. Dad's various arm- and hat-waving signals were never the same; each one seemed to mean a different thing every time he used it. By the time I was several hundred yards down the fence line, this long-range signaling exercise became just as ridiculous as it sounds. But somehow we eventually found the crooked post, one millimeter out of line, and corrected it.

For a while after we built a new fence, I dreaded for Dad to get near it. When he was driving anywhere near the fence you could see his eyes narrow as he began to scrutinize it critically. Then he'd stop and get out to check the line of posts for straightness one more time. This usually led to yet another long range arm-waving event.

Dad stretched the barbed wires "tight as a fiddle string." Occasionally when he was trying to extract some last imaginary bit of slack out of a wire, we strained the wire stretchers so hard that we actually pulled it in two. Dad would cuss loudly as the wire snapped, winged its way through the air, and rolled up in a tangled mess a hundred yards down the fence line.

Barbwire gates are normally saggy, sorry-looking things that hang loosely on the gateposts. Most people plan them that way when they build them, because the looser they are the easier they open and shut. Dad's gates were absolute works of art, and unbelievably tight. He didn't trust anyone else's artistic abilities that well, so he usually built gates by himself. Most people could build a gate in an hour, but Dad would spend half a day at one, meticulously putting it together and stretching it between the gateposts. When he finished, it did not sag. Like the taut fence adjoining it, the gate hummed in the wind. It was also the hardest damn thing to open and shut that anyone ever encountered.

Dad sound-tested a gate before he proclaimed it finished. He'd pluck each individual wire, hold his ear close, and listen to see if it hummed correctly. If it did he'd smile faintly and nod his head; if it didn't he'd tighten it some more. It never needed loosening, only tightening. When all the wires hummed perfectly, he'd stand back, look the gate over critically, and nod with satisfaction. Another masterpiece.

Dad was always concerned with his image, which seemed a little strange to me. Anyone who knew him never doubted his toughness, but I guess he was afraid somebody might get a glimpse of that soft spot inside.

He liked cats and dogs, but he tried not to let it show. We had a long-haired cat named Fuzzy, a prissy lady with a loving temperament who gained the right to come in the house, an esteemed privilege earned by few pets. Fuzzy liked to sit on Dad's lap while he read *Ranch Romances.* She'd look up at him lovingly and slowly inch closer and closer to his face as the evening went by. When she moved too close, Dad would gently tap her on the head with his book, and she'd back off a few inches. Then in a few minutes she'd start easing forward again.

Dad pretended not to care about Fuzzy sitting on his lap, but I'd hear him calling her when he thought no one was listening.

Sandy was the only dog to ever gain house privileges. Dad liked him too, but he didn't want other people to know it—not even Mom, George and me. Occasionally one of us would walk out the back door and catch him bent over Sandy, petting him and talking to him. When that happened Dad would quickly straighten up, gruffly clear his throat, and walk away. It was kind of cute to watch, and also ridiculous.

Two turkeys once threatened Dad's image and thoroughly bruised his pride. It had been my idea to buy several baby turkeys and raise them. Dad hadn't particularly cared for the idea and always referred to them as my turkeys. Two of the toms grew very large, and very mean. Those belligerent guys were always together and tried to flog anyone who came near them.

Standing in my room one afternoon, I thought I heard a distant, muffled voice outside. I looked out all the windows and, seeing no one, went back to my room. Then I heard it again. It sounded like someone hollering, but still muffled somehow. I walked outside to listen and heard it again. Louder now, it sounded like Dad's voice, but as if a long distance away or maybe inside something.

I looked at Dad's pickup, parked about seventy-five yards from the house, and saw both tom turkeys walking around it with their feathers puffed up like they were trying to flog someone. I started walking toward the pickup, and heard Dad's voice again. Then I saw his feet come out from under it, and the turkeys jump on them and begin to stomp and peck at them. Dad started hollering and kicking wildly at the turkeys with both feet.

The picture became clear. Though he knew hardly a thing about mechanics, Dad was always crawling up under the pickup to check something. The turkeys had caught him under there and trapped him.

I chased the turkeys away and looked up under the truck. Dad was lying on his back, and could barely tilt his head enough to see me. I could see that his face was red. "It's okay, they're gone," I said.

He indignantly pulled himself from under the truck, jumped up, and started dusting off his clothes. "Those damn turkeys of yours are drivin' me crazy!" he sputtered. I didn't dare look at him or say a thing; I was too close to laughing. While he was dusting off his hat he figured that out. He looked at me narrowly, stuffed his hat back on his head, stomped into the pickup, and drove away in a huff.

If he looked in the rearview mirror as he was leaving, he saw me howling.

One of our sows had a litter of nine baby pigs in the middle of winter, a bad time of year to try to raise that many little ones. Worse yet, one of them was a runt, too small and too weak to compete with the others for his mother's milk. A runt pig will soon die unless given special care. He would survive only if we fed him from a bottle and kept him in a warm place until he could grow as strong as the others.

The little pig was pink and clean, and smaller than a puppy. We took him to the house, made a bed for him in a box behind the dining room stove, and started feeding him milk from a bottle. He quickly adjusted to the good life. After he ate his fill the little pig would climb out of the box, stretch out in front of the stove, and go to sleep like a house cat.

A Landman from an oil company came to call on Dad one cold afternoon. Landmen lease mineral rights for oil companies. The Landmen who called on us were always nicely dressed, well educated, polite, and they all lived in cities. I'm sure our lifestyle surprised them, amused them, and even shocked a few of them.

The young man who came that day was clean-cut, dressed in a suit and tie, and obviously felt out of place in our house. Mom showed him into the dining room where Dad and I sat by the stove. He introduced himself, shook hands with Dad, and sat down by the stove with us.

The little pig was enjoying the stove too. He lay stretched out in front of it sound asleep, directly in front of the oil company man. A pig lying in front of a stove is pretty hard to miss, but the man didn't say a thing.

He began the conversation with small talk, the normal inquiries about our health and the weather, and did his best to ignore the little pig. Then he and Dad began to talk business, and he tried to act as though a pig in someone's dining room was an everyday occurrence. He tried, but he didn't pull it off very well.

He leaned toward Dad, speaking in an animated, educated manner and gesturing appropriately as he spoke, but occasionally cutting his eyes uncomfortably toward the pig. Dad noted the man's uneasy glances and sensed his discomfort, but he remained cool, grinning and chatting calmly as if a pig in the dining room really was an everyday occurrence.

The longer I watched, the more ridiculous the situation became. If the man had really felt comfortable, he could have pulled it off. God knows he tried. With Dad still making casual conversation, the poor guy finally felt compelled to say something about the pig.

He leaned back, folded his arms across his chest, and looked at the sleeping pig. Then with a counterfeit grin, he nodded his head, chuckled, and said, "That little pig sure likes that stove, doesn't he?"

Dad cut his eyes at me for a quick second. They danced with delight. Then he casually looked back at the fellow and replied, "Yeah, they always like a warm stove."

Chapter 14

DIFFERENCES

Dad couldn't easily admit to himself when he became too old to do something, and he certainly wouldn't admit it to us. Whatever it was, God knows we didn't dare suggest he stop doing it, unless we wanted to watch him do it again and again to prove us wrong. But when it became absolutely necessary that he stop doing something, at long last he would give it up on his own. We all knew when it happened, but nobody ever mentioned it.

He gave up riding his feisty horse, Tony, when he was seventy-five, but not before he showed him one last time who was boss. Dad had a hard time pulling himself up onto a horse at that age, but he still saddled Tony occasionally and rode off by himself.

Tony was a skittish horse, easily spooked by any sudden noise or movement. A jack rabbit jumping up under his feet, a rattlesnake buzzing nearby, or even a passing tumbleweed might make him jump or charge off unexpectedly.

I looked over on a hillside a half mile away one day and saw Tony galloping as hard as he could go with Dad on his back. "Oh God, Tony got spooked and ran away with Dad!" I thought. Then I looked closer, and saw Dad leaning low over Tony's neck, pushing him hard. I shook my head and watched them until they charged up over the horizon and out of sight.

Dad had just gone out for a leisurely ride that day, but Tony started acting up as spirited horses are prone to do. Dad put the spurs to him and ran him as hard as he could. He ran him that way until Tony became winded and had to slow down.

Tony was dripping lather when they returned to the corral. "I saw you goin' like thunder over the hill," I said. "What was goin' on?"

Dad slid off Tony's back with a scowl and said, "Son of a bitch still thinks he's boss!"

Dad bought something he'd wanted all his life after he stopped riding Tony. For years he'd talked about Morgan horses, a special breed known for their intelligence. He'd often described their physical characteristics, slightly shorter and stouter than other horses, but mostly he talked about how smart they were.

A truck came down the road one day and pulled up by the yard fence. Dad didn't say anything as I followed him out. When the driver unloaded a horse, I knew what kind he was from Dad's descriptions. "Finally got your Morgan horse, didn't ya?" I said.

Dad looked at the horse with pride. "Yeah, I did," he said. "His name is Joe."

Joe was a handsome animal. Dark gray, shiny and sleek, stoutly built, and noticeably shorter than most saddle horses. Dad beamed as he pointed out his classic Morgan characteristics.

Joe was smarter than we'd ever dreamed. He could open gates, untie knots, and perform a dozen other tricks. This unusual mental ability was interesting in a horse, but not an endearing quality. Joe studied things to learn how they worked so he could work them to his own advantage. Every smart thing he did was totally self-serving.

Our wooden corral gates fastened with hook latches. A large iron hook hung from the gate and fastened into an iron ring on the gatepost. Joe would simply stick his nose under the hook, raise it up to unlatch it, and push the gate open. We had to wire all the corral gates shut so he couldn't open them. That made the gates terribly unhandy to use, as we had to unwrap the wire to open them, then wrap it around the post again to lock them.

He learned how barbwire gates worked too, but they were harder for him to open because Dad stretched them so tightly. That didn't discourage him though. Joe tried every barbwire gate he came to, and if it wasn't too tight he would nudge the locking wire off and leave the gate lying on the ground.

We couldn't tie Joe to a post by the bridle reins like a normal horse, because he learned how to take the bridle off. He'd start by rubbing the top of the bridle against the post, and within a few minutes would slide it off over his ears and free himself. The only way to secure him was to tie one rein around the post and the other around his neck; then when he rubbed the bridle off he'd still be tethered to the post.

Tying the reins with a slip knot or a bow knot wouldn't work either. He'd pull at the loose ends with his teeth and untie the knots. Only a tight square knot would hold him.

Joe tried to rub saddles off too, but he couldn't accomplish that. He just scratched them badly by rubbing them against whatever was available.

But Joe was Dad's pride, the Morgan horse he'd always wanted, so he forgave him all those devious habits. He laughed them off and bragged about the superior intelligence they demonstrated.

Joe drove me crazy. Dad only rode him occasionally for an outing, but I had to ride him to round up cattle and sometimes to bring in the other horses. I also had to wire and unwire the damn corral gates when I did the chores.

Riding Dad around a little for fun was all right with Joe, but he hated to work. He tried every sly trick imaginable when I rode him to round up cattle. If he saw a post ahead as we were galloping along, he'd act as if he meant to miss it by several feet, then when he got close he'd quickly veer and try to smash my leg against it to rub me off his back. He scraped my leg badly a couple of times but never managed to force me off.

The first time I rode Joe near a tree I learned not to do it again. He headed for the tree as hard as he could go and ran under a limb to try and knock me off. I couldn't stop him, so I laid my head beside his neck and flattened my body enough to pass under the limb.

Joe did cute things when I wasn't riding him too. If he caught me looking another direction, he'd pretend affection by nuzzling my shoulder from behind, then open his mouth and bite the hell out of me.

I finally started complaining about Joe, but Dad didn't have to put up with as many of his antics as I did. When I complained he'd just grumble and say, "Yeah, yeah..." and that would be the end of it.

Then Joe learned to buck. One day when he was galloping I pulled back on the reins just enough to slow him down, and he threw on the brakes as hard as he could. I flew off over his head, slammed to the ground, and rolled to a stop. Joe thought that was great fun. From then on he tried to throw me off every chance he got.

I told Dad when Joe bucked me off the first time and every time he tried it after that. He wouldn't respond to those complaints either.

One day I had to ride Joe to round up the other horses. They were grazing a quarter of a mile from the house when I found them, and feeling frisky. As I headed them toward the house they all began to run and kick up their heels. Joe decided to join in the fun. He ran out of control with me on his back, jumping and kicking his heels high in the air. I could only hang tightly to his neck and mane. Then he planted his front feet and stopped short. I flew over his head, hit the ground in front of him, rolled over a couple of times, and stopped in a sitting position. Joe ran by me and kicked both hind feet in my face as he passed, his hooves missing me by inches.

I sat there for several minutes, growing madder and madder as I thought about everything Joe had done to me. Now he'd tried to kick me in the face. I picked myself up and stomped back to the house.

Dad lay on the couch reading when I walked in. "Did ya get the horses in?" he asked.

"No," I said. "Joe threw me off again and tried to kick me in the face. He almost got me too."

"What'd he do?" Dad asked. He listened as I described what Joe had done, then looked away and stared at the ceiling.

My chin quivered as I nearly broke into tears. "I've told ya and told ya what he's doin' to me," I shouted. "What're ya gonna do? Wait'll he kills me?!"

Dad rolled his head my direction and gazed narrowly at me for a moment, then looked away. I turned and stalked out of the house.

Dad fed and watered Joe himself the next morning and every morning thereafter. I didn't go near the horse. A few days after our confrontation Dad put a bridle on him, led him next to a fence so he could climb onto his back, and rode him around bareback in the corral. That was dangerous at his age, so I stood and watched, afraid he might fall off. He just looked at me defiantly and rode around in the corral until I left.

A week later a man drove up pulling a horse trailer behind his pickup. He and Dad stood in the corral with Joe and talked for a long time. Then the man handed him a check, led Joe into the trailer, and hauled him away. Dad walked back in the house, looked at me, and said nothing. Neither of us ever mentioned Joe again.

The duststorms worsened again the summer I was fourteen, and we had to shovel mud out of the tanks nearly every day as well as keep up with the normal ranch work. One afternoon when Dad lay down to rest, I asked Mom if I could ride to the creek and go fishing. "You'd better go ask Dad," she said. "I don't know what he's got planned."

I walked into Dad's room and asked him if I could go fishing. He lay there a minute, obviously perturbed at the question, then answered, "Aw, I suppose so."

I grabbed my fishing pole and hurried out the door. I bridled Champ and started to ride away, but before I rode out of earshot Dad walked out and hollered at me from the back yard. I turned and rode back.

"You don't need to be goin' to the damn creek," he said sarcastically. "You'd do better takin' a shovel instead of that pole and gettin' some more mud outta that tank we been workin' on."

I slid off Champ and stomped into the house to put my fishing pole away.

"What's wrong?" Mom asked.

"Dad told me to go shovel mud out of the tank at his place," I said.

"I thought he said you could go fishing," she replied.

"He did. Then he changed his mind and told me to go shovel mud," I said bitterly as I headed back out the door.

Mom followed me out. "I'm going to help you," she said.

Dad walked back in the house as Mom and I drove away.

At Dad's Place I stopped the pickup by the water tank and just sat there. Neither of us said anything for a few minutes, then I looked at Mom. "I'm not gonna shovel that mud," I said. "He told me I could go to the creek, then he told me I couldn't. All I've been doin' all summer is shovelin' mud."

Mom looked concerned, but she didn't differ with me. "You really aren't going to?" she asked. I shook my head.

"That'll really make him mad, you know."

"I know," I said. "I'm pretty mad myself."

We drove back to the house, and I walked through the kitchen door ahead of Mom. Surprised at our quick return, Dad asked from the dining room, "How much mud did ya get shoveled out?"

"None," I replied.

Dad stood up and stepped into the kitchen doorway with fire in his eyes. "Why not?" he growled.

To my own surprise, I replied, "Because I didn't want to."

He turned, walked into his room, put on his hat, and came hustling back through the kitchen where Mom and I stood. "Come on, let's go shovel some mud," he ordered as he stomped past me.

"I'm not gonna do it," I said, my chin trying to quiver.

Dad whirled like a grizzly, his eyes blazing. "What'd you say?"

"I said I'm not gonna do it," I spat out. "You told me I could go fishin', then you backed out on it. All I ever do around here is work."

Dad clenched his jaw tightly and pushed me against the sink with his chest, those iron fists doubled at his sides. His face inches from mine, he growled, "I oughta ..."

"Don't hit me, Dad," I said evenly. "And get out of my face."

As we stared eye to eye, something in Dad's eyes began to change. Surprise crept into them. He backed away, turned to the door, and said, "I'm goin' to dig some mud outta that tank. You comin' with me?"

Mom had stood close by the entire time and hadn't said a word. Now she said softly, "Please go with him, Gary."

"Okay, I'll go with you," I said. "Mom told me to."

I followed him to the truck, and Mom followed both of us. We all drove to Dad's Place without saying a word. Mom sat in the truck while Dad and I shoveled mud for a half hour or more, working side by side in total silence. Then Dad stopped shoveling, leaned toward me, and asked, "Why'd ya tell me to get outta your face?"

"Because I thought you were gonna hit me," I told him. He looked thoughtful, then went back to work.

My actions that day surprised me as much as anyone. I'd never dreamed I would refuse to do what he said and tell him so to his face. Why did I push it so far? Simple adolescent rebellion? That's part of the reason but not the entire answer.

Dad was the most fearsome person I've ever known, and I never saw him madder than when I defied him. At that moment, however, I discovered something that amazed me. I discovered I wasn't afraid of him.

I didn't realize the magnitude of my actions at the time, and I'll never fully understand why I forced the issue, but in reflection I know I wouldn't be the same person I am today if I hadn't defied him and discovered what I did.

Dad and I made it through that trying day with a greater appreciation of where we stood and a greater mutual respect. Life with him would still be tough to some extent, of course, but we worked our relationship out better than we ever had before. He didn't dictate orders to me in quite the same manner, and I never defied him again.

I think Dad recognized something in me that day too, perhaps the same thing I did. I hope in his heart he liked what he saw.

Jigs, Dad, and Prince

Chapter 15

SURVIVAL

The weather occasionally became so extreme as to threaten our lives. It could also threaten the livestock or both us and the livestock. Of course the wind played a lead part in those lethal storms.

One hot summer day the wind began to come and go in rapid gusts, an unusual pattern. Dad was lying down for his afternoon rest, so Mom and I took the pickup and went to shut off the windmills to prevent any possible damage.

I wasn't really concerned about the weather and neither was Mom, at least no more than usual. She just went along to enjoy the ride. Clouds were gathering by the time we left the house, but we didn't sense anything unusual. By the time we reached the windmill at Dad's Place, the wind was gusting harder and rapidly shifting direction.

The clouds gathered faster as we headed for the south pasture. They hung low, and the sky darkened. Heavy raindrops began to hit the windshield intermittently. Mom hadn't said a thing for a few minutes. I knew she was worried.

Tornadoes are uncommon on the Colorado plains, so we'd never seen weather patterns of that nature before.

The intermittent raindrops grew larger and smacked the windshield with force. We began to worry about hail. I picked up speed and glanced up again at the low-hanging clouds. They were moving rapidly now, and hung in great, black folds. They looked like hanging curtains, and despite their rapid movement I couldn't tell clearly which direction they were moving.

We stopped at the south windmill, and I jumped out and ran to shut it off. The dark sky boiled over our heads in a circular pattern. Mom was looking up at it with fear in her eyes when I got back to the pickup. "My God, Gary, let's get home!" she cried.

I dashed back to the north toward the house, planning to shut off the last two windmills on the way. Mom sat straight and stiff, terrified, as we raced through the pasture. On the nearest horizon the black clouds appeared to stretch to the ground. We were looking at a "wall cloud," a common sight in tornado weather.

The darkest, angriest sky lay to the right, where a rocky bluff obstructed our view. As we sped out from behind the bluff, I glanced to the right and practically screamed, "Look!"

I'd never seen a tornado before. It was only a quarter of a mile away, and a full quarter of a mile wide. The tornado wasn't funnel-shaped as I'd always seen in pictures; it was cylindrical, a black, boiling hulk that reached from the ground to the clouds. It looked as if a wide part of the angry sky had just extended to the earth. The huge thing whirled violently, and thousands of small funnels whirled inside it. The funnels were long and skinny, reaching to the sky, twisting and gyrating within the tornado. Fence posts, weeds, dirt, and debris spun weightless within the thing, and a million tumbleweeds whirled and bobbed inside it like so much popcorn.

To see a tornado that close was spellbinding. I stopped the pickup, stepped out, and stood on the running board to watch it. The giant mass rotated at a tremendous speed, but it moved across the ground much slower, probably fifteen to twenty miles an hour. It was heading northwest, following the draw.

Mom sat spellbound for a moment too, but she stayed in the truck. Then with panic in her voice she hollered, "Gary, look where it's going!"

I hadn't put it together, but Mom had. The tornado was following the draw, heading for the house, and had less than a mile to go. Dad was in the house and didn't know it was coming.

I jumped back in the truck and took off as fast as I could. We raced across the prairie at fifty or sixty miles an hour and outdistanced the tornado a good way by the time we reached the house. Mom said she'd run and get the Packard out of the barn while I got Dad. That way we could at least save both vehicles.

I slid to a stop, and Mom ran for the barn as I ran for the house. Dad was lying on his bed reading. I opened the back door and hollered, "Dad, there's a tornado coming!" and ran back to the pickup.

I didn't remember ever seeing Dad outside without a hat on before. He came charging out into the yard bareheaded, stopped, and looked wide-eyed at the tornado, only a quarter of a mile from the house now. Then incredibly he reached up, felt his head, whirled, and ran back into the house to get his hat.

Mom stopped the Packard beside the pickup, and in a moment Dad came charging back out of the house, holding his hat on his head as he ran. He jumped in the pickup as the tornado bore down on us. We tore off down the road with Mom following in the car.

Nearly a mile from the tornado I looked in the rearview mirror, and Mom wasn't behind us. She had turned around and headed back toward the house for some reason, and was nearly there by the time we missed her.

Dad and I stopped at the top of a hill and got out of the truck to see what Mom was doing. She was driving fast, kicking up a cloud of dust behind the car. She turned off the road and sped between the house and the tornado, directly across its path, and kept going until she reached the top of a low hill two hundred yards beyond the house. There she turned and stopped the car at a point that allowed her to watch the house and the tornado at the same time.

The big twister still moved slowly down the draw. Mom wasn't directly in its path but dangerously close if it happened to shift direction. We had no idea why she'd gone back, but it was too late to do anything about it now.

I don't know when we first noticed it, but the tornado began to slow down and shrink in size. From where we stood, a mile away, it looked like a movie scene. The twister became smaller, and now it only crept down the draw.

An eighth of a mile from the house the thing stopped altogether and just sat spinning in the bottom of the draw. Then we felt a wind begin to pick up from the southwest. When the wind hit the tornado it first distorted its shape, then dispersed it. The thing disappeared faster than it had come.

Mom sat on the hill a quarter of a mile from the tornado and watched it blow away.

"Ain't that the damnedest thing ya ever saw?!" Dad said. We got in the truck and drove to the house, still puzzled at why Mom had gone back.

She was walking slowly through the house, examining everything in it. The tornado hadn't come close enough to do any damage, but for some reason she was checking everything. Her eyes had a distant, detached look, and she no longer seemed frightened at all.

Dad looked at her curiously and didn't say anything. I watched her for a minute, then asked, "Why'd you come back, Mom?" She didn't look up, just shook her head as if she didn't know why, and continued to check everything. To this day she can't explain why she went back.

The tornado left a blackened path extending a mile and a half up the draw. It mowed the grass clean and left not a weed, thistle, or even a cactus standing in its wake. The track remained visible for two years.

Another unusual storm occurred at night. Our cattle always headed for shelter in the barns and sheds at Dad's Place during storms, or they headed there before a storm hit when they had some warning of it. One night, however, a terrific duststorm caught the herd by surprise far in the south pasture, two miles from shelter.

The cattle had a long way to go to reach shelter , and they had to face into the wind. They lowered their heads, leaned into the storm, and began to push toward Dad's Place. The wind was furious and carried a tremendous amount of dirt. They were strung out for half a mile across the prairie, fighting their way against that raging duststorm, when something incredible happened. The sky suddenly opened up and began pouring rain, and drenched the herd.

We had never seen rain during a big duststorm, nor even considered the possibility, but it rained hard that night. Its effect on the cattle was as bizarre as the storm itself. It filled their coats with mud, so thick we couldn't see the hair on their backs. Their coats looked like mortar, a smooth layer of mud an inch thick.

The rain quickly settled the dust, and sometime during the night the wind died down. The cattle made it to Dad's Place by morning, but they were exhausted from carrying all that mud. Then the mud began to dry on their backs and became heavy and suffocating. Two days later it had dragged them down until they either lay on the ground or simply stood in one place. They wouldn't eat or drink.

What a strange problem to have. We had to figure out how to remove tons of hardened mud from the backs of an entire herd of cattle. The remedy itself was hard on them, but it worked.

We rounded up all the cattle on horseback and drove them into the corrals. Then in small groups we ran them through the crowding pen, which was only about twenty feet across and enclosed by a heavy board fence. Standing on the top rails of the fence, we beat the dried mud off their backs with shovel handles. I felt sorry for the cattle in that ordeal, but we saved them. Within a day they were eating again.

No matter what summer weather had to offer, winter was always the worst. Winter brought the cold, the snow, the ice, and the blizzards. Blizzards, the fiercest winter storms—frigid winds that blow snow and ice, blind you, and freeze you to the bone.

We woke one morning to an ominous sound. A terrific blizzard had hit in the night. The wind howled from the north at fifty to sixty miles per hour as snow and ice pounded the sides of the house. The world outside the windows appeared pure white, a swirling, violent white. The temperature stood at twenty-five below zero.

I knew it was the worst storm I had ever seen. Dad walked out of his room looking grim and said it was the worst he'd seen as well. I stared out the window at the blizzard's fury, listened to its deadly howl, and knew we had to go out there. A rancher's fortune and responsibility lie in the cattle herd, and we knew they couldn't survive a storm like this without shelter. We had to get to Dad's Place to see if the herd had made it to the sheds. Four horses were there as well: Tony and Champ, the saddle horses, and Jigs and Prince, the workhorses. They were locked inside the barn, however, so we knew they were safe.

The blizzard howled and moaned around the corners of the house as we dressed to go out. We already had on long johns and several pairs of socks. Mom helped us into heavy sweaters, coats, boots, and gloves, and admonished us to be careful. Dad put on his lined leather gloves and the heaviest wrap he owned, the long sheepskin-lined leather coat that reached to his knees, but on his head he wore his hat, his old Stetson. Regardless of the weather, he always wore that old hat.

Dad moved with a purpose, grim and determined. I tried to be brave. We said goodbye to Mom, opened the back door to a blast of howling wind, and pushed out into the blizzard.

Dad was seventy-eight years old that morning. I was twelve.

The raw wind of a blizzard, filled with shards of ice and snow, cuts your face like a knife and sears your eyes when you try to open them. When visibility nears zero a blizzard becomes a "whiteout." In a whiteout blizzard the blowing snow and ice completely fill the air; you can't tell the ground from the sky. Everything looks the same—white.

The wind greatly increases the effects of the cold. The harder it blows, the more heat it pulls from your body. Wind creates the chill factor that weathermen quote along with the actual temperature. The chill factor is what your body feels. The chill factor is what freezes you.

The high wind in a blizzard generates an extreme chill factor if the actual temperature is low. A temperature of twenty-five below with a wind of fifty to sixty miles per hour creates a chill factor greater than seventy below zero. Seventy below is what we felt that morning, and what we would face in the hours to come.

We leaned hard into the storm, forcing our way across the yard. The icy wind cut my face, and the cold pierced my clothes. This was too severe, colder than I'd ever felt. We didn't even own the proper clothing for these conditions.

The pickup was parked in the barn. We were already cold by the time we reached it, but it felt good to get in out of the wind. I was glad it was a strong, four-wheel drive. The big engine cranked over hard in the cold air, but after a few anxious moments it started with a roar. I began to feel more secure as the truck idled and the heater warmed the inside of the cab.

Going south to Dad's Place, the one-mile trip would be with the wind, but coming back we would face directly into it. Visibility would be a real problem; this one was truly a whiteout.

The storm's fury rocked the truck as we backed out of the barn and found our way to the road. The four-wheel drive cut through the snow smoothly, but the poor visibility forced us to move along at a crawl. Even driving with the wind we could barely make out the snow-covered ground and the narrow two-track road ahead. Several times we had to stop and sit for a few minutes to keep from losing sight of the road.

Blizzards are loud. The howling wind and ice particles beat a frightening din against the metal cab as we inched along.

The trip to Dad's Place took about forty-five minutes, but we made it. The fenced-in lane that ran beside the barns and corrals provided a welcome windbreak as we drove in. It shut out some of the noise and improved the visibility. The wind still reached us in the lane, and the snow still blew, but the relative calm would help the chill factor a bit. The cold wouldn't bite quite so badly when we got out to feed the stock.

The cattle were all there, huddled up under the sheds, safe. Now we just needed to quickly feed them and the horses, and then get back to the house.

We opened the pickup doors and started to step out. Suddenly the engine began to sputter, and died. We looked at each other silently, and sat back down in the cab. Dad tried to start it. It turned over, but it wouldn't start. We knew we had plenty of gas and knew the battery was strong, so we sat for a few minutes and tried it again.

Again the engine would crank over, but it wouldn't fire. We got out and looked under the hood. Neither of us had much mechanical knowledge, but at least nothing looked wrong. There were no loose wires in sight and no parts missing.

The cold began to bite us quickly. We got back into the cab and tried to start it again. Nothing.

We both knew what that meant. We couldn't survive long without the heater, and we'd already used up twenty or thirty minutes trying to get it started.

Dad sat grimly silent as our breath blew steam inside the cab. He gazed out the windshield into the storm, thinking, his face a picture of determination. Then he turned to me and said, "We can't stay here. We got matches, but the old house has got no stove in it now, and we've got nothin' to burn anyway."

"Can't we burn the barn or something?" I asked him. "Or just tear some wood off of it and burn that?"

"Yeah, we could," he replied, "and that might work. And then again it might not. We might end up freezin' anyway."

"And there's somethin' else to think about," he said. "Your mother. She'll come after us ya know, no matter what. If we don't make it back this mornin', she'll take off on foot if she has to, and she can't make it in this."

He was right. Mom wouldn't know what had happened to us, and even if we did save ourselves by burning the barn she'd come looking for us, and she'd have to do it on foot. She couldn't survive that, but we knew she would try.

We thought about the four horses in the barn, though we didn't discuss them. Tony and Champ were fine mounts, but they couldn't handle a storm like this. Prince the workhorse was powerful, but he didn't have the stamina. Dad looked at me and said, "You stay here. I'm goin' to get Jigs."

I waited in the cab while he went to the barn to harness Jigs and hitch him to the big sled. Dad had built the sled for feeding the cattle in deep snow. It was low and flat with no sides, simply a plank floor resting on stout wooden runners. The floor of the sled was about eight feet long by five feet wide and sat only one foot off the ground. Dad had to stand up on it to drive the horse.

As the temperature in the cab dropped I knew Dad was even colder outside. I felt like I was freezing while I waited for him to return with Jigs.

They appeared through the blowing snow, first as a ghost-like outline, then taking shape as they drew near. Dad was standing up on the sled, and incredibly, Jigs was holding his head high and prancing through the snow as if he were leading a parade.

They pulled up beside the pickup, and Dad hollered "Whoa!" Jigs the giant horse looked marvelous. He was our only chance. But as much as I respected Jigs, I still had grave doubts that we could make it. I knew horses pretty well, and I knew how they felt about their security. Horses are extremely reluctant to leave the security of their own barn under bad conditions.

It was likely that Jigs wouldn't leave the security of the buildings, that he would simply refuse to go into the blizzard. If he refused, we were finished. And even if he did go, both he and Dad would have to face directly into that awful wind and endure it all the way.

I knew Dad could do it. I didn't know if Jigs could.

Dad had found an old tattered blanket somewhere and brought it for me. He sat me down on the sled, facing the rear with my back to the wind, and wrapped the blanket around me. I crossed my legs and sat on one end of the blanket to hold it down; the rest he wrapped completely up around my head and told me to hang onto it tightly.

Then Dad stepped up onto the sled directly behind me, picked up the reins, snapped them at Jigs, and hollered "Hee-yaah!" Jigs leaned into the harness traces and started the sled smoothly down the lane. Within a minute I felt us take a slight turn to the right as we passed out through the open gate at the end of the lane. A few more yards and we'd leave the windbreaks and head directly into the blizzard. We'd soon find out if Jigs would face it or turn back and refuse.

The blizzard roared into us, threatening to tear us from the sled. Shrieking and howling like the deadly beast that it was, it engulfed us, isolating us in its frozen violence. The wind howled around Jigs' body, around Dad's body, my body, and around the sled. It tried to tear my blanket from me, but I clung to it desperately.

Jigs was incredible. When the full force of the blizzard slammed him in the face he just lowered his head and bored into it with everything he had.

I couldn't see from under the blanket, but the snow and ice pounded me and the wind rocked me and tried to sweep me off the sled. I could hear under there though; God, could I hear! Close by, a cracking sound, the sled runners breaking through the hard crust of the snow. The wind, that God-awful wind, howling around us, screaming in our ears. And always Dad's voice, yelling, above the wind, "Hyo! Hyo!" driving Jigs on.

When I did peek out from under the blanket, I couldn't see a thing, just a swirling white mass. How could we possibly make it through this? We had to follow that little two-track road, and it was filled with snow. How could Dad and Jigs keep sight of the road in a whiteout blizzard, with that icy wind cutting their eyes all the way?

I worried that Jigs might try to make a slow turn to keep from facing the wind directly. If they lost the road for only a moment, we'd wander off onto the prairie and be lost. We probably wouldn't last more than an hour after that.

I looked out and around toward Dad once, into the wind. I could just make out his outline—that stout old frame, standing like a rock, leaning hard into the wind, and yelling, ever yelling at Jigs.

I wondered how Dad and Jigs could stand to face that cold. I still do.

Jigs faltered several times and nearly went down. Each time he stumbled Dad hollered even louder. Jigs picked up the pace again each time and fought on.

In my terror I'd forgotten all about the cold. Suddenly it came back to me. My body was freezing, and my hands and feet felt numb. I couldn't move my fingers. My hands simply felt like weights at the ends of my arms, and my feet were nearly as bad. I was beginning to freeze.

Jigs fell. He stumbled, staggered, and went down. Thrashing and pawing in the harness traces, he jerked the sled in spasms. Bawling and blowing in terror, he pawed frantically to regain his feet. Dad's steady voice became soothing, cajoling, encouraging. Then with an effort beyond belief, Jigs heaved himself to his feet, drew a long, rasping breath, lowered his head, and struggled on.

To his eternal credit, Jigs never once tried to turn away from that freezing wind. He faced it all the way. So did Dad.

I rode that sled backwards forever, listening, fearing, praying. We had to be lost. We'd been traveling too long; we should have been there by now. We could be anywhere. We probably wouldn't even know where we were when the end came, when we became just a snow-covered hump on the prairie.

The sled dipped in front, went down a slight grade, and back up the other side. Something felt familiar. Then I knew. That felt like the draw, only a couple of hundred yards from the house. Was that possible? A minute later Dad hollered, "Whoa," and we stopped.

I peered out from under my blanket. I could just make out the corral fence through the blowing snow. The corral fence. We had made it. My God—we had made it.

I stood up stiffly, stepped off the sled, and walked to the front. Dad stood by Jigs holding the reins, his tired arms hanging at his sides. The most heroic pair I've ever seen, they were an awesome sight.

Jigs looked like a giant ice sculpture. Long icicles hung from his mane and thousands of smaller ones hung from his hair, covering his entire body. His lower legs were pillars of packed snow and ice. His face was completely frozen over, and both his eyes and his nostrils had nearly frozen shut. His heavy breath forced puffs of steam from two small holes in the ice that covered his nose.

I don't know how Jigs lived through it. But as spent as he was, when I touched his shoulder he raised his head and stood tall and proud, as if he knew he'd just done something great. God, he looked magnificent.

And Dad. He looked like he wasn't alive. The front of his great sheepskin coat and the legs of his Levis were a solid sheet of ice, a quarter of an inch thick. His old hat looked like it was made of ice. Icicles hung from his eyebrows, down over his eyes, and his face had been beaten bright red by the wind. But there he stood. He'd faced that blizzard all the way, just like I'd known he would. His eyes were pained now but still grim. A spark of defiance gleamed in those old eyes too, a spark that said, "By God, we did it."

Dad pointed to the house and motioned for me to go in, then motioned that he was going to put Jigs in the barn. I found I couldn't talk, but I hugged that great horse's neck before I left them.

I trudged to the house, so frozen I could barely walk. Mom opened the door and gasped, "My God, what happened?!"

I couldn't answer. I could only shake my head.

"Where's Dad?!" she asked frantically. I pointed back toward the barn.

"Is he all right?!" I nodded that he was.

She took off my cap, slowly pulled off my gloves, and looked at my hands. Then she rubbed them gently, and asked, "Can you feel that?"

I shook my head. I couldn't feel a thing. Mom looked like she might cry, but she didn't. She pulled off my coat, poured some cool water in the wash pan, and told me to put my hands in it. I couldn't feel anything at first, but in a few minutes they began to thaw, and with that came the pain. As the pain of my hands thawing became nearly unbearable, I began to cry, and with that I began to talk. Mom stood in horror as I told her what had happened to us.

We waited a long time for Dad to come in. It seemed to be taking too long just to put Jigs in the barn. At last he limped through the door, barely able to stand. He had put Jigs in the barn before he came in, taken off his harness, and fed him. He could barely talk, but he mumbled something about Jigs having earned a good meal.

I'm sure Dad did something else before he came to the house that morning. I know he petted old Jigs and thanked him for saving our lives.

More than forty years have passed since that blizzard, yet some memory of it still returns to me nearly every day. In my mind it's often the scene of Jigs prancing through the blowing snow when he and Dad first appeared with the sled, or the two of them covered with ice at the end. I still hear the sounds too—the awful howling of the wind, and Dad's voice, yelling above the storm, driving Jigs on.

Chapter 16

FAREWELL

Colorado was still a frontier when Dad came there, young, wild, and inviting; and he had a true pioneer spirit—poor and uneducated, but daring to reach for the dream he wanted with all his heart.

One beautiful spring day when Dad was eighty-one, he and I were riding across the prairie in his pickup. He had paid the bank off by then. He owned everything.

We could see his cattle herd spread out across a grassy hillside as we drove along. Dad stopped the pickup, and sat and gazed at the cattle for a long time, saying nothing. Then he turned to me with a happy grin and a childlike sparkle in his eyes, looked back at his cattle, and said, "Lord of all I survey." His hard old face was the happiest I'd ever seen it.

"Lord of all I survey." In his joy he meant it facetiously, but the sparkle in his eyes said he knew it was true. At that moment he was the lord of all he surveyed. He had played for high stakes and paid a high price, but his face told me it had all been worth it. He had his moment.

He smiled again, then drove on.

Dad seemed not only ageless to me but invincible as well, a powerhouse that would go on forever. I never thought about losing him. I was a kid, and kids seldom think about things like that.

He was the toughest human and the hardest fighter I've ever known, but even the toughest among us and the hardest fighters all have a final battle to fight someday. Dad fought his with cancer.

It began as a tiny lump on his lower lip in late 1955 or early 1956. The lump was barely noticeable at first and wasn't painful, and like most people who have enjoyed good health, Dad wasn't concerned. But as the lump grew larger, and Mom more insistent, he finally agreed to see a doctor. The doctor in Lamar looked at it and promptly sent him to a specialist in Denver.

Dad didn't seem particularly upset when the lump was diagnosed as cancer. He acknowledged it but continued to work on the ranch the same as always. One day at the store Mrs. Lamborn handed him the opened cigar box so he could get his usual five. Dad waved his hand over it and said, "No, the doctor said I was supposed to quit smokin'." He never smoked another cigar.

I asked him later if it bothered him to quit smoking. He said, "Oh, I sure did like to smoke, but if I'm not supposed to, I won't."

He had to see doctors several more times during the following year, and he went to Denver twice for radiation treatments. The lump on his lip grew more obvious, and in time others became visible on his throat. The cancer began to slow him down, but he still continued to work as much as he could. And he didn't rage against the cancer as one might have expected; he seldom even complained.

The winter of 1956 turned to spring and summer, and Dad began to take longer naps in the afternoon. I did more of the work myself now. Mom helped me as much as she could with the morning and evening chores, as I had to look after the herd, ride fences, and keep those cantankerous windmills running.

During the time Dad was weakening, I lost my old buddy, Sandy. He disappeared one day and never returned. Someone at the store said a sheep rancher several miles to the west had shot a large dog. Mom and I saw the man at the store a few days later, and before I could say a word she confronted him. Yes, he had shot a dog, he told us, and the description sounded like Sandy.

Mom was furious. "Why'd you shoot our dog?!" she shouted in the man's face. He explained that the dog had been running with coyotes and killing his sheep. When he mentioned coyotes I knew it was Sandy. The man was embarrassed and told us he was sorry about Sandy, and I know he meant it. He also said it was the first time he'd ever seen a dog run with coyotes. Mom and I cooled off, and told him we understood. I'd have done the same thing if a dog had been killing our stock.

It seemed a terrible time to lose my buddy, but I'm glad Sandy went out doing what he wanted to do. He was a great dog, but always a little wild. He never took to civilization all the way. I know how he felt; I've often felt that way myself.

I had spotted some strange-looking coyotes after Sandy started running with them, ones that appeared larger than the others and dark brown like him. I imagine some of his blood is still running around in the coyote packs out in that country. I hope so.

Another change took place after Dad got sick. Clay Creek Store changed hands again. The Lamborns sold it to an older couple who were new to the area. They never gained the popularity the Lamborns or the Clarks before them had; they didn't even come close.

The man looked in his early to mid-sixties, and vigorous. The old lady was either older than him or had been used much harder. He was a big, husky guy who wore a bill cap, smiled often, and tried to be friendly. She was a squat bag of venom who quickstepped her dumpy little body around in a half-limp like a wounded hog pursuing its tormentor, her mouth pursed as if she perpetually ate persimmons, and her narrow eyes threatening everyone they met, especially the old man. Her squeaky, bitter voice was a thing to loathe, and she ruled the foul air she generated. The old man was only as congenial as her high-pitched orders and menacing glances permitted him to be.

When Dad went to Denver for radiation treatments, he stayed with Aunt Mary and her family for a few weeks each time. He returned the first time with visible effects of the radiation. His throat showed crimson marks, his jaw was spotted red, and areas of his face wouldn't grow whiskers anymore. He was obviously relieved to be back on the ranch.

When he left for the second round of treatments, he looked forlorn, like a child leaving home, and when he returned the effects of the radiation were worse than the first time. The lower right side of his face was uneven and discolored; purple lumps swelled his throat and jaw, darkened with red sears where the radioactive needles had pierced them. He looked sicker than I'd ever seen him, and when he walked through the yard he looked around like someone who'd been wandering lost and found the way again.

The doctors wanted him to return to Denver for more treatments, but he refused. As the cancer was visibly progressing, it probably wouldn't have done any good if he had gone back, but aside from that I never blamed him anyway. He was eighty-one years old and didn't care to spend his remaining time in hospitals far from home.

I was fifteen when the cancer started, and for several months I assumed he would recover from it. Mom explained the reality to me one evening. "I know you think Dad's going to be all right, Gary, but he's not," she said. "I'm sorry, but this is it. He won't get any better." I could see the pain in her eyes as she told me.

I sometimes wondered if Dad knew himself that the end was coming. Then one day when Jack Beatty was there I realized he did know. It happened as Jack was leaving after visiting him for a few days. Dad was sitting on the side of his cot out in the yard, the one he napped on in the summertime, and he and Jack were saying their goodbyes. Each was trying to tough it out, to act as if everything was the same as it always had been. As Jack turned to leave, Dad reached out, grabbed him, and cried, "Oh, Jack!" Jack threw his arms around him, and they both began to cry. I knew then that he knew.

The long summer dragged into fall, and I started back to school. Mom and I had an even busier schedule than normal, and as I'd never been a good student anyway, now my grades suffered even more. Dad still drove me to the school bus in the morning, and picked me up in the evening, but Mom helped him feed the cattle during the day.

I still waited in the store to stay warm until the school bus came in the mornings as I had done for years when the Lamborns owned it and the Clarks before them. Now that the Lamborn kids were gone, however, I waited alone. The old lady and her husband stayed back in their house and didn't even acknowledge my presence. I could sometimes hear her yelling at him, endearments such as, "This coffee tastes like shit!"

Mom suspected the old lady of listening in on the phone, and one day a friend of hers mentioned a strange noise on the line as they talked. Mom chuckled and said, "It's probably that old battle ax over at the store listening in." The listener hung up.

The following morning when I walked into the store, the old lady hollered at me from their living room door, "Gary, come here." I walked to the door and found her sitting indignantly in a big padded armchair. Her husband was nowhere in sight.

"Now Gary, I never minded you or your grandpa a bit," she said, tapping her fingers on the arms of the chair, "but your mother's been callin' me an old battle ax on this phone, and I don't like it."

The statement surprised me, revealing what it did of her mental prowess. "How do you know she's been calling you that?" I asked her.

That threw her a bit. "Well, I, uh, hear things around here, and find out things," she stammered. Then her eyes narrowed as she grew angrier. "My husband and me ain't got time to watch you in the store in the mornin'," she said, "and we don't want you waitin' for the bus in there anymore."

"All right, I won't," I said. I whirled and walked outside to wait.

When Dad met the school bus that evening I told him what the old lady had said. His reaction shocked me. His eyes didn't flare, he didn't get mad, raise his voice, or even look at me. He just said, "I'll wait with you till the school bus comes in the mornings then."

We changed our mail service so we could pick it up in town instead of at the store, and each morning Dad and I waited at the gate by the highway, sitting quietly in the pickup until the bus came. Then he'd say, "Have a good day at school, Son," and slowly drive away.

Dad's fire was gone. The goddam cancer had eaten it out of him.

He began to lose weight. His clothes hung loosely on him in an offense to the powerful stature he had always projected. He was quiet and distant now, often within his own thoughts when the two of us were working together. But still he worked. Giving up never occurred to him. He just went on.

The cancer on his lower lip grew larger than his thumb, and though it didn't hurt him all the time, it was extremely painful to the touch and sensitive to the cold. As winter came on and cold weather set in, he wore a large neckerchief tied around his mouth to cover his lip and help protect it from the cold.

One icy morning the snow was so deep we had to park the pickup fifty yards from the garage and carry the sacks of cake to it as we had many times before. Dad's face was red. He had a neckerchief tied around his mouth and looked miserably cold. He could no longer carry a hundred-pound sack, and was nearly too weak to carry half of one, but he still insisted on helping me.

We each grasped the end of a sack, carried it through the snow, and hoisted it up over the side of the pickup bed. As we leaned over to lower the sack into the bed I lost my grip, and my right hand slipped off. When the heavy sack fell from my grip, my gloved hand recoiled and flew upward toward Dad's face, and before I could stop it I hit him in the mouth, directly on the cancer. I saw the terrible pain flash in his eyes. He jerked his head up, grabbed his mouth with both hands, reeled backward, and sat down in the snow. He sat rocking back and forth, holding his bleeding mouth and sobbing loudly.

I fell on my knees beside him, repeating over and over, "I'm sorry. I'm sorry."

He slowly reached both arms around my neck, laid his head on mine, and sobbed through his pain, "It's okay. It's okay."

We sat there in the snow, with our arms around each other, and wept.

One could never forget the moment when a man like Dad had to ask for help to take care of himself.

He went to the outhouse that evening and stayed a long time. Mom and I began to worry, but neither of us went to check on him. We were sitting at the dining room table when at last we heard him come through the back door. He walked slowly into the room, stooped and worn. Looking at the floor, he said to Mom, "I had a hard time tryin' to clean myself up. Can ya help me?"

Mom flew into action to take care of him. I turned my head to stare out the window, and hide my tears.

Dad was the perfect patient from that moment on, a gentle person one might never have guessed was in there. But still he never complained, never despaired, and never showed the least fear of what was coming.

Now I would learn what Mom was made of. As Dad's condition deteriorated, she cared for him day and night, the bravest nurse I've ever seen. It bothered me to be near him in that condition, and for a while I avoided going into his room any more than necessary.

He eventually stayed in bed most of the time, but occasionally he still ate at the table. It always surprised me when he got to his feet, because each time he did I figured he'd be too weak to ever do it again.

As the cancer ravaged his mouth and throat, he could eat only with Mom's help. When he ate at the table I could hardly bear to eat with him, and when I did Mom kept the right side of his face covered with a cloth as she helped him.

I didn't really know what the cancer looked like at that stage, but then one day when I was sitting at the table with him, Mom walked away and left his face exposed.

His jaw was gone, from his throat to his cheekbone. The jawbone itself lay bare, exposed from chin to ear. Caught up by its awful strangeness, I couldn't stop staring at him. I wondered if he knew what he looked like.

He felt my stare, turned, and looked at me. God help me, I looked away. I couldn't do that to him. I forced myself to look back, and found him still looking at me, calmly. Then he smiled, a twisted smile that contorted his face awfully, but his eyes were the messengers. From deep in those gray eyes, a clear and knowing softness reached me. He knew it all.

That grotesque smile, at once wonderful and utterly horrible, came from the core of him, from the heart of his being. In that most awkward moment of my existence, I felt I had glimpsed his soul.

Somehow I managed to smile back at him.

Why did Mom purposely reveal his condition to me that day? I'm not sure. Perhaps it became too much for her to bear alone, and I was the only one with whom she could share it. But more likely she thought it was time for me to deal with the reality instead of hiding from it.

I wondered how Mom could stand to care for him in that condition. Years later I would ask her, "Mom, why did you take care of Dad the way you did when he was so sick? How could you do it?"

Her eyes flared a little, indignant at the question. "I worshipped my Dad," she said.

How I hated that cancer. The cowardly beast was tearing him from me day after day, destroying him before my eyes, reducing him to a horrible caricature of his true self. I'd have fought the demon if I could have. The cancer wouldn't show its face though, only its relentless damage. I couldn't fight it. I couldn't slug it, shoot it, or choke the life out of it. Hell, I couldn't even insult it. It didn't care.

His mind remained clear to the end, and he continued to direct the ranch work from his room. I went in to talk to him more often after I saw his jaw, and it didn't bother me as much as it had before. The cancer made it difficult for him to talk now; his forced speech was slurred, but I could still understand him. He'd ask about the cattle, and how certain jobs were going, but just as often he'd ask about me.

"Hi, Son. Sit down. How ya doin'?"

"All right, Dad. How you doin'?"

"I'm doin' okay, Son. Doin' okay."

One day Dad asked Mom to get him a cold bottle of pop to drink. We had no pop on hand, so she asked me to ride to Clay Creek Store with her to get some. Dad signed a blank check and gave it to Mom to take with her.

When we walked into the store, the old man was sitting down chatting with another couple. The old lady was back in the house. He stood up, smiled at us, and said, "Hello there. How ya doin'?"

"Fine," Mom said, "Dad asked us to get some pop for him."

I walked to the cooler and began to fill a carton with bottles of pop. Mom reached into her pocket, handed him Dad's check, and asked, "How much will it be?"

Before he could answer, the old lady came tripping into the store and said in her high, squeaky voice, "Lemme see that check."

"Oh, it's all right," he said, trying to smooth things over.

"Let me see it anyway," she hissed.

She grabbed the check out of his hand and began to scrutinize it closely. Mom said, "If there's any question we'll just forget it."

"I've never questioned anything of George Blizzard's," she squeaked. "But ..."

Mom stopped her cold. "Give me that check," she said. "We're leaving."

The old lady handed her the check, and as Mom turned to walk toward the door her husband suddenly flew into a rage. He charged across the store at us like a madman, wildly waving his arms and hollering, "All right then, go on, get the hell out of here!"

As Mom walked out he veered toward me, pointing at the door and hollering insanely, "Get the hell out of here!"

I turned toward him with my back to the cooler, gripping a bottle of pop by the neck like a club. He stopped a few feet in front of me, waving his arms and leaning into my face. "I said get the hell out of here!" he screamed.

He saw me raise the bottle into a more menacing position, and stopped screaming. Placing his clenched fists on his hips, he leaned forward, his head jutted toward me in a threatening posture. The old lady and the visiting couple looked alarmed. Mom stood outside, watching through the door, and said nothing.

I looked into his eyes, mentally aimed the bottle at the side of his head, and said, "Get out of my way, and I'll walk out of here." A look of surprise crossed his face. He straightened up, dropped his hands, and backed away. I set the bottle on the cooler and walked out.

Dad was asleep when we got home. I stayed with him while Mom drove to town to get his pop.

Near the end Dad told us he wanted to sell all the cattle and horses. I had two years of high school left, and I guess he knew it would be difficult for Mom and me to run the place by ourselves, even though we had done most of it for the previous year anyway.

An old friend, Raymond McMillin, helped him organize the sale of the livestock. Mom called Mr. McMillin and asked him to come to the house to talk with Dad. He was a large, prominent-looking man, a successful rancher, and a true gentleman. He greeted Mom at the door with his hat in his hand. In a low voice she explained Dad's condition to him and warned him what he was about to see. Mr. McMillin nodded gravely, knocked on the door to Dad's room, walked in smiling, and took his hand. "Hello, George," he said. "How are you, sir?"

He sat down by the bed and talked to Dad at length, and acted as if nothing was wrong with him. When they finished he told Dad goodbye, shook his hand, and walked to the kitchen. He looked at Mom with a new respect, squeezed her arm, and said, "Thanks for calling me, Lois. I'll help with everything I can."

"Thanks for coming, Raymond," she replied.

He turned to me, shook my hand, and said, "Your granddad will tell you everything to do, Son. I know you can handle it."

I rounded up the cattle for the last time and fastened them in the corrals. They would go to the livestock auction in La Junta, Colorado, sixty miles away, to be sold the following week. Two days before the cattle trucks were scheduled to arrive, Dad decided he was going to La Junta when the cattle went. He could barely stand on his feet, but he insisted on going. The old stubbornness was still intact anyway.

Mom figured Jack Beatty was the only person who might reason with Dad, and she was right. She called him at his home in Denver that evening and explained the situation. Jack left Denver in the middle of the night, drove the two hundred and twenty miles, and arrived at the ranch at daybreak.

I don't know what Jack said to Dad that morning, but he decided not to accompany the cattle trucks to La Junta the next day and instead checked into the hospital in Lamar that same afternoon.

Dad told Mom and Jack he wanted to get himself ready to go to the hospital and made it clear he didn't want the rest of us in the house. The three of us waited outside for an interminable time. At last the back door opened and he walked out, steadying himself on the door frame. He stopped in the doorway of the back porch and stood gazing around the place, alone in his thoughts, looking at none of us.

He weighed less than ninety pounds now, but he was fully dressed, in his good Stetson, his best khaki pants and shirt, his tall cowboy boots, and a clean neckerchief tied around his mouth. He walked by himself, unaided. He moved slowly down the back steps, his manner determined and resolute, his eyes clear and knowing. He walked out into the yard, turned, and looked back at the house for several minutes, drinking in every inch of it. Then he turned and slowly continued, still as if he were totally alone.

As Dad walked across the yard for the last time I felt I was dying a little myself, yet I followed his every move, spellbound. He stopped when he reached the yard fence, and looked up at the windmill. He continued to gaze around at the barn, the chicken house, and every other building on the place; then he turned, walked to Jack's car, and stepped in.

I followed them to Dad's Place, where Jack stopped so he could look at the cattle and horses. Dad got out, walked to the horse corral, and let himself through the gate. He moved slowly among them, petting them and talking to them, especially the big team, Jigs and Prince.

He gazed long at the cattle, and long at the land, the hostile landscape that he loved—his dream, that he'd nurtured for a lifetime and fulfilled by his own will and determination.

He took a last gaze across the prairie, stepped into the car, looked straight ahead, and rode away.

I stood by the corral and watched him go.

Sometime during the year and a half he'd been sick Dad told Mom he regretted not having allowed George and me to do more thinking for ourselves, but the day he went to the hospital he did a great thing for me.

He sat up in his hospital bed that evening and called me to his side. "I want you to take the pickup out to the place in the mornin' and supervise gettin' the cattle loaded onto the trucks," he said. "Then you follow 'em to La Junta and keep an eye on everything up there. Watch the unloadin' and see that the auction yard gets a proper count on the cattle. Make sure their count agrees with yours."

"You want me to drive to La Junta by myself and do that?!" I asked.

He smiled and nodded his head. "Yeah, you go up there and take care of things." Nothing could have done more for me. Dad was sending me up there to "take care of things."

I was sixteen years old. I counted the cattle as we loaded them that morning, drove to La Junta behind the trucks, watched them unload the herd, and saw that their tally agreed with mine.

The horses didn't go to the auction yard; they went to separate buyers. The man who bought Jigs and Prince kept workhorses for a hobby. I was glad they would have a good home, especially Jigs.

I'd known Jigs all my life. He'd put up with me since I was a little kid hanging on his neck, and he had stood ready to give his life for mine in the blizzard. How do you say goodbye to a friend like that? The old giant nuzzled me gently as I hugged his great head.

Dad lasted only a few days in the hospital, and he was mostly in good spirits. Aunt Mary and her family came from Denver, and Aunt Helen from the Catholic hospital in Ohio where she worked.

George took emergency leave from the navy but arrived home shortly after Dad died.

One evening Dad sat up in bed and looked at me, his eyes as alive as they'd ever been. Clenching his fists for emphasis, he said, "Gary, when you see an opportunity, grab it!" Of all the advice he ever gave me, I would remember that single statement the most.

Jack had to go back to Denver a couple of days after Dad went to the hospital. The last thing Dad said to him was, "Well, Jack, the next time you see me I'll be kickin' up my heels." Jack smiled at that, shook Dad's hand fondly, and turned away to hide his pain.

A day or two before he died, Mom asked the doctor if anything could be done to prolong his life. The doctor, an old friend of Dad's, shrugged his shoulders and said, "Yeah, but ...," and stopped, a silent, tender question in his eyes that asked, "Would you really want to do that?" Mom looked at me, and neither of us said a word. The question was answered.

The last words Dad said weren't directed at any of us. Aunt Mary and I were sitting in the room with him that evening, and thought he was sleeping. He began calling out, "Mary, Mary," his eyes still closed.

Aunt Mary walked over to him, touched his arm, and said, "I'm here, Dad."

"Not you," he replied clearly. Aunt Mary sat back down, a puzzled look on her face.

Again he called, "Mary, Mary," and several times he called, "Sam, Sam." I knew then. He was calling his wife, Mary Josephine, who had been dead for thirty years, and his brother, Sam, who had been gone for about four.

Dad was coherent when that happened, and aware. I believe he could see them—that he did see them, waiting just beyond what we could see.

He slept most of the next morning, and while Mom and I were at a friend's house, my cousin John came running in and told us the end was near.

We were too late. Dad died a few minutes before we walked into the room. I looked at him, and in spite of everything we'd been through, I wasn't prepared for it. How could I have been? He'd always been in motion, pure energy, totally alive. Now he lay motionless, all that passion, that fire, stilled.

He was my giant. We had sat in the snow and wept together the winter before. Now I wept for him, for a lifetime without him.

The morticians rebuilt his face well, for which I would always be grateful. The frail caricature was gone. Once more the strong jaw jutted under his rugged features and snowy hair. He looked as if he could open his eyes, rise up, and challenge the world again.

All manner and color of people attended his funeral, rich, prominent, and poor, but I remember the prairie folk the most. Simple men and women with rough hands and solemn, wind-creased faces; the women teary-eyed and the men sitting with their hats in their hands, looking at the floor or their wrinkled cowboy boots.

The pallbearers were ranchers, young and old. I remember their serious faces and thinking what a responsibility they had that day. They carried his casket as if it held royalty.

At the graveside service Mom stood straight and strong between George and me, staring at his casket. Dad had been Mom's security all her life, in many ways her salvation, and by her own words she worshipped him. Her grief was surely deep, but his blood ran in her veins, along with his fortitude. Standing at our sides she mustered all the strength she had, for us.

I tried to look brave as my mind raced over all the changes that had taken place so quickly. Dad, the land, the cattle, the horses— they were all a single entity—the only life I knew. Dad was gone, the cattle were gone, the horses were gone, even Sandy was gone. I didn't feel sixteen years old. I felt like a little boy, lost.

I watched them lower Dad into the hard prairie earth, turned, and walked into another life.

Gary back on the prairie in 1996

EPILOGUE

Mom and I moved to town after Dad died. She went to work, and I went wild.

Mom began selling shoes at the J.C. Penney store in Lamar, the first regular job she ever had. She enjoyed talking with customers and was happy to be among people again.

Town life was unfamiliar to me. To the other kids I was still a square, a country bumpkin, but now it made more difference to me than it had before. I was a teenager, on unfamiliar turf, filled with adolescent fears, bravado, and the need for acceptance, and I could no longer retreat to the ranch. The ranch was gone. That life was gone.

I also had a wild nature, undoubtedly nurtured by growing up half civilized on that wild prairie, and I had lost a great number of the things I valued, including my cornerstone, Dad. In an environment I didn't understand, with a principal authority figure gone, I strove to fit in.

Mom got married a year after we moved to town to a big, hard-working, fun-loving wheat farmer named Ralph Judd. With Ralph she found happiness and the companionship so absent from her life on the ranch. Though I had no reason to, I resented Ralph at first, I suppose because he wasn't Dad. I'm sure he didn't care for the antics I was pulling at the time either.

I'd only been an average student before Dad got sick, and my grades had gone downhill after that. Now they became even worse as I explored my new world and tried to become everybody's friend. Mom imposed a curfew on me, but I went out every night I could and tried to fit in with every crowd. I bought a car with my own money, customized it, and joined a hot rod club. Two wild years followed, and I became difficult for Mom to control. Driving hot cars and partying involved me in several car wrecks and could have cost me my life.

As I blew by the local police with loud exhaust pipes blaring, they'd shake their heads and say, "There goes that damn Penley kid again." But something tempered my actions during those wild years too, stopped me short of getting myself into serious trouble. Whenever anyone I knew planned to steal something, I was never asked to join. They knew I'd counsel against it and wouldn't participate. I couldn't imagine stealing something from another person.

I hadn't lost Dad after all. He was still helping me.

The wild partying, hot rodding, and disregard for school finally culminated in a painful experience. The class of 1959, my class, graduated from high school, and I didn't. I'd gone out too many nights, neglected too much homework, failed too many tests.

I had seen it coming and done nothing about it, but when my class graduated without me I was devastated. How could I have let that happen? I tried not to let it show, but inside I felt humiliated and ashamed.

I thought of not going back to finish high school the next fall. That way I wouldn't have to worry about schoolwork anymore, but mostly I wouldn't have to face a class full of students who knew I'd failed the year before. Maybe I'd just get a job and go to work instead. Ralph, my stepfather, helped me make the decision. He asked an old friend of his, Charlie Fletcher, to hire me to work for him that summer, and told me what a great job it would be. According to Ralph the work hours wouldn't be long or hard, and since I already knew Charlie and liked his easygoing ways, it sounded like a good deal to me.

Charlie's slow-talking, countrified manner belied a keen intelligence. He and Ralph conspired to teach me a lesson that summer.

Charlie was a wheat farmer and cattleman who lived in a remote corner of southeast Colorado, forty-five miles from Lamar. I drove a tractor in the field sixteen hours a day for him and slept in a rundown old bunkhouse with a bunch of foul-mouthed farm hands. Breakfast was around 5:00 A.M., I was in the field before 6:00, and drove the tractor until dark.

One evening I decided to quit. I drove the tractor to the house and told Charlie I'd had enough. I was going to town to find a better job. Charlie paid me what he owed me, and I drove the forty-five miles to Lamar, elated to be leaving the place.

When I walked in the door Mom looked up and said, "What are you doing here?" Ralph didn't say a thing. Charlie had probably already called him and told him I had left.

"I quit," I told Mom. "He's workin' me like a dog out there." I sat down and told her about the long work days, the grubby field hands, the old bunkhouse, the bad food—the whole sad story.

When I finished, Mom said, "What's the matter, can't you take it? I thought you wanted to work for a living. Well, that's what you're doing."

I looked at Ralph. "Charlie's got a lot of work to get done out there," he said, "and he's countin' on you to help him with it."

I sat there for a half hour, while nobody said a word. I knew they had me. "All right, I'm goin' back," I said with a sigh. Ralph grinned, Mom hugged me, and I reluctantly drove back to Charlie's place.

It was after midnight when I went to bed in the bunkhouse, but Charlie got me up at 4:30 in the morning as usual. He told me he was glad I'd come back, and took me to the field. When he brought my lunch later that day he said, "We're gettin' behind in the plowin,' Gary. Don't stop the tractor to eat your lunch like ya have been; just eat it on the go."

As he drove away I started the tractor across the hot, dusty field, picked up the bag of wretched sandwiches, and broke into tears. I stopped the tractor and cried long and hard, and through the tears I could see Dad's stern face. Then I cried aloud, "I'm going back to school. I'm going back to school."

I did go back to school that fall. I had classes only in the mornings that year, so I worked at a part-time job in the afternoons. I didn't study particularly hard, but I did all my homework and prepared for tests. I was so proud when I received my diploma in the spring of 1960. Mom was too, and Ralph was elated. So was my friend, Charlie Fletcher.

That fall I joined the navy as George had; I guess it was a family tradition. I'd always planned to join the military after high school and never considered any other branch but the navy.

After basic training the navy sent me to Engineman School for three months. There I studied diesel engines, air compressors, hydraulics, and related equipment. That school was the first academic endeavor at which I really worked.

I had scored high on the aptitude and IQ tests when I joined, and a year after Engineman School I was offered an opportunity to attend the U.S. Naval Nuclear Power School, one of the most prestigious military schools at the time.

Nuclear Power School was a full year long, and with a fifty percent dropout rate was known to be one of the hardest in the navy. If I accepted it I was required to extend my four-year enlistment to seven and would have to serve the seven years whether or not I made it through the school. With my high school record still fresh in my memory, it was a scary prospect to consider. But as I lay awake nights thinking about it, I could see Dad sitting up in that hospital bed with his fists clenched. "Gary, when you see an opportunity, grab it!"

I decided to try the school. When I arrived I had to stand in front of the desk of a very intelligent lieutenant who was my new division officer. The lieutenant had my high school transcripts spread out on his desk, and as he thumbed through them, shaking his head, he asked with a frown, "Do you know what kind of school this is?"

"Yes, sir," I said smartly.

"Do you really think you can get through a school like this?" he asked, with more than a little sarcasm.

"Yes sir, I do," I replied.

The officer looked me hard in the eye and said, "You've got a piss-poor background for this school, sailor. I think you'll have a hell of a time getting through it."

He was tapping my patience and prodding my determination. I clenched my jaw and said, "I'll make it through, sir. Guaranteed."

He looked me over thoughtfully, waved his hand, and said, "Dismissed."

That officer either analyzed me correctly or he got lucky. I left his office doubly determined to make it through the school after he told me he didn't think I could. For a year I focused on schoolwork to the exclusion of nearly everything else, studied harder than ever before, and graduated number eighteen of two hundred and eighty students.

I learned more than nuclear engineering that year; I learned what it took to get something done.

Following the school I served aboard nuclear submarines for four and a half years, remaining submerged for two months at a time on extended underwater patrols. After growing up in the wide open spaces, I wasn't especially adapted to submarines; some thirty years later I still have an occasional nightmare about them. I rode them though, determined not to fail. Outrageous pranks, practical jokes, and laughter became my swords against the tedium and confinement.

I didn't have to ride submarines alone, however; Dad was there with me. He could stand anything, and as long as he was with me I could too.

During the years of isolation in submarines, I dreamed of going back to the land in Colorado, which Mom still owned, and starting up the ranch again. The dream proved to be only an echo from the past, however. When I left the navy, I went back home and realized that wasn't really what I wanted to do with my life. I couldn't remake myself in Dad's image, nor could I re-create a life that lay in the past.

A year or so after my discharge Mom asked me if I still had any thoughts of doing something with the ranch. If I didn't, she said she had an interested buyer. I hated to see the old place go, but I told her I had no plans to go back. She sold it shortly after our conversation.

Nuclear Power School had given me the confidence to try college. I enrolled at Weber State University in Utah to major in a science, though I didn't yet know which science. In order to enroll I had to drag out those abysmal high school transcripts again, but I studied hard enough to earn an academic scholarship, and four years later finished number one in my class with a degree in geology. I know Dad was there the day I graduated.

From Utah I went on to graduate school at the University of Kansas to earn a master's degree and have spent my life since as a professional geologist.

During some of the most trying periods of my life, I've literally felt Dad's presence at my side. The most vivid feeling occurred in the summer of 1989. The petroleum industry was experiencing massive layoffs that year, and I was caught in one. I was forty-eight years old, and positions for petroleum geologists were practically nonexistent in the marketplace. I went back to school and took some graduate courses, and conducted a lengthy job search, but I began to fear that I would never work as a geologist again.

Sometime during that summer, when I'd been searching for a job for months and finding it harder and harder to maintain my morale, I began to wonder how much longer I could go on. In the depths of my trial, Dad came to me. I was sleeping at the time, so I suppose it was a dream. He appeared as a vision, however, or the closest thing to a vision I'll ever see.

I was an adult, middle-aged, and back on the ranch. I walked in the front door of the old rock house and there stood Dad, ramrod straight and real as life. He was dressed in his khakis, his snowy hair shining, and he looked fit and vigorous as he did in his seventies. He looked across the room with those gray eyes for which giving up was never an option, walked toward me, and held out his arms. We stood and hugged each other for a long, long time. Not a word was spoken between us; none was needed.

I woke up, and was sorry I had. I wanted to go back to sleep and recall it, recall him. I lay awake for hours, thinking about Dad and seeing him in my mind.

The following morning, with much emotion, I told my wife, Karen, what I had seen. She listened quietly then said simply, "He came back to help you." Indeed he had. It was one of the finest experiences of my life and infinitely comforting.

With perseverance and a good deal of luck, a few months later I found a position comparable to my previous one. Dad had helped me hang on until I found it.

George and I live far away now, and far apart, but we're still best friends. He pursued a career in electronics and computer technology, and retired as a manager with IBM Corporation.

Mom still lives in Lamar, happily with electricity and indoor plumbing. Recently when I took her out to the old place, on a perfectly clear day, Mom looked up, saw a tiny cloud on the horizon, and said, "There could be a storm comin' in, Gary."

Dad rests beside Mary Josephine on a hillside overlooking his beloved prairie. George and I chose the inscription on his gravestone. It simply says "Dad." That says it all.

The old rock house is still there, its walls again beginning to crumble. It's been standing there alone for over a hundred years now. It's durable, like the land, and Dad.

I still visit the old place every chance I get. As I wander over that hard land, even a rivulet of dust blowing by stirs my memory. A windmill creaks, and the sound touches my soul. I see the old road leading to the house, and I'm twelve years old again, clinging to that sled. I hear Dad's voice driving Jigs through the blizzard. I'm not afraid.

The old elm still stands, blowing in the rivers of wind

1—12-01